LEARN GRAPHOLOGY

Scriptor Books

GABRIELLE BEAUCHATAUD

LEARN GRAPHOLOGY

A Practical Course in 15 Lessons

Translated by Alex Tulloch

SCRIPTOR BOOKS, an imprint of The College of Graphology, London

First published in 1956, in France

English Edition first published in 1988 by
SCRIPTOR BOOKS,
an imprint of The College of Graphology,
75 Quinta Drive, Barnet, Herts. EN5 3DA

Editorial Office: 1B Limpsfield Avenue
London SW19 6DL

British Library Cataloguing in Publication Data
Beauchataud, Gabrielle
Learn Graphology: A Practical Course in 15 Lessons
1. Graphology
I. Title II. Apprenez la graphologie. English
155.28'2
ISBN 0–951370–00–6

Design & Production by Brigitte Froud
Cover Design by Grahame Herbert
Printed and bound in Great Britain
by Plaistow Press Ltd., London E15 3JA

CONTENTS

TRANSLATOR'S FOREWORD

When the Academy of Graphology was formed in 1985 it soon became evident that very few books were available in English which could be considered suitable for serious students who wished to make an academic study of graphology. Renna Nezos, the Principal, was in the throes of producing 'Graphology', which was to make such an important contribution to the study of the subject in the English-speaking world, but it was felt that future students of the burgeoning College of Graphology, which grew from the Academy, should have as many texts as possible at their disposal. Graphology in Britain at the time was still very much in its infancy and if we at the Academy were to nurture it and watch it flourish, there was no alternative but to turn our eyes and attention to the Continent, and in particular to France, where so much research has been conducted and progress made during the last 50 years, that it has become a veritable cornucopia of graphological information.

Once the decision had been made to make a start on translating European texts on graphology, the next step was easy. Deliberation and discussion were superfluous: Gabrielle Beauchataud's work, 'Apprenez la Graphologie' had been considered a classic of its genre and an indispensable text for beginners in France for so long that it was the obvious choice. The thoroughness with which she leads the beginner through the complexities of handwriting analysis is remarkable, but her main contribution to the science is that she bridges the gap between graphology and psychology. Mme Beauchataud was among the first to show how the theories of temperament and personality could be applied directly to handwriting and that the *theories of Jung and Le Senne could provide an invaluable additional string to the graphologists's bow. However, Mme Beauchataud's principal achievement is that she produced a work which is both a textbook for the absolute beginner and an indispensable source of reference for the more experienced graphologist.*

Unfortunately, the science of graphology has never received the recognition in British academic circles which it deserves. Continental universities have long considered it to be a perfectly respectable subject, worthy of at least as much academic interest and attention as any other branch of psychology, but the conservative British have tended to associate it with the Tarot, palmistry and other diverse branches of the Occult. This is a regrettable association of ideas, as there is nothing divinatory about graphology and I hope that this translation will contribute towards a better understanding of the value of handwriting analysis in terms of what it can reveal about the human personality.

Translation is an introverted pursuit, but not a solitary one, and there are many people whom I have to thank for their contributions in making this edition possible. I must thank Clive Carr, Lorraine Herbert and Brigitte Froud, the driving forces behind Scriptor Books. I must also thank Renna Nezos, "my friend, philosopher and guide" who led me through the labyrintine corridors of graphology, encouraging me when I got it right, despairing of me when I got it wrong and telling me to "look it up in Beauchataud!" (This I did frequently, and on one occasion the cosmic significance of handwriting dawned on me 'scripto, ergo sum').

Selectivity involves comparison and comparisons are odious. Nevertheless, I must single out for special thanks my colleague and collaborator, Olivia Graham AG (Dip), whose Nerveux Temperament kept my Sanguine Temperament under control, as she paid great attention to the detail and the finer points, whereas I was more concerned with the whole. Olivia ensured that I was consistent with translation of French graphological terminology, suggested improvements to my style and generally made an enormous contribution to the final version of the translation.

My thanks are also due to the publisher, Librairie Gründ S.A. for granting me the translation rights, and last, but by no means least, I must of course thank Gabrielle Beauchataud herself, for producing such an excellent text in the first place.

A.T.

I dedicate this book to Monsieur
and Madame Delamain and I
am happy to express here to
both of them and to Madame
Ania Teillard, my gratitude for
the valuable knowledge which
they passed on to me and my
admiration for the continuous
inspiration which they give to
French graphology.

G.B.

PREFACE

It gives me great pleasure to present to the public this second edition of Gabrielle Beauchataud's work, *Apprenez la Graphologie*. The writing of this well-known textbook coincides with the revival of the science which has taken place since 1945 under the auspices of the Société de Graphologie, which re-emerged after its decline during the Second World War.

It fell to the Société de Graphologie to rebuild French graphology from the relative neglect into which it had fallen during the preceding years through various rivalries, and also, it must be said, through the trouble engendered by the emergence of German and Swiss schools of graphology, based on principles very different from our own.

Meanwhile, a significant development in the world of psychology, of which graphology is only a part, was taking place, thanks to the discovery of the psychoanalytical theories of Freud, Adler and Jung, of Characterology and the advances in applied psychology. It was a world of innovations, in which it was necessary to establish the scope of graphology whilst making use of all the recent discoveries.

It was this task that the Société de Graphologie took upon itself, working with dogged determination. It culminated in the formation of a new doctrine, which is known as the French school of thought.

In this book, students can find the principles of modern graphology. As regards finding evidence of character in handwriting, one is first of all introduced to characterology and to the character types and the temperaments. Later comes the study of graphology itself and finally the student is shown, by means of concrete examples, the method to follow for arriving at a definition of a piece of handwriting and its interpretation.

Gabrielle Beauchataud was a pupil of Madame Delamain and subsequently, with regard to Jungian psychology, of Madame Teillard; she is, so to speak, an adopted daughter of the Society and is at present a member of the Council. That is why her introductory work on graphology is ranked amongst the best of the manuals recommended for students taking examinations. It gives me great pleasure to speak of it here.

M. DELAMAIN
Président de la Société de Graphologie

LESSON 1

WHAT IS CHARACTER?
THE HIPPOCRATIC TEMPERAMENTS
THE DUTCH-FRENCH SCHOOL (Heymans–Le Senne)

What is Character?

> *I shall certainly incur the censure of some
> people who cannot bear to have the innermost
> depths of their heart revealed and who con-
> sider that they have the right to prevent others
> from understanding them because they do not
> wish to understand themselves.*
>
> LA ROCHEFOUCAULD

Graphology is the art of assessing a person's character from
an examination of his handwriting. Therefore before
approaching the study of different kinds of handwriting we
must ask ourselves this question: *What is Character?*

According to T. Ribot: 'Character is the Self: in so far as
that Self regulates the extremely complex end-product of
heredity, physiological circumstances both prior and subsequent to birth, experience and education.'

René Le Senne, in his *Traité de la Caractérologie (1)*, assigns
a more limited significance to the word **Character**. As studied

---

(1) LE SENNE – Traité de Caractérologie (Presses Universitaires 1945).

by today's characterologists character is not the sum-total of
an individual, but merely the consequence of interacting
hereditary factors.

This concept of character excludes all that is acquired, all
that is the result of exterior events which may have influenced
the individual during the course of his life.

According to this concept character is solid and permanent,
and if a person does change during his lifetime it can only be in
keeping with the laws of his particular type. Thus, when he
reaches old age, a person of Nervous character may be quite
different from what he was twenty years before, but he will
have evolved along the lines peculiar to his type, whereas the
Phlegmatic character will grow old according to the laws of his
own particular type.

In this limited sense character is nothing more than the
skeleton of the psyche, the ensemble of inherited factors
which form man's mental structure.

Le Senne sets the *Personality* in contrast to the innate,
unchanging character. Personality includes not only character,
but all those elements in life which have played their part in
modifying an individual psyche: circumstances, education,
culture, family and social background, influences and experiences to which the individual has been subjected.

Situated between character and personality is a free and
active centre of exchange which may be called *the Self*. Le
Senne compares Character to a musical instrument, Personality to a musical composition. The Self is the musician, who,
endowed by nature with an instrument (Character), extracts
from it, with whatever art and skill he can, his own particular
melody (Personality).

But this personality will always be conditioned by its
underlying character, just as the resonance of a sonata will
vary according to whether it is played on a piano or a violin.
Character is matter, personality is form. The Self exploits and
models that matter with which nature has endowed it.

Thus Le Senne's concept of personality matches Ribot's
from every point of view, that is to say, character in the

broadest sense of the word.

It is however, necessary to bring the differences between these two terms into relief, for while Graphology can and must permit us to approach the individual as a whole, *general characterology*, whose conclusions we are about to outline, is the study of well-defined types of characters and temperaments. This will allow us to see what certain individuals have in common, how to recognise them and how to differentiate between them.

When we say that the Choleric is explosive, or that the Apathetic is placid, we are using General Characterology. But when we say that a certain Choleric is enormously cultured, or that he wastes his talents because of bad habits, we are beginning to make a portrait of a particular personality. We then examine what makes him an individual and start to think about his greater or lesser degree of merit in relation to the average member of his characterological group.

Value judgements must be excluded from characterology. One cannot assert, for example, that a Passionate has more merit than an Amorphous, for the Passionate may be intolerable, and the Amorphous full of charm. Superiority and mediocrity are to be found in every type of character; every virtue has its flaw, and every flaw its virtue. As the saying goes, 'It takes all sorts to make a world.' One person's excesses will make up for another's deficiencies, and diversity, rather than similarity, is a factor of cohesion and harmony among human beings.

Characters can be classified according to any manifestation of life; individuals can be classed according to their use of words, their gestures, their gait, or the morphology of their body, face and hands. Each starting point gives rise to a method of Characterology, but a classification according to handwriting has yet to be finalised.

Crépieux-Jamin, the master of French Graphology, accomplished an impressive inventory of all the possible aspects of handwriting and its corresponding psychological tendencies when he determined his 175 species of handwritings. It is possible that, taking certain signs or groups of signs as a starting point, he could have categorised individuals according to their handwriting; for example, the Expansive, the Taciturn, the Thinker, or the men of action. If, however, he had taken this course, he would have limited the possibilities of Graphology; for the signs which he registered, and which we are about to study, can be combined ad infinitum, since there are as many varieties of handwriting as there are of the human face.

Some people might regret the fact that a 'Typology of Handwriting' is not at our disposal, compounding some 8–12 groups of signs accompanied by their corresponding human portraits: but this is actually a blessing in disguise. As E. Mounier says in his *Traité du Caractère (1)*: 'We are only typical in so far as we fail to be fully individual. Hence typological portraits, which are pleasingly straightforward and convenient to read and to retain, are a dangerous alternative to true understanding.'

Typology is nevertheless a stepping-stone, and the knowledge of typological classifications, based upon people's main tendencies, will serve us as a guide in our research and make our portraits easier to compose. The graphologist who begins a portrait by hunting for individual signs without any notion of basic character traits and their laws of association will run the risk of creating a mosaic of qualities and defects which is lacking in any consolidating or unifying principle.

Thus the first, essential step towards understanding a character in all its complexity is to discover its basic structure and examine the interplay of inner forces which moulds it from within, brings it into relief and renders its nature explicit.

The types of character and temperament which we are about to study briefly cannot be applied wholesale to various handwritings, but they will provide the student with guidelines from which he will be able to extract several aspects of the writer's psyche.

---

(1) E. MOUNIER– Traité du Caractère (Editions du Seuil.)
   English translation by Cynthia Rowland (Rockliff. London 1956.)

Let us examine those systems of Typology currently employed by graphologists:

1) – The Hippocratic classification, which, in its relation to writing, has been revised by Hartenberg and Dr. Carton.

2) – The classification of the Dutch-French School, which has been developed by René Le Senne (in his book *Traité de la Caractérologie*).

3) – The Psychological Typology of C. G. Jung.

The Hippocratic Temperaments⁽¹⁾

In Antiquity temperaments were classified into four groups according to the preponderance of one of the four humours of which the blood is composed.

— The predominance of green bile produces the *Bilious (or Choleric)* temperament
— The predominance of black bile (or atrabile) produces the *Nervous (or Melancholic)* temperament
— The predominance of blood produces the *Sanguine* temperament
— The predominance of phlegm produces the *Lymphatic (or Phlegmatic)* temperament

These definitions may seem outdated today, but they have become so much part of our language that the types of individual they describe are still unmistakably true to life.

Bilious (or Choleric)
The Bilious (powerful temperament) is dominated by the instinct of conquest and of enterprise: this results in over-activity and a need for rich nourishment which often leads to bilious complaints. Hence the term *bilious*, in spite of the fact that this type is not particularly prone to moods.
The Bilious usually has a squarish face, matt complexion, firm mouth, decisive gestures, an imperious tone of voice and an ardent expression. People of this temperament are strong-willed, energetic and resistant: they are the war-horses. They are usually men of action, achievers, directors, explorers, conquerors, warriors. They are brave, haughty, obstinate,

---

(1) DR. CARTON – Diagnostic et Conduite des Tempéraments (Lefrançois).

tenacious, tough with themselves and with others, and ambitious. Their main defects are pride, impatience and anger. Their ideal is in action and leadership.

Nervous (or Melancholic)

The Nervous is emotional and hyper-sensitive, reacting strongly to any stimulus. He is of a more or less delicate constitution and has a prominent forehead, pointed chin, pale complexion and lively mobile eyes. His gestures are abrupt and often constrained. According to whether their nature tends towards expansion or retraction people of this temperament will be research workers, intuitive thinkers, or restless anguished spirits, over-conscientious, worried and unhappy.

Sanguine

The Sanguine is a robust expansive type of person with an open face and a broad chest. He breathes deeply, and his well-oxygenated blood gives him a florid complexion. His generous vitality endows him with a cheerful, contented nature. He is always gesticulating and showing-off. He eats and drinks enough for four. He is excessively demonstrative, and treats any newcomer as if he has known him for years. He charms one by his unexpectedly spontaneous obligingness, yet he easily forgets his promises. He has a lively intelligence and a facile, flowery way of talking. He adapts himself easily to any situation, but he is weak-willed. He is very good in attack, but bad at waiting for any length of time. His vitality is outgoing, and does not have the inbuilt solidity of the Bilious type. He is a good sort, but rather superficial.

Lymphatic (or Phlegmatic)

The Lymphatic is usually heavy and bulky. He is fleshy, has massive limbs, and his whole physique is ungainly. The lower half of his face thickens early on in life. His gestures are slow, his way of talking monotonous, and he takes a long time to make decisions: he is not very sensitive, and rather inactive. Everything about him shows passivity. At his best a Lymphatic type may be noteworthy for his patience, orderliness, fore-sight, sangfroid, and self-control. If he lacks willpower he may become lazy and greedy, and fall into negligence and inertia.

Dr. Carton sums up the main features of these four temperaments in the following way:

The Bilious (or Choleric) is enterprising, decisive, enthusiastic and exploratory.

The Nervous (or Melancholic) is restless, ingenious, excitable, and of enquiring mind.

The Sanguine is imaginative, inventive, easily moved and impulsive.

The Lymphatic (or Phlegmatic) is static, contemplative; he weighs up a situation and adjusts.

Characters which one meets in everyday life are hardly ever so clearly defined. The overwhelming characteristics of the dominant temperament are attenuated by features of the other three.

All four elements are almost equally developed in some extremely gifted people. In others there is a sort of penury on all levels, but these cases are quite rare. Usually the first and sometimes the second dominant is recognisable. These reveal themselves in the script by various signs which the student will gradually learn to recognise as he or she gains proficiency in the study of handwriting.

The Dutch–French School (Heymans - Le Senne)

The Dutch-French school of Characterology, which is represented by Heymans and Wiersma in Holland, (School of Groningen) and by René Le Senne in France, classifies characters according to three constituent factors:

Emotivity,
Activity,
Responsiveness.

We will now present a broad outline of this classification according to René Le Senne's *Traité de la Caractérologie.*

Emotivity

Emotivity is that general trait of psychological life which means that any event, thought or sensation, either within or outside the body cannot be perceived without provoking some kind of reaction in the organism. This reaction causes the release of a certain amount of energy which has been kept in reserve in the system. This energy can either disperse itself outwardly by gestures, words or actions, or it can, as it were, swim upstream, thus provoking gut-reactions such as pallor, blushing or palpitations, which will intensify the subject's awareness of his own emotion.

Emotivity is therefore a source of psychic energy which can assume very different aspects, depending on its association with other personality features and the direction which it takes. If it is associated with activity it will produce outward action. If it is combined with inactivity it will turn against the subject and become emotion. In one case or the other it will intensify either action or emotion.

We all have a certain degree of emotivity. We are all more or less sensitive to psychological disturbance, but the *Emotive*, in the characterological sense of the word, differs from the *non-Emotive* by the frequency of the shocks he sustains and by the relative unimportance of the events which provoke them. He will be exalted or moved to tears by minimal events, excited by trivia and easily moved to impulsive reaction. He may be paralysed by shyness in the most ordinary situations: these are the habitual states of the emotive.

Activity

The second constituent element of character is activity, which should not be confused with movement.

If we compare the man who is faced with danger and runs away as fast as he can to a runner training for a sporting event, we will notice that both of them are expending the same amount of energy, but the former acts because of fear, the latter because of a well-defined intention to better his performance. The athlete's will, need and taste for action comes from within, while the man who is overcome by fear is propelled by an exterior cause. Hence the definition of activity: *'To be active is to act because of an innate predisposition'*.

The *non-Active* acts reluctantly and as if under protest, and only when he has no alternative. In the best cases he may be prompted by a strict professional conscience and will do what he has to, but no more. For the *Active*, everything is an excuse for action. If he has no work, he will try to find something to do. The non-Active makes any excuse to avoid action.

The Active also differs from the non-Active in his attitude when confronted by an obstacle. Everything which hinders him in the course he has chosen reaffirms his resolution and stimulates his energy. He considers, like the moralist, that 'obstacles are made to be overcome, and not to overcome us'. When the non-Active is confronted by an obstacle he is discouraged and gives up.

These two kinds of reaction are so clear that it is possible to define a concept of activity thus (Le Senne: *Traité de Caractérologie* p.77): '*A man is active when the emergence of an obstacle reinforces his action in the direction which is obstructed by that obstacle; he is non-active when he is discouraged by the obstacle.*'

Non-activity is not the result of lack of will, but of impotence. The non-Emotive, for example, has absolutely no reason to wish to experience emotions he does not feel. But the non-Active often longs to be active and curses his own laziness and non-productivity. Sometimes, after considerable effort, he manages to get out of his rut, but once he has accomplished this effort he returns to his original stagnation. He does not have that continual drive which enlivens the Active and gives him the advantage of well established strength.

Thus activity turns the individual towards the outside world, maintaining his good humour and confidence. Non-activity, on the contrary, results in self-observation, rumination, self-doubt, pessimism and discouragement. Emotive-Actives will be men of action, enterprising and efficient, while Emotive-nonActives will more often turn towards the inner life and be poets, artists and dreamers.

Responsiveness

Everything which we perceive has either *immediate* or *long-term* effects on us. Le Senne gives the example of a Professor who glances at a clock on the wall of the lecture room while he is giving a lecture. He notices the time and is worried that it is later than he thought. The effect which this glance at the clock has on his mind constitutes an initial response which is called the **Primary function of Responsiveness**. But what the Professor has just noticed could have a deeper and more long-term implication for his future behaviour. He may now try to get through the beginning of his lectures more rapidly, or he may cut down on their content. All the effects which his noticing of the time continue to produce, after his original glance at the clock has lost its immediacy, constitute the *Secondary function of Responsiveness*.

Let us take another example: a young woman sees a hat that she likes in a shop-window. She wants to buy it, and immediately begins to imagine how well it will suit her, and checks to see if she has enough money on her. But as she is about to push open the door of the shop, she remembers that a few days ago her husband scolded her about her extravagance and that she promised to resist buying anything frivolous or non-essential in future; so she goes on her way, forcing herself not to look at other tempting shop windows.

Until the moment that she began to enter the shop, the young woman was under the effect of primary responsiveness; her subsequent inner debate was the result of her secondary responsiveness. Superimposed on her spontaneous immediate wish to acquire the tempting hat were the memory of her husband's past admonishments and the anticipatory image of their future economic hardship.

Primarity and Secondarity are like two poles of psychic immediacy and continuity between which we are constantly oscillating. Primarity causes us to particpate in the present, secondarity to organise ourselves for the long term. One of these functions is nearly always more prevalent than the other. The young woman could have forgotten her former good resolutions and given in to her immediate desire; in that case she would have behaved in a primary way. In the circumstances she acted in a secondary way by repressing the call of the present, and by respecting what she had learned from the past.

Perfect balance between these two attitudes is rarely achieved. Some people are more subject to the power of the present than others: *they are called* **Primary**. Those who take past experience more into account, and who take more precautions about the future *are called* **Secondary**. The former react in a strong, visible, immediate manner. The reactions of the latter are delayed, subdued or inhibited. Primarity is illustrated by impulsiveness, Secondarity by deliberation. For the Primary type life presents itself as a series of images or moments without any co-ordinating links; the subject surrenders to the demands of the present moment. The Secondary, on the contrary, is always bridging the gaps between past, present and future.

The Primary has intense yet short-lived perceptions with a corresponding intensity of reaction; the more subdued perceptions of the Secondary are sometimes made more intense by the trials of time. Nothing could illustrate Secondarity better than this self-portrait by Jean-Jacques Rousseau quoted by E. Mounier: 'I have studied Mankind and consider myself a fairly good observer; nevertheless I do not know how to see anything of what I am seeing. I only truly see what I remember; through memory my wits are brought to life. Of all that is said, done, or happens in my presence I see nothing, feel nothing, there is nothing I can penetrate. But afterwards everything comes back to me; I remember place, time, mood, expression, gesture and circumstance; nothing escapes me. Then, from what has been said or done, I divine what has been thought'.

It is evident that this kind of character is governed by the lasting nature of impressions. The Secondary, unlike the Primary, remains under the effect of impressions for a long time. He is difficult to console, and does not find reconciliation easy. He is less spontaneous, but more profound than the Primary and as constant in his affections as in his enmities. He can do without companionship quite easily, as he is self-contained. He is methodical and persevering in his undertakings, caring more about the future than about immediate results; he is patient and obstinate. He is usually more punctual than the Primary, more trustworthy and more attached to principles. He is more economical because he is less inclined to succumb to the temptation of the moment, but he knows little of that life-force, the powerful enthusiasm and total participation in being of which only the Primary is capable.

* * *

The three constituent facts which have just been explained can be combined to make eight types of Character:

The Emotive-nonActive-Primary	(EnAP)	or	Nervous
The Emotive-nonActive-Secondary	(EnAS)	or	Sentimental
The Emotive-Active-Primary	(EAP)	or	Choleric
The Emotive-Active-Secondary	(EAS)	or	Passionate
The nonEmotive-Active-Primary	(nEAP)	or	Sanguine
The nonEmotive-Active-Secondary	(nEAS)	or	Phlegmatic
The nonEmotive-nonActive-Primary	(nEnAP)	or	Amorphous
The nonEmotive-nonActive-Secondary	(nEnAS)	or	Apathetic

The nomenclature assigned to these types is a guideline which does not always correspond to the exact image which they bear in current language. In order to avoid confusion it is therefore better to designate characterological types by their determining formula (Emotive-Active-Primary, Emotive-nonActive-Secondary, etc.). For the sake of linguistic simplicity and factual accuracy, it is a good idea to retain both nomenclature and formula. Let us now sum up the main features of each of these types.

The Nervous Character (EnAP)

Because of the combination of Emotivity and Primarity, the Nervous Character reminds one of, to use Le Senne's description, a 'non-stop combustion engine'. Every instant supplies people of this character with a succession of perceptions and emotions which follow each other disconnectedly, and have no lasting effect. Hence their extreme mobility of feeling, their need for change and for new impressions — since past impressions leave no mark — and their unstable moods.

Because the energy released by emotivity has no activity to
channel it usefully, the Nervous often tire themselves out in
pointless agitation, going from one project to another, from
wild enthusiasm to despondency.

They are more prone than other types to impulsiveness and
instability in everyday behaviour, to infidelity, wastefulness,
and falsehood. Of all men, they are the least attached to
principles. They are the original anarchists and bohemians;
but it is also among them that most artists are to be found. The
vivid sensitivity which is the result of their emotivity,
combined with the spontaneous high spirits which come from
their primarity, gives them great riches of imagination and
expressiveness.

They are not active enough to complete epic works and will
not be found among such dedicated workers as Balzac, Victor
Hugo, or Alexandre Dumas, but among poets such as Musset,
Rimbaud, Verlaine and Baudelaire.

Inactivity often makes them suffer from a feeling of
impotence and inferiority which they conceal beneath a mask
of vanity and extreme susceptibility. In some cases this frame
of mind gives them a tendency towards bitterness, melancholy, pessimism, systematic disparagement and persecution
mania. Of all the characters they are the most liable to
neurosis and mental illness.

The Sentimental Character (EnAS)

The Sentimental has the combination, Emotivity-
nonActivity, in common with the Nervous, and like him he has
maximum sensitivity and receptivity. But his sensitivity, unlike
that of the primary types, does not disperse itself in the
present, but penetrates deeper and is longer lasting because of
the effects of inhibitions and secondarity. Sentimentals are
true victims of their emotions. They are denied the relief and
optimism produced by activity, and are the most vulnerable of
all the characters. Feelings of sadness affect them more than
any of the other characters.

They are extremely subjective and self-conscious, often living enclosed within their own thoughts. They pursue solitude, not only in order to escape their fellow-men (of whom they have a low opinion), but to search for themselves and to pursue their own souls, for they are more interested in their inner life than the outside world. Poised between dream and introspection, their purest form of expression is the Diary (Amiel, Biran, Jean-Jacques Rousseau's *Confessions*).

Because of their lack of activity they tend, like the Nervous types, to be self-doubting, anxious and pessimistic. Secondarity diminishes their presence of mind and they are often shy and awkward, always thinking of a retort when it is too late, and as our enjoyment of company is in proportion to our social success it is not surprising if they are misanthropic.

The Nervous is a boisterous prodigal child whose emotion is constantly released and renewed by primarity. Restrained emotion, pent-up by secondarity, makes the Sentimentals serious, conscientious and dignified; they have profound moral feelings, are faithful in their affections, but they also harbour resentment. They are, together with the Apathetics, the most inconsolable of all characters.

Sentimentals, like all the emotive types, have high aspirations, but their initial drive is impeded by debilitating inactivity, making them indecisive and self-doubting. Hence a painful inner conflict between excessively high ideals and the powerlessness to achieve them. An imbalance between aspiration and achievement makes them dissatisfied with themselves and with the world in general.

The Choleric Character (EAP)

The combination, Emotivity-Activity, is a doubly dynamic factor which makes the Choleric character an ardent being with great powers of achievement. One can compare these characters to powerful machines of high productivity, but hungry for fuel. They have a generous nature, an overwhelming vitality, vigorous instincts and a demanding sexuality.

Emotivity makes them sympathise with their fellow beings, activity makes them efficient. They are helpful, enterprising, daring and resourceful.

Their activity expresses itself mainly in the social field. They are voluble, and masterly orators (Diderot, Victor Hugo, Mirabeau). Emotivity gives them direct contact with their public, and primarity enables them to improvise: they are ring-masters, leaders. They are often attracted by politics and like to be in the front line so that they can test their powers of influence on the masses. Whether painters, poets, or novelists, they require the drama of a drum-roll, of the sort that stirs up crowds. They are in too much of a hurry to be discriminating and like to fraternise with people of any social group. They are good sorts, happy to be alive, and although they do not always stick to their opinions (primarity being a factor of inconstancy) they are well loved for their affability, open-mindedness and charisma.

The Passionate Character (EAS)

Le Senne says that the Passionate character is the most highly charged of all. Emotivity gives him propulsive energy, activity tempers him for struggle, and secondarity brings him method and continuity of action. The combination of these 3 positive factors makes the Passionate the most forceful of all the characters and it is not surprising that it is among this group that we find the most men of genius (Louis XIV, Bossuet, Napoleon, Foch, Beethoven, etc.).

They are conscious of their power and are the most ambitious of all the characters, but unlike the Sentimentals their ambition goes beyond mere aspiration.

More consistent than the Choleric — who may be caused to waver by his primarity — the Passionate does not deviate from the path he has chosen. He is compelled to achieve what he has set out to do. He concentrates on his goal and will motivate anyone who will be useful to him. He is persevering, obstinate and relentless, but not pig-headed or inflexible, because the will to attain the goal he has chosen makes him learn how to adapt himself to circumstances.

A particular feature of this group of characters is their taste for greatness. Their ambition is directed at a social, economic, political or religious ideal which goes beyond their personal interests.

They will willingly sacrifice comfort, possessions or even life for an ideal. Dedicated philanthropists have been known to end up destitute. Relentless tycoons intent on making millions which will be of no real benefit to themselves have lived on sandwiches, denying themselves the leisure and the pleasures that life can provide. In both cases the pursuit of higher interests reduces personal need to zero. They are among those most given to sobriety and asceticism. They seem to thrive on stress and ambition and, as they need very little sleep, their work capacity is enormous.

The trouble is that they often treat others as they treat themselves — in extreme cases they consider people no more than a means to an end — the businessman exhausts his personnel, the industrialist his workmen and the statesman makes a whole people slave to an ideal which he forces them to accept as their own.

When he is not blinded by ambition, the Passionate has great virtues: he is faithful, serious, patriotic and a family man; he is compassionate, lucid, modest and without affectation. He does not care much about having a good time because his greatest enjoyment in life, indeed his 'raison d'être', is his work.

The Sanguine Character (nEAP)

We now come to those characters whose emotivity is minimal or attenuated. All of the groups we have studied up to now are greatly stimulated by above average emotivity, and are therefore sensitive to the environment and in a perpetual state of sympathy or antipathy towards other people. The non-Emotives prove to be more objective and generally more detached from their fellow beings.

Commonsense is the Sanguine character's main feature. The combination Activity-Primarity makes the Sanguine realistic and ready to take advantage of any opportunity. They like money and all the pleasures it procures. Primarity makes them quick-witted and flexible, and they know how to adapt themselves rapidly to circumstances. They are diplomatic and clever manipulators. Sanguines are fluent speakers who express themselves well and are convincingly logical. They are often successful lawyers, tradesmen or sales representatives. For them immediate results take precedence over long-term objectives. When they are in a position of authority they are good at reconciling their own and the common interests.

The Choleric, bursting with emotivity, goes whole-heartedly into action, but the Sanguine knows how to get out of awkward situations because he is cool-headed and objective. His attitude towards the demonstrativeness of the emotive types is condescending, amused and rather sarcastic.

His inner or personal life is somewhat lacking in ardour. Non-emotivity diminishes his sensitivity and primarity makes him liable to the influence of external events. He can easily control his feelings in matters of the heart. His ideals are aesthetic rather than moral. He likes women more for their bodies than their minds, and is generous with them (he knows how to make money), but he is inclined to be fickle and sometimes cynical.

He is often sceptical about religion, more from lack of natural enthusiasm than from sectarian opposition. On the whole he is tolerant and well meaning. His non-emotivity prevents him from being over enthusiastic. He demands moderation from other people and makes himself useful to society in his capacity as an intermediary and conciliator.

The Phlegmatic Character (nEAS)

There are few characters easier to recognise and more difficult to fathom than the Phlegmatics. Their formula places them in a position diametrically opposed to that of the Nervous (EnAP), in contrast to whose impulses and restlessness they show calm, impassivity, self-control, even-temper and sobriety of gesture and speech.

Secondarity makes them level-headed, prudent, methodical, attached to the past and to habit. Because of the combination, non-emotive secondary, they tend to be rather cool towards their fellow beings. They are more interested in theory than practice. They like intellectual activity, scientific research and theoretical subjects, in which they are sometimes a bit too systematic. They are interested in everything which pertains to the mind. They are not usually very creative artistically, as they do not have the vibrant sensitivity and imagination of the emotives.

They are often broad-minded, so that in spite of their attenuated emotivity they have an intelligent understanding of others which shows itself in a discernment and attentiveness surprising in such seemingly cold individuals. They have good manners, sometimes to the extent of over-formality, but they are never vain. They are the most tolerant of people. They are courageous, stoical when put to the test, and resigned when faced with death.

They have extreme respect for the law. They are men of passionless virtue, having great integrity and truthfulness. They are attached to principles and their sense of duty is not only confined to patriotism and family, but is also social and professional.

They always keep themselves busy and work with regularity and rigorous punctuality. They are provident, persevering, tenacious and patient to the highest degree. They are unaffected, modest, disinterested, usually economical and disdainful of power and honours.

Despite so many virtues, they might seem boring if it were not for their sense of humour, which relieves the monotony of their ways with the discreet sparkle of a subtle intelligence.

The Amorphous Character (nEAP)

As they lack both the enthusiasm and sympathy for their fellow beings produced by emotivity, and the wide interests resulting from activity, people of the Amorphous character, having no higher distractions, remain subject to the satisfaction of their organic needs. Statistical surveys by Heymans and Wiersma show them to be the most intemperate and sensual of all the characters.

In some ways they are like the Nervous because of the combination, nonActive-Primary. They are spendthrifts, unable to resist immediate temptation, but their desires remain on the inferior level of a concern for food and the instinct of self-preservation. They are also colder than the Nervous, who is excitable because of his emotivity, and are therefore less easily discouraged, but this is also probably due to the fact that they seldom undertake anything. They are lazy, careless, indecisive and liable to postpone any undertaking or obligation which concerns them.

They are impractical, may easily live in a makeshift way or become accomplished spongers. They are extremely attracted to gambling. In order to modify this very unflattering portrait it must be said that the Amorphous, like the Phlegmatic, is often courageous when confronted with danger and can be objective and tolerant.

Because primarity endows them with a certain spontaneity of expression they succeed quite well in the interpretive arts, particularly in the field of music. They are way out in front of all the characters when it comes to acting talent; their passivity and plasticity allows them to be animated by others, and as they lack the contrasts which would grant them a fully individual personality they can faithfully reflect the moods of those they are asked to portray.

The Apathetic Character (nEnAS)

The Apathetics are like the Sentimentals in their sombre, melancholy moodiness: like them the combination, non-Active-Secondary, makes them withdraw into their shells. They do not talk much and hardly ever laugh, but while the Sentimental broods on inner dramas which gnaw at him, sometimes forcing him to let go and pour out his soul in a heart-rending way, the inner life of the Apathetic is of a desperate emptiness. If he likes solitude it is not, like the Sentimental, to protect any thin-skinned sensitivity, but because of sheer indifference to other people. Everything bores him. Children and animals disturb his peace of mind, and he makes very little allowance for them.

The Apathetics are more sober and continent as regards sexual matters than the Amorphous, because absence of primarity lessens the intensity of their desires.

They are not as sulky as the Sentimentals, being less vulnerable and susceptible, but their secondarity makes them terribly vindictive. They are more obstinate than persevering (perseverance being a form of activity, obstinacy often only a reinforcement of passivity) and are firmly entrenched in their habits, fanatic in their own opinions, sticklers for principle, and cautious and economic to the point of avarice. They are known to be severe educators. They are not of an enquiring mind and are unattracted by intellectual activities. They often lack initiative, but on the other hand they are very well suited to carrying out orders. The combination, nonEmotive-Secondary, endows them with appreciable qualities of moral probity, orderliness, honesty, rectitude and fidelity.

Le Senne sums up the dominant features of each of these characters in the following way:

The Nervous	is characterised by		Instability
The Sentimental	"	"	" Vulnerability
The Choleric	"	"	" Cordiality
The Passionate	"	"	" Achievement of Ambition
The Sanguine	"	"	" Practicality
The Phlegmatic	"	"	" Devotion to Law and Order
The Amorphous	"	"	" Subjection to organic needs
The Apathetic	"	"	" Submission to habit

LESSON 2

Jung's Typology

Extraversion — Introversion

Jung defined the two directions that psychic energy (or libido) can take through his concept of extraversion and introversion. *(1)*

Extraversion is an attitude which directs us towards the outside world, either as an outlet or as a means of enjoyment or conquest. In this context the world of things and the world of beings are of equal importance.

Introversion, on the contrary, is an attitude which holds us in and drives us back into our inner selves.

The extravert is possessed with a need for outward expression. He is spontaneous, lively, exuberant, always on the move,

---

(1) C. G. JUNG – Types Psychologiques (Georg et Cie, Ed. Genéve)

and inquisitive about everything. His eagerness about people and things is boundless. Everything attracts and interests him.

The introvert is only interested in and concerned by what happens within himself. Unable to show his emotions, he dwells on them, continually turning them over in his mind. The only value the object has for him is the one he himself bestows upon it. He turns his back on the outside world and retires within himself.

Jung's portrait of the extravert is rather like that of the Active-Primary group of characters (in particular the Sanguine): adaptable, sociable, resourceful, outgoing, enterprising and fond of novelty and adventure. His inner life is very sparse, and his existential motivations are only to be found in the outside world. He is characterised more by expansion than by intensity, and is superficial, light-weight and easily distracted.

The introvert is closer to the nonActive-Secondary types, in particular, the Sentimental. He is basically subjective and vulnerable, finding it difficult to adapt to the outside world. He has the same cautious reserve as the Sentimental character and is withdrawn, hesitant and shy. He is attached to the past and to habit, is frightened by the future and rather suspicious about anything new. This frame of mind may create a distance between the introvert and his fellow-beings, but it helps him to increase his mental concentration and enriches his inner world.

Nobody is either totally introvert or extravert. Both tendencies exist in every person and we usually go from one to another according to the requirements of particular moments in life. The extravert has times of introversion, and the introvert is sometimes forced to come out of his shell. But in the end everybody automatically reverts to the attitude which is most natural to him and which determines his type. Thus it is easy to distinguish the expansive, talkative extravert from the more reticent and self-effacing introvert.

The Psychic Functions

Jung defined the two directions which psychic energy can take as centrifugal, which corresponds to extraversion, and centripetal, which corresponds to introversion. However, this energy can also manifest itself in four different ways which he called the Psychic Functions. These are: *Thinking,*
Feeling,
Sensation,
Intuition.

Thinking

Thinking in Jung's sense of the word, i.e. as a psychic function concerning adaptation to life, is that capacity (usually more masculine than feminine) to establish relationships between ideas and things and to discover the logical link which unites them. It is an instrument of both analysis and synthesis; an organisational faculty.

Feeling

Feeling is more feminine than masculine and it is a function which proceeds either by acceptance or refusal of the object without the intervention of intellectual judgement. The person who obeys his Feeling function will say 'I like this', or 'I hate that' without being able to explain the reasons for his liking or dislike.

Sensation

Sensation is direct perception of what touches the senses. It is also called 'the reality function'. If we say: 'This carnation is red', we express what our Sensation function has just established. If we add: 'I adore red carnations', we demonstrate our Feeling function.

Intuition

Intuition does not perceive what exists, but what could exist. In a sense it is a function which defies barriers of time and space. The object we perceive has not always been, will

not always be what it is now; it has a past and a future. Its
present state as we see it represents only one point in a line of
successive transformations. So Intuition does not isolate the
object and does not limit it to a present instance. Intuition
perceives things in a continuum, in accordance with their
possible evolution, and instantly predicts any situation which
may arise from a given circumstance.

If he is near a cool river the person whose dominant
function is Sensation enjoys a sense of well-being, admires the
translucency of the water and thinks how pleasurable it would
be to go for a swim. The Feeling person will be overwhelmed
by the charm of the place, will imagine himself there with his
girl friend and conjure up the memories which make him feel
happy — the joys or sorrows he once experienced on the
banks of a similar river. The Thinking type will examine the
geological structure of the river bank, calculate the depth of
the water, criticise the construction of a nearby bridge, and
look at a map in order to find out the exact location of a village
he has just caught sight of. The Intuitive type does not even
notice which particular part of the river-bank he is sitting on,
but as his gaze wanders upstream and downstream an idea
may flash through his mind. He may imagine damming up the
narrow end of the valley: a dam and a factory suddenly appear
in his mind's eye, the river is transformed into a lake and a
dilapidated town 200 kilometres away becomes prosperous
because of new supplies of water and electricity.

Jung calls *Thinking and Feeling rational functions*, because
both of them make value-judgements: *Thinking judges things
as real or unreal, exact or inexact; Feeling judges them as good
or bad, right or wrong*.

These functions cannot operate simultaneously in our mind.
We are unable to reason and to feel at the same time; if feeling
tries to manifest itself while we are reasoning we brush it aside
as importunate, forbidding ourselves to give in to it, knowing
that it will disturb our reasoning. In the same way, at the
actual moment when we feel either attraction or revulsion

towards an object, we do not know how to analyse the motives for our attraction or disgust. Thus thinking and feeling are like two poles of an axis, between which the value-judgments which we apply to the world fluctuate. These judgements are more or less objective and cool when they are the result of our Thinking function, more or less subjective and charged with emotion when they are the result of our Feeling function.

According to Jung, *Sensation and Intuition are irrational functions* because they are both purely perceptive. Like Thinking and Feeling they are in opposition to each other. It is, in fact, impossible to give one's whole attention to a person's physical appearance and at the same time to try and imagine various aspects of their way of life, their past, or their character. As soon as our mind drifts into speculation it loses that total concentration or contact with reality which is peculiar to the Sensation function, so that reality has in fact only served as a springboard for intuition.

The individual adapts himself to the world about him through the play of these four functions, but one of them is always more developed than the three others, and is called the *main function*. This is the one in which the individual is most secure and which he makes use of most spontaneously. This main function is usually associated with a second one which is called the *auxiliary function*. A rational main function can be linked to and aided by an irrational function, and an irrational main function can have an auxiliary rational function, but no two rational or irrational functions can ever operate simultaneously.

For example, Thinking can have either Intuition or Sensation as an auxiliary function but it can never operate in conjunction with Feeling, because as we have just seen, the mechanism of Thinking can only work if it pushes Feeling into the background.

In the same way an Intuitive type can be aided in his intuitive process by either Feeling or Thinking, but never by Sensation; for, if he is to give free rein to his intuition, he must escape from reality.

The following diagrams were set up by Jung and will help us to understand the play of the functions:

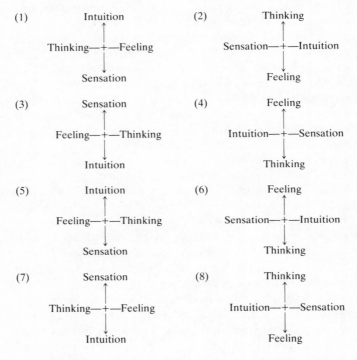

(1)   Intuition   (2)   Thinking
                    ↑   ↑
       Thinking—+—Feeling   Sensation—+—Intuition
                    ↓   ↓
              Sensation   Feeling

(3)   Sensation   (4)   Feeling
                    ↑   ↑
       Feeling—+—Thinking   Intuition—+—Sensation
                    ↓   ↓
              Intuition   Thinking

(5)   Intuition   (6)   Feeling
                    ↑   ↑
       Feeling—+—Thinking   Sensation—+—Intuition
                    ↓   ↓
              Sensation   Thinking

(7)   Sensation   (8)   Thinking
                    ↑   ↑
       Thinking—+—Feeling   Intuition—+—Sensation
                    ↓   ↓
              Intuition   Feeling

The dominant function is always to the North. If Intuition is the principal function then either Thinking or Feeling can be auxiliary. Sensation will be the Inferior function, the one which is least developed and least used.

If we turn the circle through 45° to the right we shall have Thinking as the main function. If we move the circle half way round, Sensation will be dominant, Thinking or Feeling will be auxiliary and Intuition will be in the inferior position. If Feeling is to the North, either Intuition or Sensation will be auxiliary and Thinking will be relegated to the inferior position.

An individual's character type depends on his main function.

The Thinking Type has the kind of mind which tends to operate in an abstract way. He looks for the unifying principles which connect various phenomena, his actions are regulated logically and methodically and are uninfluenced by either his personal feelings or by those of his entourage.

The Feeling Type submits himself wholly to his surrounding environment, but distorts it because he confuses his knowledge of things or beings with the pleasant or unpleasant feelings which they arouse in him. His pleasurable or painful memories overpower him, and he not only relives his perceptions, but still feels the impact which they have made upon him. These memories regulate his conduct by virtue of the negative or positive values which they represent for him.

The Sensation Type is acutely perceptive of everything which is communicated by the senses. His mind lingers on subtleties of form, colours, tactile perceptions, tastes and smells. He is in tune with all the manifestations of his own organism.

The Intuitive Type seems to absent himself from the real world and from his own body. His perceptions only serve as a starting point for his imagination to pursue endless possibilities.

Our main function plays a vital role in the orientation of our destiny. Our vocation usually depends on this function because it determines a whole area of interests. Outside this area the subject will do what he has to do inadequately, and will meet the demands of his profession in a half-hearted manner.

Le Senne makes the following statement about the constituent factor of character: 'Emotivity gives rise to the subject's attachment to the element which moves him. In order, therefore, to assess an individual's degree of emotivity, it is of prime importance to know what is of interest to him'.

The application of graphology to Jung's typology will permit us to know just that. Once we have learned to recognise the signs of emotivity in handwriting, and the signs by which a prevalence of Thinking, Feeling, Sensation or Intuition are revealed, we shall be able to predict what the subject will be most sensitive to, and in what field his activity will express itself most effectively and willingly.

*   *   *

An attitude of either extraversion or introversion differentiates each of the psychological types we have just reviewed.

The Extraverted Thinking Type

This type is in his element when he can organise, classify and make arrangements and plans. He is capable of creating order out of chaos. He has a critical, constructive mind and clear judgement. Business and administrative posts will suit him better than those of public relations or salesmanship. In these jobs an Extraverted Feeling type will do much better. Women of this type are capable career women. They seek intellectual jobs or ones which require initiative. However, their lack of Feeling impoverishes their femininity, creating a distance between them and men of their own type. These women attract weaker men in whom they inspire confidence with their seriousness and competence.

The Introverted Thinking Type

This type is more interested in what is within himself than in the external world, and cultivates the intellect for its own sake. He will be a philosopher, theoretician, or an intellectual devoted to logic and debate. He is tenacious, uncompromising and often stubbornly opposes those who disagree with his ideas. External things interest him only insofar as they confirm his own ideas and bring grist to his own mill. He is often excessively systematic, intolerant, dogmatic. He is sometimes harsh with his enemies, but he is more faithful and profound than the Extraverted Thinker. It is because his Feeling function is extremely deficient that he has little sympathy for his fellow-beings, who usually adopt a similar attitude to him. He is often more respected than loved.

The Extraverted Feeling Type

This type is the most companionable and endearing of all the types. He is very like the 'Choleric' of Heymans-Le Senne's classification. He is warm-hearted and welcoming, he is capable of putting everyone at their ease and of discussing everything under the sun. He introduces people who would never have met each other without his intervention. Like all extraverts he abhors solitude and his need for social contact is intense. If he is deprived of companionship he feels that he has been left high and dry. The Extravert Feeling type is rich in sentiment, but poor in original ideas. It is in this area that his lack of Thinking function makes itself evident. He also conforms to the existing viewpoints of his era and his social class. It is not unusual to see a Feeling type woman who adheres blindly to her husband's ideas, or a militant of this type who submits entirely to a cause, identifying himself unquestioningly with the aims of a political party or the views of a newspaper.

The Introverted Feeling Type

This type has much in common with the Sentimental (Emotive-nonActive-Secondary) of Heymans-Le Senne's classification. He has the same egocentric, painful sensitivity, the same tendency towards disparagement and misanthropy. People of this type are incapable of considering things objectively. Because of their subjectivity and vulnerability they are difficult to put up with, tyrannical and deaf to others' pleas. They are single-minded, obstinate and intransigent, capable of the deepest attachments, but very exclusive in their affections. The bond of love which ties them to one person and makes them capable of total sacrifice for the beloved can also isolate them from the rest of the world for whom they feel only indifference.

The Extraverted Sensation Type

This type needs tangible reality. He only believes in what he sees. He is a positive sort of character who is well adapted to the real world and who settles down into existence as into a comfortable arm-chair. His keen sense of observation makes him successful in technical professions or in the kind of business which requires careful appreciation of commodities through the faculties of taste, sight and touch. He likes good food and pretty women. If his taste for pleasurable sensations is cultivated in a civilised way it can evolve into a feeling for art, but he will always be almost devoid of intuition, his judgement of others will be awkward and he will not be much of psychologist.

People of this type are pleasure-seekers. They have both zest for life and solid common-sense, but are often lacking in subtlety.

The Introverted Sensation Type

The world of external things makes a profound and intense impression on the Introverted Sensation type. His introversion makes him sensitive. He is of a more cautious and delicate disposition than the extravert of his type. He is always dissatisfied with the quality of things, because he would like them to be perfect. He is fastidious, meticulous, demanding and indecisive, the kind of person who will be unable to make a choice even if the whole contents of a shop have been unpacked for his inspection. He will also refuse to eat a meal, if he does not think that the food he has been given is perfectly prepared and presented. He closely observes everything which concerns his own organism, and is irritatingly careful about his health.

In spite of their extreme keenness of perception people of

this type seem to be blinkered about anything which does not have a direct effect on their senses. Their intuition is very poor, and they are easily frightened in anticipation of the future, about which they have no inkling. They are mentally short-sighted, like ships without radar. Because of this they are more dependent on the security of habit than most people, and everything which upsets their routine makes them painfully anxious. The unknown seems full of threat for them. As the cause of their anguish is nearly always of a material or personal kind, they tend to be particularly egotistical. But if culture or even good taste imbues them with a true sense of beauty, they may become meticulous artists or painstaking craftsmen who develop their art to the point of perfection. Introverted Sensation types are often drawn to professions in which their refined taste for material things is a great asset: they may be experts in perfumes or fabrics, antique dealers or art collectors.

The Extraverted Intuitive Type

The Extraverted Intuitive's faculty of seeing beyond what actually exists to what could exist, of being able to envisage future possibilities, is extremely highly developed. We find people of this type originating those activities which have changed the world: navigation, exploration, invention, strategy, statesmanship, diplomacy, philosopohy, economic or political leadership etc. Everything which has transformed humanity springs from a flash of intuition. Of course, all intuitives are not geniuses and all geniuses have not been beneficial to humanity.

People of Extraverted Intuitive type share a taste for adventure. They like change and novelty. Reality bores them, for they are really only interested in new possibilities. They are driven outside themselves by curiosity and love of risk, and as soon as they achieve some success in one thing they abandon it for something new. Their actions are guided mainly by their intuition, like the financier who has a hunch that certain shares are about to rise and risks his fortune because of a presentiment, or the explorer lost in the desert who has a feeling that he will find water in a certain direction and does so. The intuitive woman will say to her husband: 'So and so doesn't make a good impression on me — you had better not do any business with him', and nine times out of ten her prediction will be confirmed by events. The Intuitive type will certainly make mistakes sometimes, but he is not easily discouraged, and always thinks that he will be proven right in the future. The Intuitive is rather detached from things, and even from his fellow beings. He goes through life without seeing what is around him, or only notices what really interests him. Sometimes he will search endlessly for something which is in reality very near at hand. This inattentiveness to reality and contempt for material things sometimes leads him into mishap. Fascinated by a distant objective, he may neglect substance for shadow, fall into obvious traps, and not pay enough attention to fundamental issues. He is liable to become the victim of an eclipse of his sense of reality. He could be, for example, an audacious architect, who, carried away by his revolutionary techniques, plans a marvellous new building but forgets to provide either lift shafts or a stair-well.

The Introverted Intuitive Type

The Intuitive Introvert is, according to Jung, an original sort of individual; a dreamer, a mystic, a fantasist, or an artist. He is not interested in exterior reality, more in the metamorphosis of what he perceives.

Alphonse Daudet tells the story of how he was inspired to write his novel, *L'Arlesienne*, when he heard a distant, poignant woman's voice calling the name 'Frédéric' one evening across the fields. The testimony of a sentimental and intuitive writer helps us to understand the workings of intuitive creativity; one small event may give rise to a whole world of resonances which are only perceptible to the artist himself, which he then proceeds to develop and organise in his work, sometimes guiding his characters and sometimes being guided by them as if he were the prisoner of his own creation.

Mystics or visionaries who communicate with God or with the beyond may sometimes receive revelations which are only valid for themselves. When no rational function counterbalances their intuition they may become victims of their hallucinations or their dreams. They are often considered to be excitable or of unsound mind by more ordinary people who rely on common sense.

Whether he is an artist, a visionary, or simply a harmless dreamer, the Introverted Intuitive is the most impractical and the least resourceful of all the character types. He does not suffer unduly from the insolvency often caused by his inability to cope with life because he does not care much for worldly things. He may even forget the existence of his own body and neglect its needs. But this body of which he is so disdainful, sometimes takes its revenge, and he may be overwhelmed by sudden and incomprehensible instinctual excesses. These are the uncontrollable volcanic eruptions of the inferior function (in the Intuitive's case the Sensation function), which, contained, acts directly and independently through the unconscious.

*   *   *

The student who has just read these brief portraits has certainly recognised several acquaintances to whom they seem to apply. However, in order to recognise more complex characters it may be necessary to take elements from two, three, or even from all four of the character types into account. This is because absolutely pure character types are very rare. Those defined by characterology are in fact theoretical compounds of tendencies, bearing the same relationship to living characters as caricatures to reality; mere prototypes which help us to understand the mental mechanisms of various characters. In real life the individual is usually situated at the crossroads of several types, with however, a

predilection for certain attitudes and ways of reacting which
enable one to relate him to such and such a group with which
he has much in common, even if he does not possess all its
characteristics.

It would also be unrealistic to try and find a perfect
correlation between Heymans-Le Senne's and Jung's typolo-
gies. Their respective points of view correspond to different
aspects and levels of the psyche. Le Senne says that the Dutch-
French method of characterology is 'on the borderline of the
organic and the mental', that is, at the lowest level of
psychological life, and that its subsequent development
depends on investigation and deduction. The three constituent
factors which form the basis of his classification, Emotivity,
Activity and Responsiveness, are, in fact, common both to
human beings and to animals. Jung's study of the psychic
functions enables us to acquire understanding at a higher level
of human evolution.

Combining the information provided by both methods will
help us to differentiate between individuals of the same basic
temperament. For example, we may consider a group of
individuals of the Nervous Character. The behaviour of each
member of this group will be oriented towards a zone of
interest determined by his or her main psychic function,
whether it is Thinking, Intuition, Feeling or Sensation, but at
the same time the individual will retain those characterics
common to the Nervous Character — inconstancy, spontaneity, restlessness, inactivity, etc.

*The art of the graphologist consists in being able to pick out
the predominant tendencies among all those which reveal
themselves in a handwriting, in understanding the play of forces
which create either strength or conflict within an individual, in
assessing the unifying power of the Self which either dictates
these forces or is unable to co-ordinate them: in a word, in being
able to understand what constitutes the richness or the poverty,
the balance or the imbalance of an individual, and in
discovering the why and wherefore of his or her particular state
of being.*

LESSON 3

1. The History of Graphology

The first known graphologist was Camillo Baldi who, in 1622, published a short book entitled *The Means of Recognising the Habits and Qualities of a Writer from his Handwriting*. His work, which was a collection of random observations, remained virtually unnoticed.

At the beginning of the nineteenth century the German, Lavater and the Frenchmen, Edouard Hocquart and Abbé Flandrin developed the art of interpreting handwriting. However, it was only in the second half of the last century that the true doyen of graphology, Abbé Michon, appeared on the scene. His first works, *The Mystery of Handwriting* (1870), *Graphology, or the Art of Understanding People from their Handwriting* (1872), and then *A System for Graphology* (1875), all of which laid the foundations for this new science, enjoyed considerable success.

Michon's system was attractive because of its very simplicity. The author studied the following elements of handwriting in their different aspects: the i-dots, the stroke, the letters, the words, the baseline, paragraphs, free movements (t-bars), flourishes, punctuation, paraphs.

A fixed sign, that is, a constantly repeated feature of the handwriting (thinness or thickness, firmness or softness, angularity or roundness) corresponded, according to Michon, to a particular character trait. His interpretations are, to a great extent, the basis of modern graphological interpretations.

A further element in his system was the negative sign. For Michon, 'the absence of a sign was a positive indication of the presence of the opposite quality'. For example, the absence of a sign for kindness implied unkindness in the writer's personality.

Michon's successors, in particular Crépieux-Jamin, disagreed with this theory and also with the practice of attributing rigid interpretations to single signs.

Crépieux-Jamin (1859-1940), the uncontested leader of French graphologists, relying heavily on Michon's works, which he expanded with his own research, did for graphology what Linné did for botany. He defined all the different elements or signs *(1)* to be found in handwriting and divided them into 7 categories with 175 species. The seven categories are:

Dimension	*Form*	
Pressure	*Speed*	
Direction	*Layout*	*Continuity.*

---

(1) The term 'sign', which is used in place of the word 'species' seems badly chosen. We would rather talk of aspects of the writing but the word 'sign' is already established and therefore we have to use it. The student must understand what is meant by sign, species or general aspect: e.g. large, small, round, thick, meagre writing etc. A Particular Sign is only an accidental aspect (the bizarre form of a letter, an isolated small hook etc). When a Particular Sign is repeated, for example regressive hooks at the end of words, needle pointed t-bars etc., they become a general sign and constitute a species. For example, left tending hooks are known as the regressive species. One must only take account of a sign when it is repeated. An isolated sign may be a slip of the pen, a wrong movement, momentary fatigue etc. and tell us nothing about the character.

To every species Crépieux-Jamin attributed a range of possible meanings, insisting that the value of any given sign is not fixed and that its significance and interpretion can vary depending on the other features in the writing. This theory is supported by all graphologists: thick (species) handwriting for example, in conjunction with a clear layout, harmonious forms, and well maintained direction will indicate a sensuality and warmth of feelings. But together with muddy, ink filled letters, poorly maintained direction of letters and baseline, inordinately large, vulgar formations this same pressured handwriting will have a very negative significance and will probably indicate the writer's total abandonment to his instinctual drives.

As we can see from the above, thickness of the penstroke reveals, in both cases, a strong sensuality, but the adjoining signs in the two types of handwriting allow us to vary the interpretations which are vastly different and show greatly differing personalities of the writers.

It should never be forgotten that: before interpreting a sign one must always take account of all the other features in the handwriting.

Crépieux-Jamin and Michon both sought to discover clues to the writer's behaviour in features of his handwriting, the exterior manifestations of character which they evaluated positively or negatively according to moralist tradition. These positive and negative qualities were often only the result of more deeply rooted tendencies than the psychology of the day could reach. Michon, for example, believed that an initial loop on a capital 'M' was a sign of talkativeness, whereas we now recognize it is a symptom of extraversion, and an urge on the writer's part to exteriorise his thoughts in ways other than just abuse of the power of speech.

The German graphologists (Preyer, Meyer and Klages) as well as the Swiss graphologist, Pulver, made greater attempts than their predecessors to understand the inner, psychological causes of graphic movements. They were able to draw on a more highly developed understanding of a psychology and

characterology which attempted to penetrate to the very
source of the human personality.

The findings of modern graphologists do, with some slight
variations, agree with the interpretation of handwriting
features reached by Michon and Crépieux-Jamin. Klages, who
developed the concept of the expressive value of movement
and Pulver, who combined the significance of letter formations and the direction of handwriting with the Symbolism of
Space, both may be said to have rediscovered what the first
graphologists knew instinctively. Furthermore, modern
graphologists who attempt to explain graphic movements, find
themselves in almost total agreement with those psychologists
who try to understand the workings of the human mind and its
exterior manifestations.

There is no doubt about the value of graphology, but one
must discuss its limits. It would be presumptuous in the
present state of our knowledge, for example, to expect to find
physical illness or deformities, as some people claim. The
success of some graphologists in this area says more about
clairvoyance and chance than about scientific graphology. To
work backwards from a written movement to the mind of the
writer is to work backwards from the effect to the cause. There
can only be a logical connection between the two and it is
these connections we are about to study.

2. The Basis for Interpreting Graphic Movement

The Symbolism of Space (Zones and Directions)

What is handwriting?

For the graphologist, handwriting is a physical act and one which is only mastered after several years of practice.

Experience has shown us that a man reveals himself in what he does — from his simplest gesture to his most accomplished task. Our gestures do not only obey our intentions and desires of the moment but are the result of a combination of conscious and unconscious inner forces which constitute the essence of our being.

The shrewd observer can tell much about a person's psychological make-up from the way he raises his hat, from his walk, how he holds his pipe or cigarette, and many other apparently insignificant actions which nevertheless reveal a person's psychological make-up.

But such mannerisms are fugitive and last for a fleeting moment and then are lost, whereas the movements produced by the pen leave an ink-trail which records even the minutest gesture or movement. *'Handwriting'* said Pierre Janet with considerable justification, *'is an act which leaves its own print-out. It is the film record of the writer's sensibilities'*.

Every act reveals the relationship between the individual and the outside world. The moment the writer places his pen on the paper he comes into contact with the universe represented by the blank page. In this universe the roads and invisible landmarks are already marked: they are the form, dimension, slant, the baseline and margins such as they were taught in school. This school model, of course, may vary according to nationality and educational background, but an experienced graphologist should be able to recognise immediately:

— *The English of Rollin* (fig. 1), now used even in primary schools
— *Sacré Coeur* (figs. 2, 3) which used to be taught in convents
— *Simple script,* in use in certain British schools and to some extent in French local state schools.

No matter what style of writing a person is taught at school he will always modify it according to his own temperament. One person may increase the general movement towards the right, whereas somebody else may rein in the handwriting with movements tending towards the left. Some writers project their writing away from themselves and develop the upper zone, whereas others prefer to emphasise the lower zone area. Some handwriting spreads out and occupies more space than is taught in the copy book. On the other hand, some writers, who are more timid, produce a handwriting which occupies as little space as possible. Even the speed of progress across the page differs from one writer to another — some writing is slow and heavy and some seems to fly from one end of the line to the other.

Let us try to explain the significance of these deviations from the copy book in terms of character.

In European handwriting which progresses across the page from left to right, the left represents the origin of action and the right, the destination or goal. At whichever point we stop the pen, everything which is on its left represents actions already committed and, therefore, the past. Everything to the right of the pen represents actions still to be completed and, by extension, the future. In the same way the left, the origin of actions, represents the writer himself from whom movements originate and everything on the right symbolises the exterior world or whatever he is striving towards.

Consequently all movement which accentuates or exaggerates the direction of the handwriting towards the right reveals a need on the part of the writer to exteriorise his thoughts and to move towards other people. In fact very progressive handwriting (figs. 5, 6) belong to extraverted personalities, dominated by a taste for action, a spirit of enterprise, confidence in the future and an interest in the external world.

On the contrary, all movements which slow the handwriting down or contain penstrokes which move to the left when they should move to the right, are introvert and reveal egocentrism (fig. 7), difficulties in 'forgetting oneself', attachment to the past, taste for introspection and meditation, as well as a dislike of external action (fig. 8).

Irrespective of whether the handwriting dashes towards the right or retreats to the left it can also, with the symbolically unlimited space of the page, tend towards the top (fig. 9) or stay near the bottom (fig. 10), depending on subconsciously obeyed imagery.

Man has always, in effect, thought of himself as the centre of the world and represents his environment as:

Above him: Heaven, authority (spiritual and temporal), power, grandeur, free air or the spirit, which liberated from matter, rises or becomes dissipated.

Below him: Earth, the eternal symbol of life and power, the source of hidden treasures mentioned in legends, the source of material riches, carnal pleasures and the domain of instincts.

The middle: The Ego with its content of impressions, emotions, its capacity for joy and suffering, the self amidst other people and in daily life.

Depending on how our interests are orientated to one or other of these regions our handwriting movements will be directed naturally towards the relevant area. 'When one defines the inclination of movement' said Bergson, 'one is not speaking metaphorically. In the presence of several pleasures conceived by the intelligence our body orientates itself spontaneously towards the area of preference.' The frequency with which we allow certain tendencies to appear, and give rein to aspirations, influences the general direction of physical movements and dictates directions and formations over which we have little conscious control. *These movements, whether conscious or not, are recorded by the handwriting faithfully and can be interpreted by the graphologist.*

From the very beginnings of graphology it has been recognised that ambition, enthusiasm, zeal, exaltation and pride manifest themselves in the *Upper Zone* of the handwriting (the upper extensions and capital letters).

On the contrary, the power of vital instincts, motivation and materialistic tendencies is shown by greater development of the *Lower Zone* (the lower extensions) and by a tendency for movements towards the area below the baseline.

The development of the *Middle Zone* (that is the area occupied by letters without upper or lower extensions) is, as we will see in the chapter on dimension, relative to the writer's emotional make-up and his social awareness (fig. ll).

Movements which shoot off to the *right and upwards*, show independence, courage, an unwillingness to be fettered, indiscipline, insurrection. Movements towards the *right and downwards*, show dumb obstinacy, sometimes pessimism and discouragement.

If the movements veer to the *left and upwards*, they reveal a contradictory nature, restive obstinacy and inhibition of desires. Towards the *left and downwards*, they show egoism and a desire to monopolise.

The diagram opposite shows the zones and directions where our principal tendencies are indicated. This picture is not complete, but it shows the direction and interests associated with it.

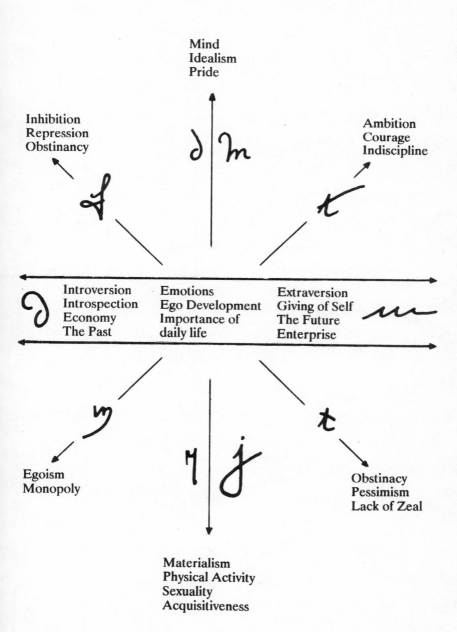

LESSON 4

1. Preliminary Advice for the Study of Handwriting

Materials

The equipment needed by the graphologist is very simple: a good magnifying glass, a centimetre ruler and a transparent protractor are all that are needed for an examination of a sample of handwriting.

Choice of Documents

The best documents for analysis are those which have been written spontaneously under normal conditions. It is as difficult to analyse the character of somebody who has disguised his handwriting as it is to get a clear idea of what a person looks like from a photo in which he is pulling a face.

Michon recommended that every graphological report should
start with the words 'If this handwriting is truly that of this
person and has not been disguised or altered, but is his
spontaneous and usual style, then it shows us that . . . ' We no
longer adhere to the formula, but nevertheless we should not
forget its underlying idea.

In addition to deliberate disguise, there are other causes
which can alter the appearance of handwriting: a poor pen, a
spongy paper, an uncomfortable sitting position. Cold will
reduce the size of handwriting, emotions can increase the
irregularities and fatigue can reduce the tension of the stroke.
There are also writers of a sensitive nature whose handwriting
varies from day to day and only by examining several samples
of their writing can the permanent characteristics of their
writing be determined.

When we are dealing with a very irregular handwriting
which seems to have been written in a hurry or in adverse
conditions it is wise to ask for additional samples. The same
applies if the handwriting appears particularly constrained or
if the writer may have deliberately altered his style.

All graphologists have always insisted on the necessity of a
reasonable amount of documentation. Sometimes, however, it
does happen that the person seeking an analysis can only
produce a single, small sample of writing. In such cases, the
graphologist should decline to do an analysis or express
serious reservations about any conclusions he makes. *The
absolute minimum should always be a signed letter and its
envelope*. The former reveals the writer's real self and the
envelope, destined to be read by a third party, will reveal the
face which the writer shows in society.

Rough copies can serve as supplementary documents, but
the graphologist should guard against attempting a full
analysis based on hastily produced scrawls. Writing found on
invoices and bills is often abbreviated, impersonal and it does
not allow free expression on the part of the writer.

It is certainly possible to say quite a lot about an individual's
character after examining a single line of his writing. But if we

are attempting to capture the whole personality, then it is wise to obtain the greatest possible number of graphological indicators. In this respect the layout, the signature, the differences which frequently occur within the handwriting between the beginning and the end are all sources of information far too important for the serious graphologist to ignore.

A letter submitted for analysis must be written *in ink*. In fact, all samples written in pencil should be refused and those written in ball point should be approached with caution. The ball point is too liable to produce extra pastosity due solely to an irregular ink flow. Accurate assessments can be made on the basis of form, dimension and slant, when a sample has been written in biro, but definite assessments of pressure should be reserved for samples written in fountain-pen as it alone is capable of registering all the nuances of pressure.

The Graphological Analysis

How should a graphologist approach an analysis?

1 — *General impression*. He should examine the sample passively, so that the writing will speak to him. General first impressions should be noted down.

2 — *Form Level*. An evaluation of the Form Level should be made.

3 — *Definition*. All the features of the writing should be noted down in order of decreasing importance, that is to say beginning with the most striking features and progressing to the particular signs and those of least importance. This *list* is known as the *Definition*.

4 — *Interpretation*. Opposite each feature the most probable interpretation should be entered, always keeping the writing as a whole in mind.

5 — *Profile*. He drafts the profile,

During this course we will return to these various stages.
But first we have to:
- learn to appreciate the overall quality of the handwriting
- study all the graphic features and the character traits they reveal.

2. Evaluation of Form Level

As the value of any feature depends on the overall picture of the handwriting it is essential to be able to evaluate the quality of the writing at first glance. When we are reading a letter we can sense immediately whether or not the text was written by a child or an adult, by an educated person or an illiterate. We can tell, by the command of language, if the writer is capable or incapable of expressing his thoughts well. Ease or awkwardness, maturity or childishness are revealed through the linguistic style.

The actual handwriting though also has a *style* of its own which is made up of the elegance or otherwise of the letters and the grouping of words and lines on a page. This style does not only address itself to our intelligence but also to our eye, our taste and our aesthetic sensitivity. When we say, 'Oh, what beautiful writing!' we are making a value judgement of a personal style. It is on this style that the Form Level depends.

What is 'beautiful' handwriting to the layman is not necessarily so to the graphologist. The graphologist's eye needs to be trained by comparison with many other handwritings just as an artist's appreciation becomes more refined through studying and comparing many paintings. A master trains his disciples how and from what angle a picture should be observed and, in the same way, we must learn to evaluate handwriting by considering in turn its degree of:

Organisation
Dynamism
Harmony
Rhythm and Originality.

The Degree of Organisation

Before we make any sort of value judgements concerning a handwriting we must first of all ascertain whether or not it was written under conditions conducive to spontaneity.

Unorganised

When a child begins to write he attempts to imitate the model of instruction as faithfully as possible. While he is forced to fix his attention on the letter formations and word composition his writing will remain awkward, constrained, hesitant and will contain trembling strokes. The term we use for writing at this stage is unorganised (fig. 12 is from a sample written by a six year old child. Notice the twisted strokes, the false connections of the lower zone loops and the 'm' and 'n' of 'maman'. The stroke, although concentrated, shows more or less the same amount of unsteadiness throughout).

As the act of writing becomes more spontaneous the movement of the pen shows fewer stoppages and the strokes, although still not dynamic, show more confidence (fig. 13 written by an eleven year old). It is still too early to make any kind of prognosis concerning the child's future personality: nevertheless, certain dominant traits in his temperament can already be detected.

Organised

Between the ages of 12 and 14 the graphic movement achieves almost total spontaneity. Letter formations and their association within the words now flow quite naturally from the pen. The child thinks less about his writing and more about the thoughts he wishes to express. His writing is freer and more personal. When the writing reaches this stage we call it organised (fig. 14, written by a fourteen year old).

Many individuals, who are illiterate or retarded, never reach this stage and their writing remains unorganised throughout their lives. In such cases there is usually an increase in pressure and overall heaviness. At times we may come across confident or aggresssive strokes which allow us to distinguish it from the timid writing of the very young (fig. 15 is from a sample written by an uneducated man of 20. Note the firmness of the letter 'V' on the first line and the 'f' in 'fautes' in the third line).

Combined

Handwriting continues to evolve as an individual's thinking becomes more organised and developed. The highest level is reached when the writing is combined (figs. 16, 17).

'Combined writing is that in which the formations, connected and simplified to whatever degree, are harmoniously constructed' (Crépieux-Jamin). Such writing depends on fluent simplifications, harmonious unity of the strokes, a variety of suitable movements and, above all, on the choice and appropriateness of the forms of connection, which should differ from those taught in the copy book. This type of writing should not be confused with exaggeratedly connected writing (in which all the letters or all the words are connected). It is originality in the forms of connection which makes for combined writing. There are forms of connection which are showy and exaggerated, which show nothing more than the writer's desire to stand out. Ingenious connections, simplifications which quickly bring together all the elements of the writing, are the best indicators (see fig. 16, the combination of 'a' and 'd' in 'Madame' in the first line, and between 'd' and 'r' of 'voudrais' on the last line). Combined writing, by the cleverness of its movements, is indicative of a *supple and inventive* mind. It is one of the clearest indications of culture and intelligence. However, we must not conclude that the absence of combinations means a lack of intelligence. Louis de Broglie's handwriting (fig. 18) is not combined, but it contains other features indicating intelligence which we will discuss later on.

Disorganised

Finally, age, general debility and weakening of the nervous system all have an effect on the suppleness of our movements and are detrimental to handwriting. Disorganised writing is characterised, depending on the case in question, by weak or very irregular pressure, trembling, breakages, false connections, pastosity in the loops and ovals, general progressive diminishing of the writing, imprecision etc. (figs. 19, 20).

The student should not be afraid of confusing this regressive stage of the writing with the unorganised writing of children, because in the case of sick or old people there is always some evidence present of the former organisation. In fig. 20 we can recognise, despite the breaks, a handwriting which was formerly elegant and simplified. In fig. 19 the word 'de' in the first line, could never have been written by a child, any more than could the first three downstrokes of the word 'interest'.

The main signs of disorganised writing are: *trembles, breakages, fragmentation, shakiness and false connections*, all of which are evidence of a diminution of the faculties and activity of the writer stemming from physical debility or old age. (See the end of the lesson for a recapitulation).

Age and Sex

We cannot ascertain with any degree of accuracy the age or sex of a writer from the degree of organisation or disorganisation in the writing. Some forty year old men are decrepit and many old men preserve much of their youthful vigour. The handwriting reflects the degree of psychic vitality, but not chronological age.

It is the same with sex. Many people are surprised that it is impossible to tell the sex of the writer from a sample of handwriting. Here again, it is the character of the writer which reveals itself in handwriting and many women are quite masculine in their attitudes, just as many men have feminine personality traits. As handwriting reveals character traits, even the most experienced graphologists can be wrong in their attempts to discern sex from handwriting. For this reason, when an analysis is requested, *the graphologist must always be given the age and sex of the writer*. This information will allow him to judge whether or not the handwriting contains the appropriate features for the age and sex of the writer. Good combinations and firm strokes in a young adolescent will indicate a maturity of mind or will power beyond his years. Awkward or infantile formations in a handwriting in which the spelling is correct, indicating a good level of education, will indicate, in a thirty year old man, a childish nature. Signs of disorganisation in a thirty five year old woman's writing will indicate a premature onset of old age or poor physical health. Finally, a firm, precise handwriting in a seventy year old will show great vitality and well preserved faculties.

Dynamism or Inhibition

When we have satisfied ourselves of the ease or otherwise with which the writer handles the pen and ascertained his degree of co-ordination, we should then turn our attention to an assessment of his potential energy.

Dynamism

Strength of character, although often associated with good physical equilibrium, is not necessarily connected with an individual's muscle power. We often see men of powerful athletic build whose handwriting is organised, but inconsistent, and others who look as if the slightest breeze would blow them over, yet have handwriting composed of iron bars! The point here is that what the handwriting reveals is *psychic energy*, and this energy is revealed by *dynamism* (fig. 21) *firmness* and *resoluteness* (fig. 22). Dynamism of character, strong desires and willpower are all exteriorised in gestures charged with intensity.

Inhibition

On the other hand, weakness, apathy and 'softness' are revealed in handwriting which is *soft*, *slow*, *flat* and *without relief* (fig. 23). Hesitation, timidity and fear show up in what we call **inhibited** writing.

Inhibition is more difficult to detect in handwriting because it does not always show up as a weakness (such as in soft or jerky writings as in figs. 23, 24), but rather as a constraining force whose élan is restricted. This élan, it is true, is frequently timid but it can nevertheless be misinterpreted by the novice. Fig. 25, for example, is full of retouching, superfluous strokes and unhealthy hesitation in a character which can, at certain moments, see things on a grand scale. In figs. 26, 27, 28 the inhibition stifles all possibility of expansion.

In order to decide whether or not a handwriting is inhibited, the best thing to do is to follow the movements with a fine pointed instrument. Doing this with figs. 26, 27 and 28 will convey an idea of how constrained and cramped the movements are, whereas in dynamic writings (fig. 21) the movements flow along freely and result in an easy and agreeable fullness.

In the evaluation of the Form Level, inhibition should be considered as a negative quality, as it represents a hindrance to the free development of latent forces. Dynamism, however, is always a positive quality as it reveals freely flowing energy and a good ability to achieve one's aims.

Harmony — Inharmony

The dynamism in a handwriting allows us to arrive at an appreciation of the writer which is *quantitative* but still not *qualitative* because we do not yet know how or to what ends the psychic energy of the writer is directed.

Harmony

It is at this point we should turn our attention to the concept of Harmony. For Crépieux-Jamin harmony was the most favourable sign to detect in a sample of handwriting. He said:

> 'Harmony is comprised of good proportion, clarity and an agreeable balance between all the elements of the writing. Handwritings which are simple, sober, and easy-flowing are the most harmonious and harmony in the handwriting corresponds to that of the character'. (1)

Indeed, nothing could be more logical. Movements recorded by the handwriting are a direct expression of elements of the writer's character and it is clear that harmonious agreement between all the elements in the handwriting reflects a similar association between the component elements of the personality.

The handwriting of the novelist, Jules Claretie (fig. 29), is a pleasing combination of ease, grace and sobriety, all features perfectly in keeping with harmonious handwriting. The prolonged stroke of the 'r' in 'Monsieur' is somewhat excessive, but it is in perfect harmony with the climbing direction of the baselines. It is a sign of graceful élan which bears no resemblance to the aggressive t-bars in fig. 30. Fig. 29 is a well constructed assembly of component elements totally devoid of discordances, but fig. 30 contains sharp points which are immediately noticeable to the extent that we notice almost nothing else.

Inharmony

If we compare fig. 29 with 31 (an English text) we are immediately struck by the discordances of the latter. Violence and cruelty leap out at us from every trait in the writing. As for figs. 32 and 33 they are inharmonious because they are so vulgar.

---

(1) J. CRÉPIEUX-JAMIN – A.B.C. de la Graphologie (Alcan, Ed.)

Harmony in handwriting should be assessed in the same way as one would assess the harmony of a painting which, if it is to be aesthetically pleasing, has to have all its composite elements arranged in a balanced manner. *Disorderly baselines, sudden increases of pressure, enormous loops or vulgar embellishments, disproportions of dimension or spacing* make the finished article look chaotic and charmless.

In the same way that harmonious writing corresponds to harmony of character, writing which is inharmonious, vulgar and discordant reveals an imbalance of personality traits and a lack of harmony between the different areas of the psyche.

Crépieux-Jamin went even further in his interpretation of harmony and inharmony in the writing. He stated: *'Harmony is an indication of general superiority, inharmony is an indication of general inferiority'*.

As has already been pointed out, the master of the French School defined superiority as being of the highest moral value. However, an individual's worth can be measured against a scale of values other than that of civic or social virtues. Many illustrious men had less than harmonious personalities yet we have to recognise them as being 'superior' in some way.

We should really think of harmony as an expression of equilibrium of psychological tendencies and of 'serenity of character'. For an appreciation of other characteristics such as the nuances of personality, creativity, originality etc., Klages introduced yet another concept into graphology — rhythm. *(1)*

Rhythm and Originality

Rhythm is the periodic reproduction of similar phenomena. Examples of rhythm in Nature are the succession of the seasons, the ebb and flow of the tide, the migration of birds,

---

(1) L. KLAGES – *Expression du Caractère dans L'écriture (Delachaux et Niestlé, Ed.)*

the rise and fall of the sap, the rhythmic flow of blood through our veins, inhalation and exhalation of air and the alternation of sleep and wakefulness. These changes of state, which resemble the oscillations of a pendulum, testify by their very continuity to the presence of life. At the very moment when a phenomenon ceases to reproduce itself, life comes to a halt.

The intensity of life which radiates from an individual's personality animates his movements in such a way that his writing will be impregnated with this vital rhythm. *A rhythmic writing is one which flows and which resembles the rising and falling movements of the waves which follow on, one after another, in continuous movement*. A river may subside or be in full flood, it may meander or be a raging torrent but, whatever its state at any given moment, there are no breaks in its continuum. In order for a writing to be rhythmic, therefore, it must appear to be carried along by a kind of flowing movement which animates it, unifies it and gives it its own personal style.

César Franck's writing (fig. 34) offers a magnificent example of rhythmic writing.

It is important not to confuse rhythm with metric rhythm. The rhythmic motion of a pendulum or the tick-tock of a clock are examples of *artificial rhythm*, regulated by man. Natural phenomena are never reproduced with perfect similarity. Our pulse beats with almost imperceptible variations in its rhythm. Could any one of us breathe in perfect time with a metronome? A Chopin Sonata, played with no fluctuations of rhythm, would sound as if it were emanating from a mechanical piano.

Natural rhythm means the repetition of similar, but not identical phenomena, and rhythm in handwriting depends:

1 — *on a balanced distribution* of the writing on the page, a harmonious balance between the width of the margins and the positioning of the text and spacing between words and lines. Too rigorous a layout, margins and paragraphs which are as straight as a die and perfect baselines give a mechanical

appearance to the writing and create an impression of rigid control (figs. 26, 28). Spacing which contains too many irregularities, words which are at times cramped and at times widely spaced out, sudden increases in pressure which attract attention, as in fig. 31, excessive lower extensions (fig. 10) make the writing arhythmic.

Obviously the concept of rhythm in writing is closely allied to that of harmony since any rigidity or discordance detracts from the rhythmic quality. However, a sample of writing may contain elements of disproportion, but still be rhythmic (fig. 34: the 'p' of 'partir' is very large in comparison with the other letters) provided that the disproportions are reproduced in accordance with the writing's own law of renewal and therefore are in keeping with the overall flow.

The rhythmic interchange of the ink-trail and the white background and the homogeneity of the writing correspond to the radiance of the personality and equilibrium of the character.

These qualities are not only found in writers of genius. For example, we see in fig. 35 a rhythm which is absent from figs. 24, 27. It could be argued that the small, fine writing of fig. 35 reveals a level of intellectual development which is greater than that suggested by the other two examples. If we now compare fig. 27 (Je connais parfaitement . . .) with fig. 36 (Les récoltes sont rentrées . . .), we see that both handwritings reveal a modest level of education and an equal attempt to adhere to the school model. We detect, however, far more homogeneity in fig. 36 than in fig. 27. In fig. 36 the vivacity of the small movements forming each letter does not detract from the serenity of the whole. This writing, which belongs to a country dweller, retains a simplicity, sincerity and tranquil ease which we do not see in fig. 27. In this latter sample every capital letter is designed to create maximum effect, whereas the rest of the writing is squeezed, lacking in confidence and completely devoid of signs of ease. The letters seem to clash into each other like the footsteps of a man whose movements lack co-ordination. When the writer succeeds in tracing a graceful letter (as the 'R' in Roumanie) he cannot sustain the effort and the rest of the word slips back into an impersonal and banal style.

We must conclude that the writer of fig. 36 is of a much more balanced personality and, in his simplicity, has greater depth to him than the writer of fig. 27. This writer is capable, on account of his refinement, of creating a temporary illusion which in due course may be recognised as cruel deception.

2 — *on a rhythmic production of original formations.* An aptitude for spontaneous creation implies an ability to reshape, to recreate letter formations in an entirely personal style, either by simplification or transformation (see fig. 29: the 'M' of 'Monsieur', the 'V' of 'Voulez', the 'z' of 'onze' on the last line). But these forms which are so different from the school model are of value only when they are spontaneous. Calligraphic skill in forming perfect capital or small letters suggest inauthentic expression in behaviour (fig. 91 and the last part of the word 'amitié' of fig. 21). The results of the writer's efforts here are more or less ornamental letter formations, but the writing as a whole does not present a succession of unexpected forms which come periodically from chance movements of the pen as in figs. 16, 21, 29, 34, 35, 37.

Originality of letter formations reveals the creative originality of the writer. The more numerous and repetitive the personal forms in a writing sample, the greater is the creative imagination of the writer. One original letter formation repeated from time to time suggests the possibility of occasional flashes of inspiration. But writing such as that of César Franck (fig. 34) which is so personal that it seems to have nothing in common with the school model (yet it remains totally legible) reveals a creative genius of exceptional power.

On the other hand, what are the personal qualities of the writers of figs. 23, 33? The first is content to gently reproduce those forms he was taught. The second, far more dynamic, makes additions to the school model, but in such a manner that they appear heavy and the vulgarity of almost every letter is striking. The lack of taste and moderation in conjunction with such an overbearing ego make for anything but a likeable character.

Fig. 38 is quite devoid of originality, but there is a certain mark of distinction running through the writing as a whole. Here there is a liking for elegance and an idealism which is revealed in the tall upper extensions and the delicate pressure.

Apart from those writings containing originality of form we also come across those which are more or less 'distinct' or more or less 'conventional'. These variations in writing, which can be detected intuitively even by a non-graphologist when he sees a piece of writing for the first time, have to be borne in mind when we evaluate the form level. They form part of the first impression a writing makes on us before we get down to specific considerations.

*   *   *

All the foregoing, in particular the explanations of how to assess rhythm, may appear very complicated to the beginner, but he should not be discouraged. A 'global' appreciation of a writing sample will become easier with experience and as his eye becomes more accustomed to the graphic elements.

We have seen that, besides the degree of organisation in writing, the main criteria which allow us to make an assessment of the overall quality of any writing are: Dynamism, Harmony, Rhythm and the Originality of the letter formations. In some writing the dynamism is the striking feature, whereas in others it is the harmony, and in others the rhythm or degree of originality. In yet others the striking feature may be the exact opposite of these qualities i.e signs of inhibition, weakness of character, inharmony, a lack of rhythm or indications of banality. The vast majority of writings will be slightly above or slightly below an average form level.

It should be obvious that any writing which combines a high degree of dynamism, harmony and rhythm will be classified as high since the writer possesses force of action, equanimity, moral superiority, personal magnetism and creative originality. But these are very rare. Crépieux-Jamin said at the end of his life (he was just over 81 when he died) that, during his long career as a graphologist, he had never encountered more than 10 writings with a high degree of harmony. No student of graphology should be surprised if his files do not contain many examples of 'superior' writings.

The important thing for the beginner is to compare several writings and to learn how to arrange them in hierarchical order, and to classify them. He has to learn to recognise, for example, out of 10 writings, which is the most dynamic, or the most harmonious, or the most banal or the most discordant, or rhythmic. Later on, with more experience, he will be able to tackle the more difficult problem of arranging them in descending order according to an overall assessment of the form level of each.

RECAPITULATION

GRAPHIC FREEDOM

DESCRIPTION	INDICATION
UNORGANISED writing (figs. 12,13,15) Awkward style showing an insufficient degree of spontaneous movement which prevents a detailed character analysis.	The writing of children or uneducated adults.
ORGANISED writing (fig. 14) containing a sufficient level of spontaneity.	Of no significance by itself as regards character, but permits a full analysis.
COMBINED writing (figs. 16, 17) contains ingenious or original connections not taught by the school model.	Intelligence, culture, supple and inventive mind. Speed and originality of thought.

DISORGANISED writing (figs. 19, 20) in which a once organised style has deteriorated through age or illness.

Of no significance as regards the character of the writer but an indication of reduced activity in general.

BROKEN writing (fig. 20) in which letter formations contain small breaks or interruptions.

Great physical debility, exhaustion, old age.

STICK writing (batons) (fig. 39) is that in which the letters are formed with a succession of isolated downstrokes.

Emotivity very strong. Hypersensitivity. Activity slowed down by strong impressionability.

TREMBLING writing (figs. 12, 20) is produced by an unskilled or shaking hand.

Seen in writings of children or old people. Lack of co-ordination, asthenia, fatigue. Also appears when there is a nervous illness present (paralyses) and intoxication.

FALTERING writing (fig. 24) contains fragile strokes and lacks assurance of direction.

Debility, lack of vitality, lack of physical and moral resilience.

TWISTED writing (fig. 40) is that in which the downstrokes of upper and lower extensions show deviations.

Weakness, exhaustion, temporary lack of vitality. Frequently found in the pre-puberty stage (between 9 and 13 years) and during menopause. However this feature may accompany any signs of physical weakness. Fig. 40 was written by a 15 year old girl suffering from tuberculosis. (Another interpretation of TWISTED writing will be given in the chapter on DIRECTION.)

DYNAMISM

DYNAMIC writing (fig. 21) is characterised by élan, fullness and vigorous movement. The stroke is nourished and free of all signs of constraint.

Strong vitality and energy directed to specific goals. Ardour. Euphoria. Love of life. Good health. Activity. Quick thinking. Persuasiveness. Impatience. Infectious enthusiasm.

RESOLUTE writing (fig. 22) contains firm strokes, accelerated speed and good proportions.

Decision, drive, daring. Self-confidence. **With signs of pride:** presumptuousness.

FIRM writing (figs. 18, 33, 37) is more or less angular, resolute with precise strokes and pressure which is regular and maintained to the base of the downstrokes.

Energetic character. An achiever who is not given to outbursts of temper. Will power. Backbone. Suitability for positions of authority. The 'man of action'.

If the writing is also large and angular: courage, self assurance.

With very angular writing: intransigence, stubbornness, resistance to outside influences, brutality.

INHIBITED writing (figs. 25, 26, 27, 28, 39) is characterised by sudden retraction or stopping of the graphic movement. Contortions, restricted movements, squeezed formations, hesitant and suddenly truncated movements.

Feelings of inferiority. Lack of self confidence. Timidity. Nervousness. Irritability. Repressions. Inner tension. Inability to adapt. Anxiety and feelings of confusion.

HESITANT writing (fig. 25) is comprised of movements which lack confidence and decisiveness. Movements which do not progress to the right. T-bars which sometimes curve upwards and lower extensions ending without vigour.

Lack of decision. Timid nature. Hesitation.

When the signs of vacillation are only occasional they indicate a reflective mind, wisdom and consideration of the pros and cons.

WEAK OR PALE writing (figs. 23, 24) contains slow, anaemic strokes which seem to lack boldness. This is noticeable in the curves or an overall lack of vigour.

Lymphatic (Phlegmatic) temperament. Spinelessness, slovenliness, inactivity, laziness, indifference, lack of precision, weakness of will, lack of initiative, apathy, heaviness.

With angular writing: stubbornness through weakness.

With round writing: impressionability.

HARMONY

HARMONIOUS writing (figs. 29, 35) contains proportion, order, clarity, simplicity, sobriety and ease of movement.

Harmony of tendencies. Well balanced character. Sociability.

INHARMONIOUS writing (figs. 31, 32, 33) contains disproportions, discordances, exaggerations, vulgar forms, confusion, complications and coarseness.

Imbalance between tendencies. Vulgar taste and feelings.

RHYTHM AND ORIGINALITY

RHYTHMIC distribution or HOMOGENEOUS (figs. 35, 37) writing shows a good equilibrium between black and white, a harmonious agreement between margins, the text and the spacing.

Harmony and magnetism of the personality, intensity of the psyche. (This should not be confused with organic vitality.) Good co-ordination of energy and abilities.

RHYTHM in the letter formations (fig. 34). Original formations spontaneously reproduced and with continuing rhythm.

Creative imagination. Inventive mind. Capacity for artistic creation.

BANAL writing (fig. 32) is a lifeless copy of the school model.

Lack of personality. Banality. Conformism.

ORIGINAL writing (fig. 16) contains spontaneous deviations from the school model.

Originality of thought and individuality.

LESSON 5

Layout

The Choice of Paper

If we could be sure that the writer had complete freedom of choice in his writing materials every time he jotted down a few lines, the quality and colour of the paper he uses would provide us with a good deal of information concerning his character before we even began to look at the writing itself.

The writer who shows a preference for large pieces of paper and who may even turn the page sideways to gain a greater expanse for progression towards the right, expresses drive, a spirit of enterprise and a greater degree of confidence than the person who carefully folds the paper in two or even in four. Expansive personalities need space to breathe and plenty of room in order to feel at ease. Economical people, on the other hand, frequently experience a kind of vertigo when confronted with open spaces and prefer to direct their activity towards predetermined set goals. They need a framework which is in keeping with their immediate needs. A small-sized page, however, does not necessarily exclude ambition, but the ambition of such people proceeds in stages rather than from an initial burst of enthusiasm towards a distant goal.

Sometimes a writer will show a preference for lined paper, and this can be very significant from a psychological point of view. The lines and grid pattern of Continental notepaper undoubtedly make the writing look unattractive and to prefer such paper to the virginal clarity of unlined paper reveals a strong need for support and guidance. The choice of ruled paper, furthermore, reveals a tendency to follow entrenched habits and to rely on well-established principles. The spirit of submission, self discipline, and a lack of improvisation and personal initiative are character traits generally attributable to writers who habitually opt for lined paper.

Writers also exercise a choice over the actual texture of the paper. Combative individuals, always seeking to gratify their desire for conquest, prefer slightly embossed paper which offers some resistance to the pen, and avoid soft or 'slippery' paper. Gentle, indolent, passive or superficial people prefer smooth surfaces over which the pen can move without effort. This is a preference which may also be shared by people in a hurry, impatient, or nervous, who cannot tolerate any delay in putting their thoughts into action or in satisfying their wishes.

The colour of the paper, also, should not be overlooked. It is a known fact that sensitivity to colours is directly connected to a person's emotionality. If women tend to use coloured writing paper far more than men it is because the softness of a coloured background reflects their sensitive souls. A cold man prefers a white background. A sensitive man who is afraid of appearing effeminate by choosing blue notepaper, for example, may betray his gentle nature by choosing very pale grey or light yellow.

Some people are as careful about choosing their notepaper as they are about choosing a new tie or pair of gloves. Others always write on scrappy bits of paper torn from the first pad which comes to hand without the slightest concern for the person who will be the recipient of it. A person who conducts himself in his correspondence in this manner will reveal the same attitudes in his everyday dealings with others. Respect for oneself and for others, taste, attention to detail, courtesy and manners, as well as negligence, rudeness, and inattention to detail all reveal themselves in our most insignificant actions. Whether or not a writer has taken the trouble to smooth off the jagged edges from a piece of paper torn roughly from a pad will be of importance to the graphologist.

The above indicators are of psychological rather than graphological significance, but they can nevertheless be of considerable assistance to a graphologist because they can often confirm indications seen in the writing. They should never be considered in isolation as they are only *secondary indicators* which should only be considered when they are constant. Conclusions concerning writing material can only be made over a considerable period of time when there is absolutely no room for doubt that the pen, paper etc. represent a personal choice or habit and are not the result of circumstances or what was available at the time.

Layout of the Text

When confronted by a sheet of paper of whatever size, shape or colour, what does the writer do? How does he occupy that part of the universe which is, for the moment, his domain? Some writers will invade every inch of space, but the majority will use margins and their shape, size and position on the paper will provide the graphologist with interesting information.

Invading
Among 'invading' writings which cover the whole page with no right or left margin, we must distinguish between:

— those which progress in extended movements right across the page (diagram 1 in 'Recapitulation') exploring the

available space, or gathering it up. Such writings belong to
expansive individuals who are both extravagant and mono-
polistic, whose presence, personal life story and Ego puts
everbody else into the shade. They can also be overbearing
and make exhausting demands on others. For all that they
can be generous and hospitable, sympathetic, extravert
with an ease of social contact. They can be at home
anywhere, can put others at their ease and cheer them up
with their infectious vitality and
— those which crawl across the white surface in tiny little
movements, using up all the available space (diagram 2).
These writings are every bit as invading as those described
above, but they show a meanness or pettiness in the writer.
People who write in this manner are determined to profit
from everything and everyone: from friends, influence,
pieces of junk, bits of string. Like indefatigable rodents
these people will find a use for virtually anything. Fig. 41 is
an extract from Léon Bloy's 'Letters to his fiancée' (Stock.
Ed.) in which the author himself admits 'I could call
anybody who would give me money my friend'.

Whether the writing is large or small, the act of 'invading'
the whole page and covering it with writing from edge to edge
shows, in all cases, expansion of the personality and a need for
change. The writer, feeling cramped within the confines of his
own four walls, will knock at his neighbour's door, talk about
himself and try to win a sympathetic hearing by expressing his
opinions, even when they have not been asked for. The
dividing line between his world and that of others is not clearly
defined in his mind. He can easily overstep the realm of his
authority or property without any feelings of embarrassment,
because he lacks a sense of proportion and discretion.

Typographic
It is quite a different story, however, if the text is framed
with careful margins, particularly if the right hand margin is
noticeable. (See diagram 3). A certain control of graphic

movements is necessary if the text is to be firmly fixed in the centre of the page. In such cases the writer seems to withdraw onto his own little islet. He maintains a distance between himself and others, a distance guaranteed by the strip of white paper. This type of layout is particularly noticeable in the writing of hypersensitive introverts who are repelled by the promiscuity of their fellow men and strive to protect their own retreat and inner life. There is a certain aristocratic spirituality associated with those writings framed by large margins, which is why such a layout is often favoured by poets, artists and literati who transport the typographical order of the printed page to their own writing.

The Margins

Invading, and typographical layout are, in reality, rather rare. Convention dictates that we leave a margin at the top and on the left when we write a letter. In official correspondence the custom is to increase the margins in accordance with the relative importance of the recipient's position. To reduce the margins to such an extent that they virtually cease to exist is to exhibit a disrespect of formalities and an insensitivity to any hierarchy. An attentive respect for margins, on the other hand, is indicative of the writer's respect for established conventions and of his own ability to conform.

It is also usual for the writer to turn over the page before he reaches the very bottom of the paper. But the impulsive writer, driven by his feelings, does not let go easily. What he has to say or do is more important to him than obedience to conventions. His enthusiasm is too great to be contained by the size of the page and it is all he can do not to finish on the table what he began writing on the paper! This overspilling into the space on the right and at the bottom of the page is a sign of an ardent, impulsive or passionate nature. Carried away with their own enthusiasm these writers rush into action or towards any object that attracts them and only apply the brakes at the last moment in order to keep to the line, i.e. exercise prudence or consideration for the rules (diagram 4).

The writer who is cautious, sensible or pusillanimous, on the other hand, keeps a safe distance between himself and the unknown. He always stops himself before reaching the edge. This same cautious movement also occasionally causes him to begin each new line a little further to the left, making his left margin decrease in width (diagram 5). This characteristic is typical of mistrustful, reserved people who dislike taking risks and who are constantly on the defensive, whereas impulsive or overactive people begin every line a little further to the right than the preceding one, producing a left margin which gets progressively larger (diagram 6).

The Spacing

Quite independently of the form and dimension of the margins we often come across texts in which the words are distributed over the page like seeds in a well planned plot of land (fig. 42). The writer dominates the area without getting lost in it or spreading out all over it. Each letter sits comfortably in the vicinity of its neighbour, and the air circulates between the lines. Such writing is termed *aerated*, and suggests an ability on the part of the writer to overcome problems, to view matters dispassionately and in perspective without allowing his personal feelings to affect his judgement. The writer views the world objectively from the sidelines and can grasp essentials without getting bogged down by superfluous detail. He faces up to reality with a clear mind or even, at times the cold over-simplification conferred on him by keen intelligence and a well developed Thinking function. He will generally be a man of few words because he is predominantly interested in ideas. Impressions and sensations which are of such importance to sentimental natures are of little concern to him. He takes a broad view of the universe, judges events from a universal standpoint and for their long-term implications. The general, for him, is more important than the particular and this bestows an air of personal authority on him, making him suitable for command.

Exaggerated spaces between words and lines produces *spaced out* writing (fig. 45). In this type of layout the writer loses contact more and more with life as he proceeds towards a world of abstraction. Spaced-out writing, particularly when vertical, denotes a cold, distant and reserved character.

We must not, however, interpret in the same way those spaced out writings produced through lack of skill by, for example, a child or illiterate adult. Widely spaced words in an unorganised writing is a sign of intellectual impoverishment and defects of co-ordination.

Compact writing, containing letters, words and lines cramped close together (fig. 41) belongs to spontaneous, impulsive individuals who are far more dependent on the outside world than the people described above. They 'cling', so to speak, to those things whose minor details hold their attention. Usually talkative, they give the impression that they are afraid of not having enough space to accommodate all the words flowing from their pen. They are indiscriminate and reveal to all and sundry the content of their minds or hearts without stopping to consider or to weigh up what would be best left unsaid. Less capable of restraint than people with aerated writing, they are more biased and frequently blinded by personal feelings, envy or jealousy when exercising their judgement. But they can be passionately attached to those they love as they can also be to their belongings.

In some writings we find that the spacing between the words is normal *but between the lines it is compressed* (fig. 43). If we accept that the baseline represents everyday reality whereas the page itself symbolises abstract reality in a time/space continuum, we may conclude that the writer can cope with the problems of everyday living, but lacks the breadth of vision necessary to raise him above the pots and pans of the daily grind.

Order and Disorder

The layout of the writing on the page, considered as a whole, can create an impression of order or disorder.

An orderly writing, in which the lines and paragraphs are well arranged and everything fits together in a way which will assist the legibility and comprehension of the text, is an indication of a clear mind and a faculty for organisation. A few slight irregularities of spacing will not affect this interpretation; in fact, quite the contrary. If order is based on absolute rigidity it is seen as an absence of flexibility and adaptability and may indicate an obsessive concern with tidiness.

There are two aspects of *disorderliness* to be considered. There is *active disorder* which contains vehement, excessive or precipitated movements of the pen (fig. 21), revealing hasty or unco-ordinated activity, and *passive disorder* in which all the movements are slower and more flabby. Badly formed, incomplete words, uncontrolled baselines, large and randomly produced gaps which serve no specific purpose are an indication of carelessness, negligence and lack of foresight (fig. 24).

A *confused layout*, such as that in fig. 44, is a sign of a confused mind.

Mental illnesses frequently manifest themselves in writing by unco-ordinated layout, sentences grouped together in all four corners of the page, and the repetition of words or syllables. We must point out here that Graphology, at its present stage of development, cannot provide conclusive diagnoses on the mental state of a writer. *(1)* Perfectly formed, careful and regular writing can often be produced by people who are mentally disturbed, and the writing of many mentally healthy people can be so shocking at times that it resembles the scribblings of an idiot. What we can detect in any writing, including that of the mentally deranged, is the writer's

---

(1) Translator's note: In 1956, when the book was written.

personality, but we cannot determine his pathological state.
No matter how discordant a writing may seem to be, as long as
the text remains coherent we can detect any imbalance of
tendencies, but we cannot specify mental ailments. An
individual may be somewhat unbalanced in his behaviour, but
that does not necessarily mean that he has lost his reason.

The Address

The layout of the address on the envelope should be
interpreted in the same way as the layout of the text on the
paper.

An address which covers the whole envelope reveals an
obtrusive personality who has little consideration for others.

An address which is cramped together in the middle of the
envelope and surrounded by a vast expanse of white indicates
voluntary isolation and a withdrawn personality.

If the address is placed very near the top edge of the
envelope, with pen strokes shooting upwards, it is an
indication of idealism. When positioned very low on the
envelope, and accompanied by heavy pressure or long lower
zone projections, it should be considered as an indication of
materialism.

The address in the left half of the envelope shows prudent
reserve and, at the same time, a certain distance the writer
likes to maintain between himself and others. If it is pushed
over towards the right it is an indication of extraversion,
spontaneous communication with others and/or hyperactivity.

The overall layout of a sample of writing can confirm or help
to determine the significance of indications seen in the writing.
But here again, the reader should be warned of the dangers of
making fragmentary interpretations. One should never, for
example, draw any definite conclusions from the width of the
margins alone. The size of a sheet of paper may make a writer
condense his writing or overshoot the margins. Before any
conclusions can be drawn the graphologist must examine the

writing itself and decide whether or not it is narrow and cramped or, on the other hand, if the writer feels restricted writing on a piece of paper which is too small for him. In the latter case, another sample should be asked for.

To be able to vary the layout and size of one's writing in accordance with the writing area at his disposal is a sign of flexibility and adaptability.

To make alterations for no reason, on the other hand, reveals a degree of instability, a need for change and a possibily idiosyncratic nature.

RECAPITULATION

DESCRIPTION

INDICATION

INVADING writing (diag. 1) Without margins. The text covers the whole page.

With large writing or with extensive movements: Extraversion. Generosity. Hospitality. Prodigality. Taste for luxury. Great materialistic demands.

(diag. 2).

With compact writing: Extraversion. Communicative nature. Curiosity. Intrusiveness. Lack of tact. Profiteering nature. Egoism. Overbearing personality.

TYPOGRAPHIC LAYOUT (diag. 3) Text positioned in the middle of the page preserving surrounding margins.

Search for isolation. Introversion. Discretion. Coldness. Independence of mind. Aesthetic sense. Culture. Feelings of one's own worth. (See also the right margin.)

ORDERLY LAYOUT

Order, method, punctuality. Respect for conventions. Politeness.

DISORDERLY LAYOUT (fig. 21)

With lively, vehement movements: Impulsivity and uncontrolled activity.

(fig. 24)

With weak or pale writing: Carelessness. Lack of foresight.

CONFUSED OR INCOHERENT
(fig.44)

Confused mind. Lack of organisational ability.

AERATED writing (fig. 42) Good distribution of black and white between words and the lines.

Intelligence. Clarity of mind. Objectivity. Loftiness of vision. Independent judgement. Spirit of synthesis.

COMPACT writing (fig. 41) Cramped within the words and between the lines.

Impulsivity. Spontaneity. Talkativeness. Lack of reserve. Concentration. Attentiveness. Memory for detail. Subjectivity. Egoism. Partiality. Narrow mindedness. Pedantry. Parsimony.

SPACED OUT writing (fig. 45) with large spaces between words and lines.

Lack of spontaneity. Tendency towards isolation. Introversion. Timidity. Critical mind. **With vertical, narrow and sober writing:** Coldness. Fear of life.

WORDS SPACED OUT (diag. 7) but no margins.

Independence of character. Need for space and solitude. The writer distances himself from others and shows little consideration for them. Prodigality.
With a low form standard: Poverty of the mind. Exaggeration. Spendthrift tendencies. Slackness of character.

WORDS NORMALLY SPACED (fig.43) but lines crowded.

Writer copes with day-to-day affairs but lacks loftiness of vision.

VERY IRREGULAR SPACING (fig. 24)

Instability of thought and feelings. Lack of concentration.

MARGINS

LEFT:

BROAD

Generosity. Spontaneity. Extraversion.
With good layout: Respect for conventions.

TOO BROAD (diag. 8)

Bad taste. Extraversion taken to excess. The writer seeks refuge in extravert activity.

NARROW

With full writing: Familiarity. 'Bonhomie'. Laxity of manners. **With compact writing:** Economy.

INCREASING (diag. 6)

Impulsiveness. Vivacity. Hyperactivity. Tendency to overspend. Haste. Generosity. Extraversion. Impatience. Enthusiasm.

DECREASING (diag. 5)

Prudence. Distrust. Suspicion. Fear.

REGULAR

Order and self-discipline

IRREGULAR (diag. 9)

Lack of order and discipline. Sense of fun.

RIGHT:

BROAD (diag. 3)

Introversion. Reserve. Fear of the future. Little entrepreneurial spirit. Hypersensitivity. Impressionability. Desire to keep others at a distance. Pessimism. Restless mind.

NON-EXISTENT (diag. 4) Words reach the right-hand edge of the paper.

Extraversion. Vitality. Courage to face life. Verbosity. Need for social contact. Precipitate activity. Lack of foresight.

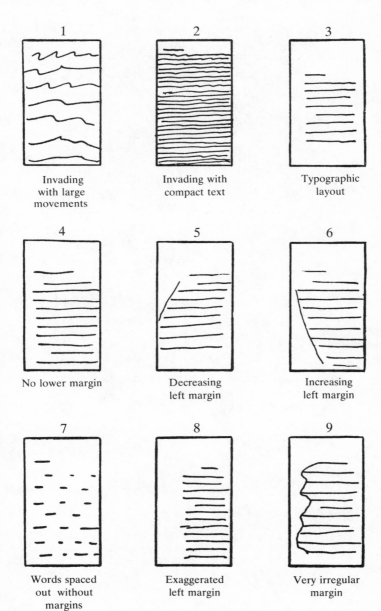

1
Invading
with large
movements

2
Invading with
compact text

3
Typographic
layout

4
No lower margin

5
Decreasing
left margin

6
Increasing
left margin

7
Words spaced
out without
margins

8
Exaggerated
left margin

9
Very irregular
margin

LESSON 6

Irregularity and Regularity

All modern systems of teaching handwriting insist on, among other things, regularity of the size of letters and parallel downstrokes.

However, as we saw when we were dealing with rhythm in writing, no natural phenomenon is ever repeated with absolute regularity. A well regulated machine can reproduce perfectly identical articles, but any living movement which repeats itself always introduces variations, however slight, on the preceding one.

Why is it that human movements can never occur with the absolute regularity of a clock? Basically, because the rhythm of our bodily functions (respiratory, circulatory etc.) has an effect on all our movements, whether they are voluntary or involuntary.

Human beings are endowed with a sensitivity and emotivity which machines do not possess. As soon as we awake from the unconscious state of sleep, we immediately become aware, once again, of those objects which surround us and our sensitivity is there as protection against possible danger and traumas. It stands guard and keeps us permanently in a state of apprehension which identifies with fear.

The philospher insists: 'It cannot be repeated too often that fear is natural to and permanently present in humans. The variations of emotion which we experience are nothing more than variations of fear . . . all living creatures, from the smallest amoeba to the birds of the sky, are in a perpetual state of wariness. Man's first efforts were to guard against fear. Civilisation evolved through people clustering together to protect themselves against fear. It is impossible to suppress fear, but it can be tamed, bit by bit, and eventually turned into a virtue. Prudence may be considered as rationalised fear; activity as agitation co-ordinated by intelligence, and courage as flight into the future.'

In hypersensitive people sensitivity and emotivity manifest themselves in shaking and visible vibration of the whole body. The effect of this is transferred into our writing and can be seen in oscillations of varying importance and frequency, depending on the degree of emotivity in the writer. Emotive people have a more agitated, and more irregular writing than their non-emotive counterparts, with corresponding differences in personality. Knowledge, intelligence, self-discipline and activity reduce or modify the effects of emotivity. On the other hand, emptiness of mind and spirit or the absence of will power leave the whole person at the mercy of his emotions.

Irregularites in writing, therefore, can have many interpretations depending on the signs accompanying them.

An example of the above is provided by a comparison of figs. 46 and 47. Both samples contain considerable irregularities of size. In fig. 46 the 'z' of the word 'veuillez' is disproportionate to the other letters of the same word. In 'serviteur' (last line) the third letter is four or five times smaller than the first. However, despite these discrepancies of proportion, the text remains coherent, homogeneous, rhythmic and similar throughout. The vibrant sensitivity which emanates from this writing is of the type that enriches life and an individual's work. Here we have a fruitful abundance of emotions and impressions.

In fig. 47 the differences in size are perhaps less noticeable than in the previous example, but there is little similarity between the different parts of the writing. These four lines are just about as discordant as possible. Emotivity, in this case, is a disturbing influence on the personality. The writer does not possess the strength of mind to resist the attacks on his nervous system. He is at the mercy of his emotions, impulses, desires and instincts.

Irregularity can affect all the elements of writing: height, width, thickness of stroke, slant etc. For each type of irregularity there is a corresponding zone of interests in which emotivity will be particularly evident.

Irregularity of Height

For example, when the irregularity is in the height of the letters in a writing with a dominant middle zone (the middle zone, as we have already seen, is associated with the writer's emotional tendencies), (figs. 48, 49), it is an indication of sensitive feelings, emotionality and that gift of spontaneous sympathy associated with people of a sentimental nature. With these people, their concern for others is always uppermost in their minds, so it is not surprising that their sensitivity is most evident in anything concerning human relationships: an interest in children, concern for a spouse, friend or neighbour can lead them to exaggerate insignificant details relating to the object of their concern, whereas an event of world-shattering importance may leave them totally unmoved.

Irregularity of Slant

Irregularities of slant frequently go hand-in-hand with the sombre, small, combined writing of a thinker or intuitive person to produce *nuancée writing* (see fig. 50: the writing of Henri Baür, taken from his 'Nouvelles Epitres' and also fig.

51, the writing of a 15-year-old, the winner of many competitions). In writings of this type the emotivity changes direction: interest in people yields to an interest in ideas. Here we are no longer dealing with the primitive sensitivity of an open-hearted person, but a sensitivity which has been intellec-tualised. The writer lives primarily by his intellect, he is attracted by those things that appeal to his mind, logic, intuition or his facility for analytical thought. Rather than trust to his feelings he makes comparisons and orientates himself in the world with the curiosity of a thinker, not through emotional zeal.

Irregularity of Pressure

Irregularities of pressure, which we will examine in greater detail when we study the characteristics of the stroke, are the main indication of differences in energy output. Their presence is indicative of emotional responses on the part of the writer: outbursts of temper, meaningless gestures, over-excitability etc. (fig. 31). They can also be an indication of physical, circulatory or respiratory troubles.

Irregularity of Speed

Irregularities of speed, which will be dealt with in the chapter on speed, indicate irregularity in activity.

A sample of writing may show irregularities in one or more of the above areas, while preserving a high degree of similarity with other samples written by the same person, and without affecting the overall style unity of a sample written at any one time. The samples shown in figs. 46, 50, 51, 52 are more or less constant in their irregularities. It may happen, however, that a person's writing will show considerable variations from one sample to another and sometimes the different parts of the same document will vary considerably in style. In fig. 53, for example, the word 'dirigeant' (2nd line) seems not to have been written by the same person who wrote the word 'pessimiste' (third line). Apart from the missing t-bar in both samples, there is an appreciable difference in the general fluidity of the movement of both. In the word 'dirigeant', the letters pull to the right, and the finishing stroke is an almost aggressive movement. In the word 'pessimiste' however, the pull towards the upper zone affects the breadth of the letters and the finishing stroke is abrupt and inhibited.

Such alterations in the general flow of the writing reflect complete changes in the writer's attitudes. The type of writing which we classify as **unstable** is characteristic of fickle, undisciplined, or versatile individuals whose reactions and behaviour cannot be anticipated. In such writing we find some words which slant to the right alongside others which are perfectly vertical and spacing which can be wide in places and narrow in others. The text may begin with large writing which subsequently becomes small and then reverts to a large size again at the end. We must accept that such variations often occur if the writer wishes to stress some part of the text. In unstable writing the movements fly off in all directions without rhyme or reason and they express in varying degrees, depending on the seriousness of the instability in the writing, inconsistency, mobility of feelings, weakness of concentration or an inability to maintain a logical train of thought.

Writing which is **irregular, unstable or discordant** is the opposite of that which is **calm, regular or monotonous**.

A **calm** writing, in which the writing trail progresses without jerkiness or contortions, with a high degree of regularity in the size of the letters, is an indication of weak emotivity. Fig. 54 provides an example of writing which is both ponderous and regular. The letters are more or less of the same height and width throughout, the i-dots are perfectly round and well placed, and the brackets are symmetrical. The ordered ensemble reminds one of a well regulated life style in which everything is in the right place at the right time. When the writer of writing like this embraces an opinion, espouses a principle or acquires a habit, he keeps to it. Thoughts, feelings and actions are all classified and labelled in tidy compartments where fantasy is denied access.

In *irregular* writing a lively receptivity on the part of the writer to outside stimuli and influences is indicated. This sensitivity and receptivity entails perpetual rejuvenation of the soul.

The writer of a **regular** script will tend, on the other hand, to force everything into the framework of his own systematic concept of the order of things and to reduce Nature to a clearly defined system of pigeon-holes. Anything which disturbs his orderly way of thinking throws him off balance. There is nothing unpredictable about him; he lacks the ability for renewal. His impoverished imagination, his living by the rules, self-discipline and devotion to habit frequently make him a crashing bore. On the other hand he will be stable and faithful to a degree which the preceding type would find impossible.

Depending on the other indications in the writing accompanying the regularity, we will be able to tell if this consistency is allied to an active will power and directed towards a specific goal or if it is merely the result of passive obstinacy, as is the case with weak, monotonous writings. In any case, regular writing always indicates order, punctuality, methodical activity and a sense of discipline.

Care must be taken not to confuse simply regular writing (figs. 43, 55) with **automatic** writing (fig. 56). The latter is a caricature of the former. In fig. 56, 'l'annonce parue . . . ' every change of direction involves a sudden interruption in the stroke. The regularity here is the result of constraint. Emotivity is great, but it is repressed. The writer lacks flexibility and is incapable of adapting to his surroundings. He can be easily irritated and hurt and, in situations where he finds it impossible to conform or reconcile his instincts and wishes with the discipline his upbringing has imposed on him, he reverts to an attitude of rigid conventionalism. His reactions are artificial and totally unspontaneous. The same rigidity of behaviour can often be seen in the behaviour of obsessive people who withdraw into their manias and obsessions.

While discussing regular and irregular writing, special

mention should be made of *cadenced* writing. This is a 'mobile' writing which progresses consistently towards the right in a procession of regular hand movements and rhythmically timed extensions and flexions of the fingers. Such writing contains a considerable uniformity in size, thickness of stroke, slant and letter spacing (fig. 48, 49, 57). Cadenced writing never possesses the serenity of calm, regular writing. Slight tremors in the continuity of movement, a certain angularity at the base of the letters and some irregularities in the height of the middle zone will always be present to distinguish this writing from calm writing.

People who habitually write with cadenced writing possess an emotivity which produces regular activity. This type of person is both sensitive and productive and his feeling of well-being is a stimulus to action, and action a refuge in times of trouble. This type also possesses qualities of consistency, perseverence and frequently a strong sense of duty.

Below is a list of definition and meanings of the principal species, ranging from the greatest degree of regularity to the most discordant irregularities. The student will notice that the signs with the highest personality values are those associated most closely with moderation and harmony.

RECAPITULATION

DESCRIPTION	INDICATION
AUTOMATIC writing (figs. 2, 56) The movement looks mechanical, forms are simple and stereotyped and follow on in a monotonous sequence.	Deviousness. Repression. Lack of flexibility. Neurasthenia. Tendency to obsessions. Mechanical activity. Lack of will power and/or personality. Obstinacy.
MONOTONOUS writing (fig. 23) Uniform style without any variation.	Routine. Lack of imagination. Apathy, Indolence. Melancholy. Resignation.

REGULAR writing (figs. 4. 54, 55) Regularity of forms, dimensions and spacing.

Equilibrium. Stability. Regular habits. Punctuality. (These interpretations do not apply in artificial, constrained, automatic or complicated writings.)
Depending on other signs: Sense of order. Discipline. Over-simplicity. Lack of finesse. Poverty of feeling.

CADENCED writing (figs. 48, 49, 57) Regular in size and slant, speed and pressure.

Stability. Regular working habits. Consistency of feelings. Perseverance. Fidelity. Courage. Honesty. Firmness. Resistance to fatigue. Sense of order and duty.

HOMOGENEOUS writing (figs. 46, 49, 50, 54, 57). Unified style which does not differ from one document to another, or within the same script.

If in combination with originality of forms and RELIEF (figs. 46, 50) and if spontaneous, it is an indication of a firmly established personality.
With very regular writing (fig. 54) it reflects a lack of flexibility and receptivity, a tendency to preach. Need for systematic arrangement of things.
In all cases: a good sign of reliability and equilibrium.

NUANCÉE writing (fig. 50) Slight irregularities of size, spacing and slant in letters and words. Ink-trail remains regular overall.

Sensitivity. Delicacy of perception. A lively mind. Flexibility. Tolerance.

IRREGULARITY:

(1) OF HEIGHT OF LETTERS (figs. 48, 49)

Sensitivity. Emotivity. **With angular writing:** sensitiveness, touchiness.

(2) OF WIDTH OF LETTERS (fig. 53)

Alternating enthusiasm and inhibition. Variations in self-confidence.

(3) OF SLANT OF LETTERS (figs. 16, 46, 51, 52)

If the irregularities are only slight: Intellectual sensitivity. Curiosity of mind. Ability to see things from different angles. Broad mindedness. **Very irregular slant:** see following chapter.

(4) OF PRESSURE (fig. 31) Sudden increases of pressure which increase the width and thickness of the stroke.

Variations in energy output. Irritability. Anger. Violent gestures. Over-excitability. Temper.

(5) OF LAYOUT AND SPACING (figs. 47, 53)

Instability. Difficulty concentrating and 'getting things done'. Impressionability. Lack of self-discipline. Unpredictable reactions. Dissipation.

AGITATED writing (figs. 44, 5l) Discordant irregularities. Animated with imprecise forms.

Hypersensitivity. Nervousness. Impatience. Suggestibility. Fickleness. Difficult character.

JERKY writing (fig. 52). Sudden changes of direction, forms and size which produce angles or 'jerks' throughout the ink-trail, particularly in curved strokes.

Extreme nervousness. Hypersensitivity. Irritability. Grumpiness. Cantankerousness.
With sharp points: Aggression.

UNSTABLE writing (figs. 47, 53) Contains differences in direction between one document and another, or within the same document.

Indiscipline. Inconsistency. Variable moods. Fragility of attention and feelings.

DISCORDANT writing (fig. 47) Total lack of proportion and harmony, striking exaggerations and lack of agreement between the different elements.

Depending on the Form Level: Impulsiveness. Impressionability. Instability. Inconsistency. Lack of discipline. Lack of co-ordination in behaviour and effort. Irresoluteness. Agitation. Absence of morals and respect for rules.

Handwriting Slant

The Degree of Slant

Some text books recommend a vertical style of writing, whereas others teach a form in which the words and letters slant to the right. Vertical writing has to form an angle of 90° to the baseline and slanted writing an angle of 54°.

As it is usually impossible for us to know how the writer of a sample we are analysing was taught to write, we do not pay undue attention to this feature if the writing is more or less vertical or if it slants only slightly to the right. We only need to pay more than passing interest to the slant in cases where it is rigidly vertical or unusually slanted, because such features would reflect the writer's preference for one kind of attitude above all others.

The degree of slant is a general indication of the writer's emotional tendencies, the degree of sympathy he feels for others, his reserve or distrust of his exterior surroundings.

The writer who keeps all his letters *vertical*, as if attempting to emphasise the extent of isolation between them, resembles the man who cannot relax in company and who never seems to fit in with the group. The vertical movement may be interpreted as a deliberate attempt to assert oneself and preserve a certain distance from everybody else. Generally speaking, vertical writing reveals an individualistic nature, independence of mind, indifference, or an insensitivity to others which can develop into pure selfishness (figs. 9, 45).

On the other hand, a writer who has a lively interest in his surroundings leans towards things and people with intense curiosity, desire or sympathy. His body follows the impulses of his soul quite naturally, and his attempts at entering into closer contact with people and things are revealed by a *right slant* in his writing. We may also say that the greater the degree of slant, the greater are the writer's impulses and the less his control over them. To a certain extent cold reason holds the writing in check and produces a higher degree of verticality. Passion, on the other hand, increases the angle of the writing until it resembles a fiery steed charging at a target, or an obdurate man who uses his head like a battering ram to overcome obstacles. (figs. 58, 59). Whether or not he fights actively or is dominated by his impulses and external influences, the writer who slants his writing to the right always moves ahead, forgets himself and looks to the future.

On the other hand there are some people who meet any suggestion with an automatic refusal, distrust or recoil. This attitude of rebellion, contraction or disregard for his surroundings is illustrated mainly by a *left slant* in the writing (fig. 60). This feature is often found among adolescents who rebel against school discipline or family authority. It is also frequently found among hypersensitive people who cannot accept the world as it is and whose instinct for self-preservation produces a certain defiance and a systematic refusal to consider anything new or unfamiliar.

Between the extremes of very right slanted and very left slanted writing the whole gamut of behaviour is revealed from impulsivity to extreme reserve, from passion to voluntary withdrawal.

Variations of Slant

Anybody's writing can vary according to the day, the moment or even the nature of the subject matter. We often hear people say 'I can change my writing at will' and more often than not this means nothing more than that the person concerned can change the angle of slant. It is very rare, however, for a person who normally produces a right slanted script to alter it to a vertical style and maintain it for a whole page. The minute the attention flags the writing will revert to its normal slant and, moreover, where this has been consciously changed, the writing will always contain signs of fatigue or slackening concentration to alert the graphologist.

Nevertheless, we have to recognise that there are some people who unconsciously write now with a vertical and now with a slanting style. This is an indication that they react differently depending on who they are talking to or the milieu in which they find themselves. It is not uncommon to find people who write vertically in anything to do with their business or professional matters, but adopt a right slant which reveals a greater spontaneity and warmth when writing to people on a more intimate basis. As is so often the case, we have here a perfect example of why a graphologist should ask for as many samples as possible when doing an analysis.

By studying a person's writing at different stages of his life it is possible to follow the evolution of his character, and, by examining the slant in particular, to determine those periods which were most favourable for his development or the circumstances which caused him to withdraw into his shell. It is possible to ascertain the degree of difficulty caused by the need to adapt and to what extent this was achieved.

Irregularity of Slant

When we were dealing with *nuancée* writing we saw that slight fluctuations in the slant were an indication of a flexible mind capable of grasping various shades of meaning, of making comparisons and understanding the different aspects of a problem, the various faces of truth.

When these fluctuations are so great that they disturb the writing (figs. 52, 61) they no longer signify a delicate, receptive mind, but a personality torn between contradictory impulses. The individual lives in a state of perpetual dissatisfaction and his behaviour reflects his internal ambivalence.

Too intelligent not to see the advantages or otherwise of a given situation, he does not possess sufficient moral fibre to make a decision. He wants to hunt with the hare and run with the hounds, he always looks for compromise and undoes today what he did yesterday. He exhausts himself and everybody else with his moodiness and unpredictability.

It sometimes happens that, while preserving an overall unified appearance, the writing may become progressively more upright or more slanted in the course of the same document.

When the writing begins with a right slant and gradually becomes more vertical it signifies a tendency in the writer to embark on projects impulsively, but subsequently to exert greater control over himself.

Conversely, a document in which the writing starts off by being more or less vertical, but gradually acquires a greater slant as it progresses down the page reveals a character whose initial reserve decreases as a result of greater involvement.

Absolute rigidity of slant, whether the writing is vertical or slanted (figs. 62, 63) reflects a corresponding inflexibility of principles, a lack of suppleness and a refusal to change a decision once made.

The opposite of ***rigid*** writing is ***slack*** writing. This is writing which just seems to drift along without observing any rules of direction. When found together with an incisive stroke (fig. 61) it is an indication of a lack of moral sense, varying will power and an obedience to impulses, whether good or bad. With a weak stroke the indication is one of indolence, laziness and slovenliness.

*   *   *

Any conclusions we may draw from the slant of a writing will be confirmed or modified by other signs. We cannot repeat too often that ***all graphic indicators must be considered along with the Form Level and in conjunction with all their accompanying signs***.

For example, a vertical writing in which the letters are close together, the pressure is nourished and the forms are full (these terms will be explained later on) will suggest a rich emotional life, but also a selectivity on the part of the writer concerning the objects of his affection. In this case the verticality modifies the interpretation of the other signs.

Another writing, which may show the same verticality, but accompanied now by dry pressure, poor letter formation and spaced out words (fig. 45) will indicate a cold-hearted nature. Here, all the signs support each other and point to one interpretation.

The student should not take flight at the complexity of sign combinations. When he has learned to recognise them all and can make a list of 10 or 15 signs present in any given sample, he will quickly learn to separate the features of primary and secondary importance. The most striking features allow us to determine the skeleton of the personality. The less striking features tell us how to modify and be more specific about our portrait and which details to add to, or subtract from, our initial overall impression. Therefore we must not be put off by apparent contradictions between the writing of a person we know well and his behaviour. All will become clear as the student learns more about graphology.

RECAPITULATION

DESCRIPTION	INDICATION
VERTICAL writing (fig. 63) Forms an angle of 90° with baseline.	Stability. Strength. Reserve. Self-possession. Lack of spontaneity. Self control. Reflection. Coldness. Heart ruled by head. Pride. Distrust. Egoism. **With firm writing:** Will power.

RIGHT SLANTED (figs. 57, 59) Writing forms an angle of 54° with the baseline.

Desire. Impulsiveness. Spontaneity. Ardour. Passion. Need to express feelings. Sociability. Strong sympathies or antipathies. Entrenched convictions. Often profound partiality. Subjectivity. Lack of self-control.
With light pressure: Impressionability. Weakness.
With pasty stroke and pronounced right slant: Ruled by one's passions.

LEFT SLANTED (Fig. 60) Writing inclines to left of vertical.

Opposition to society. Opposition to authority. Opposition to established conventions. Negative tendencies. Rebelliousness. Fear. Timidity. Repression. Flight from life's problems. Dissimulation. Affectation. Refusal to be affected by one's own sensitivity. Avoidance of suffering.

RIGID (figs. 62, 63) Writing shows inflexibility of graphic direction.

Inability to adapt. Lack of social sense. Egoism. Severity. Obstinacy. Intransigence. Stability. Correctness. Moral strength.
With small irregularities: Hidden sensitivity and emotion.

SLACK (fig. 61) Writing contains limp strokes, uncertainty of direction and uncontrolled movements.

Instability. Amorality. Impulsivity. Disorderliness.
With weak strokes: (fig. 47) Laziness. Slovenliness.

IRREGULAR SLANT (fig. 52)

'Tug of war' between contradictory inner feelings and tendencies. Indecision. Avoidance of responsibilities. Energy dissipated by inner conflicts. Difficulties of concentration and seeing a job through to the end.

LESSON 7

The Dimensions of Handwriting

The dimensions of modern writing are more or less as follows:

Height of small letters (those letters without upper or lower extensions)

2mm to 2½ mm

Height of upper and lower zone extensions and the capitals

with small letters of 2 mm : 4½ mm

with small letters of 3 mm : 6 mm

(The letters 't' and 'd' are exceptions in that they are usually shorter.)

Width between two downstrokes: More or less equal to the height of a small letter. (The letter 'u' for example, should be capable of being contained in a square.)

Any writing in which the small letters are taller than 3 mm is deemed to be *large*; from 4-6 mm *very large*, and above 6 mm *exaggerated*.

Any writing in which the small letters are less than 1½ mm in height is *small*.

The terms 'large' and 'small' when applied to handwriting refer only to the middle zone. Abnormal length in the upper or lower zone extensions is simply termed ***prolonged***.

Large and Small Handwriting

Large

The extent of the hand movement which produces a *large* writing can have several causes. The first possibility is an *excess of vitality* which forces the writer to use up his energy in exterior movements. Robust and extravert temperaments and characters (Sanguine and Choleric, for example) generally have a larger writing than the weaker ones such as the Nervous or any of the introverts. Proof of this can be seen in the way the size of writing always decreases when vitality diminishes, for example, in an invalid or old person.

But vitality is not always expressed by extensive movements. There are some very dynamic people whose energy, rather than expressing itself on the surface, as is the case in large writings, shows up either in the pressure on the paper or in the greater acceleration and speed.

The most usual cause of enlarged writing is ***increased consciousness of the Self***. We saw when dealing with the symbolism of space that the middle zone, the body of the writing, represents the Self. The greater the awareness of the Self the more this zone will increase in height. The person whose nature impels him to exaggerate his feelings, experiences, desires, expectations or undertakings will have a tendency to lay claim to as much space as his wish for expansion requires. Amplification of the writing is, to a certain extent, principally an act of occupation.

The amplitude of the writing is connected with the strength of feelings, enthusiasm, ambition, taste for grandeur and, in the case of exaggerated writings: pride, presumptuousness.

But the dominant characteristic of such writers is the sense of their own worth, the importance or superiority of their social role, no matter in which milieu they move. Thus, it is the same faith in their own personal dignity, the same belief that they are fulfilling a grand mission that caused Louis XVI to say 'I am the State', and our concierge to say 'I have to be informed about anything going on here'. The writing of Cécile Sorel (fig. 64) is an example of the overdeveloped Self which is so common among the famous.

This feeling of importance is not without a certain appreciation of one's obligations. Rank has its responsibilities: the respect we pay to others is the consequence of that we pay ourselves. If we believe we should make a gesture it will be a broad gesture, a gesture of a 'grand seigneur'. Large writing, in effect, corresponds to pride, arrogance or repugnance for anything on a small scale.

When *large* writing is at the same time *firm* and *resolute* the same expansiveness can be seen in the writer's *need for activity*. He has a need for space in which to be active. It would be difficult for us to picture him working in a laboratory, for example, bent over a microscope studying the evolution of infinitesimally small life forms. He was born to be seen, to travel and to sacrifice himself. Wherever he may be, his personality, audacity and vitality emanate from him and his personal authority is unmistakable. This type of person 'gets on' by sheer force of character as much as by the refinement of his intelligence and he is frequently lacking in objectivity and critical ability. He is motivated by the conviction that he is doing the right thing and is following the right lines. He keeps no record of time or the effort he devotes to what he has undertaken. He reacts quickly and with enthusiasm, becomes involved in many projects and demands that others follow him, showing no pity for anyone who does not share his convictions or reserves of vital energy. He is the knight who exhausts his steed, the driver who drives his car into the ground. Blind to reality, he hears only what his own wishes say to him. He does not ask, he demands, and usually he gets what he wants.

A whole world of activity and restlessness is contained in large writing and the range of interpretations is from the complimentary to the uncomplimentary. Among large writers we find the conqueror and the adventurer, the woman of the world and the common schemer, and all temperaments have their faults as well as their saving graces. Pride, lack of judgement, excessive subjectivity which represent the obverse side of the coin, could easily, in an unbalanced personality, pervert his moral values and cause him to sink into excesses.

Whatever else we may say about large writing, if it is accompanied by firm pressure, it can never come from the pen of a shy or retiring writer.

If *large size* is accompanied by **weak strokes** and **monotonous forms** it should be taken, mainly, as an indication of vanity, superficiality, and 'emptiness of the soul' although these negative qualities do not diminish the personal vulnerability of the writer.

Small

Small writing reveals a more modest appreciation of the writer's own importance. If the height of the middle zone corresponds to the writer's appreciation of his Self, then obviously the person with large writing will have greater feelings of self-importance than the small writer.

Less obsessed by worry about what he owes himself and what other people owe him, the *small* writer is capable of making judgements based on reason and objectivity. His horizon is not blotted out by his own ego and he is more suited to the role of an impartial observer than the large writer.

Small writing particularly if it is also *regular*, is the sign of the observer, the patient investigator, and the man who is good at 'fiddly' work. This is the writing of introverts who are more inclined to sedentary occupations or cerebral activity than physical action. The effort involved in the concentration of mind and attention leads to a parallel concentration of movements in general and the writing in particular.

This does not mean that there are no small writers among

men of action. In General Leclerc's writing, for example, the reduced height is compensated for by the overall impetuosity and rapidity. Leclerc's writing was small, but very progressive. Courage, zeal, confidence are all indicated by the progressive nature of his writing, and in his case the smallness is a sign of modesty. He shunned honours, was somewhat retiring and made few demands on others. He was embarrassed rather than intoxicated by glory.

When *small* writing is allied to signs of **great activity** the writer is capable of activity guided, directed and co-ordinated by intelligence. If large writing shows a dominant Feeling function, small writing, on the contrary, shows that the writer's dominant function is Thinking.

Small writing, if combined with **squeezed, inhibited movements**, is an indication of self doubt, feelings of inferiority, timidity and/or pettiness.

We should always be very careful when we see **superelevated** capitals together with tiny middle zone letters. Such a discrepancy in height is virtually always a sign of an inferiority complex overcompensated by excessive pride.

Variations in Height

When considering the size of a sample of writing we must not only consider the overall dimension, but also the relative size of individual letters and, in particular, the degree of proportion between the capitals and small letters.

It frequently happens that the capital letters of a writing tower above the middle zone letters and exceed the relative proportions prescribed by the school model. The 'J' may describe an arrogant curve (figs. 65, 66) or the initial stroke on a capital 'M' may be projected high above the rest of the letter (fig. 64). Sometimes letters may appear on a kind of pedestal (see the 's' of 'Mademoiselle', fig. 64 and, in fig. 67 the 'S' at the beginning of the last word of the second line) so that the letter stands out from its neighbours. The same effect is often produced by inflating the lower loop of a 'D' or capital 'L' (see the 'D' of 'Du', fig. 64). Or again, the t-bar may be placed high above the stem. All of these features come under the heading of *superelevated* writing (figs. 64, 66, 67, 68).

Superelevated writing expresses, depending on the nature and intensity of the sign: conceit, pride, pretentiousness or a despotic nature. It is no longer the perfectly natural self-esteem of large writing. The need to be admired by others or to dominate them is in direct proportion to his feelings of mediocrity. The fear of being undervalued may stimulate his pride and exacerbate his vulnerability.

When the writing reduces in size in the last letters of a word or the last lines of a page we have what is called *diminishing* writing (words which taper like a fine rapier fig. 69). This progressive diminution of the writing may be caused by overextended fingers and be a sign of fatigue or effort which cannot be sustained.

Diminishing writing, with the economy of movement which it represents, can also be the result of precipitation. Some graphologists (after Michon) have tried to interpret it as a sign of lying and deceit. However, we believe that this is only the case when the ends of words are written with ambiguous forms or in evasive, indecisive movements and are definitely not due to exhaustion or haste.

One must always be careful, particularly when assessing loyalty or honesty from writing, not to draw any conclusions on the basis of just one sign. Any character trait will always reveal itself with several graphic indicators. Just as no doctor would ever make a diagnosis on the strength of one symptom, so in graphology we must always make sure that our interpretations can be supported by several indicators or the Form Level of the writing.

The opposite of diminishing writing is *enlarging* writing (fig. 70). Here the letters increase in height towards the end of the words. It represents an ever increasing degree of effort which the writer puts in to his work. It is a style of writing which we come across more among children than adults. In an organised script it denotes a certain childlike candour and a tendency to reveal one's deepest thoughts with only minimal encouragement. It may also be an indication of a tendency to 'fly off the handle' — a characteristic of Sanguine temperament types.

Upper and Lower Extensions

As we have already seen the upper zone in writing corresponds to the writer's intellectual tendencies and the lower zone to his sense of reality and materialism. Any amplification in these zones reveals increased activity in the relevant area.

In writing which is *prolonged upwards* (fig. 71) we will detect, depending on the Form Level: curiosity of mind, mysticism, illusions, exaltation. Mysticism is frequently expressed in a final stroke of a 'd' shooting upwards (fig. 72).

When the writing is prolonged downwards (fig. 73) it indicates great activity, a desire for movement, a need for physical exercise, materialism, practical sense and realism.

Crépieux-Jamin *(1)* frequently noted lower zone prolongments in the writing of accountants. He explained this as a result of an obsessive fear of travel, or of being transferred which is typical among people of sedentary occupations.

When the writing *is prolonged both upwards and downwards* (fig. 74) it expresses, according to Klages *(2)*, a state of unease or dissatisfaction which can be a constant incentive for activity. The writer is searching in very different spheres of activity for ways to excel. However, as he takes on too many things at the same time, he dissipates his energy without accomplishing anything. Alternatively he may immediately begin dreaming of other areas of activity after an initial success. Long upper and lower extensions are very common

---

(1) CRÉPIEUX-JAMIN – *A.B.C. de la Graphologie (Alcan Ed.)*

(2) KLAGES – *L'Expression du Caractère dans l'Ecriture. (Niestlé et Delachaux, Ed.)*

among young people. They express at the same time the
illusions, the elation and the need for movement associated
with youth. Long extensions usually become shorter as the
writer gains in maturity and learns how to limit his energies to
activities in which he is sure of success. The opposite of writing
prolonged upwards and downwards is *low* writing (fig. 75).
This type of writing is not necessarily of smaller dimensions,
but the upper and lower zone extensions will be less than half
the height of the middle zone letters. Such writing reflects
modesty and moderation of aspiration. The writer concentrates his energies on the realities of everyday living. With a
high Form Level such writing reveals an inner harmony and
serenity. If other signs contradict this interpretation the
indication will be apathy, a lack of drive, indifference or
laziness.

With signs of emotivity, a reduction in the upper and lower
extensions accentuates the signs of hypersensitivity, inactivity,
and an exclusive preoccupation with the Self. These writers
lack the intellectual curiosity to take an interest in what is
going on around them and seldom experience those feelings of
relaxation which greater physical activity produces.

Width of the Letters

The length of the upstrokes and the distance between the
downstrokes are what make the writing progress. The more
the pull to the right takes precedence over movements into the
upper zone, the more the letters will tend to spread out at their
base. This is typical of what we call *wide* writing (figs. 76, 77).
If we retrace the ink-trail of fig. 76, for example, with a sharp
point, we will not encounter any resistance to the impulse
which pulls the writing to the right: the writer allows the pen to
move freely across the page. We have already seen that these
rightward movements express extraversion, confidence in
oneself and the future, and an interest in exterior objects.

Wide writing expresses an exaggeration of these tendencies which reveals itself in superficiality, lack of depth, lack of consideration for others, uncontrollable talkativeness and self display.

In *narrow* writing (fig. 78), the opposite type to the above, we detect a restriction in the movement towards the right. Narrowness between the downstrokes indicates reflection, prudence, the capacity for concentration — or a fear of moving forward. People who write like this are generally not noted for their élan, nor for their generosity.

When a writing presents letters which are now wide, now narrow (fig. 79) we detect in the writer's character alternating confidence and distrust, reserve and a lack of control, generosity and meanness. Movements which advance and then hesitate reveal periods of courage and timidity, and are frequent among emotive people. The differences in letter width constitute a kind of irregular writing.

Expansion and Inflation

Expanded writing results from an amplification of the movements which are not only detected in the height, as in large or prolonged writing, nor in the width, as in wide writing, but in all directions at the same time. This produces a slight inflation of the loops and ovals (the letters 'o' and 'a'), a broadening of the letters and increased spacing between the words. It is a more or less round writing, ample and aerated (fig. 77).

As with all expansive writing, this type indicates extraversion, love of life, a state of euphoria, a happy personality, a lack of concern, and gaiety.

In *inflated* writing the expansion is exaggerated in a few loops without affecting the writing as a whole (figs. 65, 80), unless the writing is both expanded and inflated at the same time.

Inflation is a sign of vital exuberance. Dr. Carton *(1)* states that in such writers 'the need to gesticulate, to talk, to stress their own importance, to talk about themselves, to seek attention, to exhibit their bodies and express their ideas is their main concern'.

---

(1) DR. PAUL CARTON – Diagnostic et Conduite des Tempéraments

RECAPITULATION

DESCRIPTION	INDICATION
LARGE writing contains small letters of 3mm-4mm in height.	Extraversion. Ardour. Enthusiasm. Strong feelings of self-importance. Need for social contact. Need to play a role in society. Love of splendour. Great vital needs. 'Feeling' function. **With firm pressure and well maintained size:** Strong activity. Authority. Independence. **With weak and monotonous writing:** Superficiality. Vanity. Inner void.
VERY LARGE OR EXAGGERATED From 4mm-6mm and above.	Inflated ego. Excessive emotivity. Excitement. Insatiable demands in everyday life. Caprice. Lack of respect for others. Partiality. Subjectivity. Lack of judgement and critical ability. All the interpretations of large handwriting remain valid for very large and exaggerated writing also.
SMALL writing m/z letters no taller than 1½mm.	Introversion. Modesty. Finesse. Concentration and attention to detail. Observant nature. Objectivity. Easy adaptation to surroundings and circumstances. 'Thinking' function

VERY SMALL writing
Less than 1mm and inhibited.

Weak vitality. Lack of enthusiasm. Pettiness. Timidity. Pedantry.

SMALL MIDDLE ZONE LETTERS WITH LARGE CAPITALS

Inferiority complex, overcompensated by excessive pride. Vulnerability.

PROLONGED UPWARDS (fig. 71) with upper extensions taller than 1½ times the height of the small letters.

Excitability. Tendency to self-delusion. Lack of firmness of character. Lively mind. Idealism. Mysticism.

PROLONGED DOWNWARDS (fig. 73) with lower extensions equal to more than 2½ times the height of the small letters.

Realism. Practical mind. Objectivity. Positive character with an appreciation of the material things in life. Feet firmly on the ground. Materialism. Ability for organisation. Sensuality. Sexual needs. Need for physical activity.

PROLONGED UP & DOWN (fig. 74)

Extraversion. Sanguine temperament. Need for activity. Taste for change. Dissipated energy.

LOW writing (fig. 75) in which the upper and lower extensions are barely equal to the height of the small letters.

Simplicity. Timidity. Modesty. Rejection of activity in favour of the inner life. Introversion.
With signs of weakness: Lack of moral strength and initiative. Indolence. Apathy. Inactivity.
With ordinary, enlarged writing: Predominant ego. Egocentricity.

SUPERELEVATED (figs. 66, 68) Increased height in the first part of a letter or the first letter of a word, particularly in capitals.

Extreme conceit. Dignity. Pride. Despotism.
With small writing: Inordinate pride as over-compensation for an inferiority complex.
With narrow capitals: Vulnerability

SOARING writing (fig. 67) This species resembles writing which is prolonged upwards. Some movements, at the beginning, end or in the middle of words, seem to shoot upwards.

Excitement. Idealism. Ambition.

DIMINISHING OR TAPERING (fig. 69) in which the words become progressively smaller. The term applies also to reductions in height at the end of a line or page.

Susceptibility to fatigue. Exhaustion. Overwork. Unsustained activity. Sensitivity. Finesse.

ENLARGING writing (fig. 70) in which letters and words become progressively taller.

Open-heartedness. Naïvety. Frankness. Tendency to 'fly off the handle'. Increased will power.

WIDTH OF LETTERS

WIDE writing (fig. 76) Small letters wider than tall. Letters with increased width at the base.

Extraversion. Superficiality. Tendency to uncontrolled verbosity. Lack of inner life. Lack of thought.

NARROW writing (fig. 78) Small letters taller than they are wide. Minimal space between the downstrokes.

Reflectiveness. Concentration. Prudence. Lack of self-confidence. Egoism. Parsimonious nature.

CAPITALS TALL & NARROW

Social timidity. Professional envy. Ambition frustrated by lack of ability.

EXPANDED writing (fig. 77) Expanded in all directions, ample and aerated.

Extraversion. Frankness. Euphoria. Generosity. Communicative and/or sentimental nature. Dissipation. Talkativeness.

INFLATED writing (fig. 65) Exaggerated inflation of upper and lower loops. Increased size of ovals and knots.

Sanguine Temperament. Self contentment. Lack of discernment. Over-active imagination. Boasting. Need to grab the limelight. Need to exhibit one's body (lower loops) or expound one's ideas (upper loops). **Lower loops inflated and with heavy pressure:** Hyper-excitable sensuality.

Direction

Direction of the Ink-Trail

In the preceding chapter we considered the slant of letters in relation to the baseline. Now we should consider the direction which the writing itself can take while evolving to make the letter formations. Depending on whether the writing shows a more spontaneous pull to the right or left, we can talk of *progressive* or *regressive signs*.

Progressive

'Progressive writing (also known as *right tending*) is that in which the writing moves towards the right by any means compatible with greater economy of movement.' (Crépieux-Jamin, *A.B.C. de la Graphologie*). It is writing which gives the impression of hurrying towards the end of the line.

The letters are more or less simplified, the ovals sometimes slightly open (see fig. 58). Any connective form or combination likely to increase the speed is utilised (see fig. 81: the 'd' of 'devez' which, despite a slight turn to the left, connects with the following letter; the simplified 'z' at the end of the same word, the 'p' with lower zone 'v' formation in the word 'occupée').

We saw in the second lesson that any movement to the right expresses a tendency to exteriorisation, a need for action, an inclination to spend and a facility for contact with the exterior world.

Depending on the Form Level, originality in the connective forms which favours progression to the right reveals intellectual gifts, an openness of mind, intelligence, rapid comprehension and quick reactions. On the emotional level it shows altruism, sociability and a willingness to help, and on the physical side, activity, easy adaptability to the environment, and courage.

Regressive

Regressive writing (or *left tending*) is that in which there is a tendency to amplify some loops or graphic movements which move in a direction which is contrary to the general direction of the writing. (See fig. 82: the capitals 'L', 'H', 'M', the lower extensions of the 'g' and the 'y', fig. 83: the 'M' of Mon', the 'A' of 'Ami'.)

The retreating movement counteracts sponta- neity, trust, activity or self-denial. It is a gesture which returns towards the writer. It indicates, *in the intellectual area* (in particular when the upper extension of the 'd' turns towards the left without any connection to the following letter): introversion, imagination, taste for introspection, intellectual 'rêverie', contemplation. *From the point of view of the emotions:* egoism, indifference to others, individualism, lack of generosity, and, in certain cases, flirtatiousness (a gesture of a man or woman who refuses in order to be even more desirable) and dissimulation. *On the physical side:* instinct of self-preservation, inactivity, economy of energies.

When the regressive movement is combined with a reverse angle at the base of the 't' for example, or at the bottom of lower zone extensions (see opposite and fig. 82) it is a sign of a restive, stubborn or undisciplined character.
Whereas progressive writing shows élan, zeal, confidence in the future and, occasionally, a kind of escape from oneself and the shackles of the past, regressive writing is a mark of dependence on the past, distrust, apprehension in the face of anything new and unfamiliar and a fear of not being able to adapt to circumstances.

There is a bond between regressive writing and certain kinds of *twisted* writing such as that seen in fig. 82. Instead of breakages in the upper extensions, so characteristic of certain types of debility (fig. 84), we see in fig. 82 a kind of mannered sinuosity. The movement of the pen is directed first to the left, then to the right and then back again to the left. This evasive type of movement would appear to express all that is contrary to sincerity.

Direction of the Baseline

The lines on which the writing stands is connected with the writer's mood.

Rising lines (rising from left to right) show enthusiasm, optimism, zeal and ardour.
Falling lines show depression, melancholy, pessimism and discouragement.

The above can be easily explained: excitement, drive, 'joie de vivre', enjoyable activity etc. cause us to 'bounce', as if lifted by a surplus of energy and this in turn produces increased extension in our movements.

In sadness, depression or fatigue our exhausted arms tend to fall towards our sides and all movements, including those responsible for producing writing, are affected by this 'heaviness'.

However, the direction of the baseline (rising or falling) does not always proceed regularly from the beginning of the line to the end.

In writing known as *galloping upwards* (also as rising tiles), individual words rise, but the baseline itself does not. It is an indication that the writer is subject to short-lived enthusiasms which flare up and immediately die down again (fig. 85).

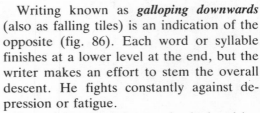

Writing known as *galloping downwards* (also as falling tiles) is an indication of the opposite (fig. 86). Each word or syllable finishes at a lower level at the end, but the writer makes an effort to stem the overall descent. He fights constantly against depression or fatigue.

Sometimes the line may begin by rising and then start falling, thus producing what is termed a *convex line*. What we have here is a sign of vivacity. But the writer's reserve of energy is not equal to the initial burst of enthusiasm and there is a tailing off after the prematurely reached maximum.

With a *concave line*, which begins in a downwards movement and then starts to climb again towards the right, we have an indication of little zeal at the beginning of activity, but energy which increases progressively.

Horizontal lines show stability, even temper, possibly originating in a placid nature or great self control. The sum of the other signs will help us to decide which is the correct interpretation.

Lines which change direction in the course of the same document are an indication of moodiness. It is a good idea to check the variability over several documents, particuarly if the writing is otherwise regular. In the case of irregular writing, diversity in the line directions is merely another sign of general irregularity.

Sinuous lines, finally, show a wave-like sequence of letters, syllables and words, and reveal a versatile and sly character. According to the Form Level and the association of signs, we should be able to choose between interpretations of: dexterity, agility of mind, diplomacy, ruse or dishonesty.

RECAPITULATION

DESCRIPTION	INDICATION
PROGRESSIVE (figs. 58, 81) writing in which all the strokes move as quickly as possible to the right.	Rapid reactions and thoughts which are also well co-ordinated. Intelligence. Activity. Sociability. Adaptability. Confidence. Extraversion. Enterprising mind.
REGRESSIVE (figs. 82, 83) writing in which certain strokes move in an exaggerated manner to the left.	Lack of spontaneity. Inadaptability. Egoism. Egocentricity. Tendency towards dissimulation. **Left tending l/z extensions:** restive, stubborn, undisciplined nature. **Large regressive movements:** shameless monopolizing. **Small regressive hooks at the end of words:** Egoism. Avidity. Greed.
RISING BASELINE	Elan. Enthusiasm. Optimism. Ambition. Aggression. Agitation.
FALLING BASELINE	Fatigue. Overwork. Dejection. Depression. **If it is a constant feature:** Melancholy. Pessimism. Discouragement.
GALLOPING UPWARDS (fig. 85)	Optimistic character, but physical weakness. Intellectual zeal which is not supported by physical resilience.
GALLOPING DOWNWARDS (fig. 86)	Fight against depression. Persistent effort. Energy constant, but lacking vigour.

CONVEX LINES
(higher in middle)

Unsustained ardour. Vivacity. Energy, and above all, persever-ance, are not equal to the initial impulse.

CONCAVE LINES
(lower in middle)

Initial lack of enthusiasm, but energy eventually reinforced and goal achieved.

HORIZONTAL LINES Regularly parallel to the horizontal edge of the paper.

Calmness. Evenness of temper. Self-control. Order. Method. Punc-tuality. Constancy. Discipline.
or: Coldness. Indifference. Apathy.

SINUOUS LINES The base of the words follow a more or less serpen-tine direction. (This can easily be detected by placing the edge of piece of paper under the writing line.)

Changing moods. Instability. Hesi-tation. Lack of firmness. Dexterity. Ruse. Diplomacy. Depending on other signs, it may confirm dishon-esty.

LINES NOW CLIMBING NOW FALLING

Sensitivity. Moodiness.

LESSON 8

Speed

In order to be able to assess the pace at which a sample of writing was written we have to be conversant with the effects which the speed or slowness of movement can have on various graphic elements.

We will now examine the most obvious effects produced by a quickened or retarded graphic movement, effects which the student graphologist, pen in hand, can demonstrate for himself.

Speed and Regularity

)))|)))

The first thing to do is to draw a vertical single stroke with a rapid movement of the pen. Then, with the same speed, draw several similar strokes in the same manner. None of the lines produced will be exactly the same length as the others. Any pen stroke, if quickly executed, will always be longer or shorter than its model. On the other hand, if we slow down the pen movement it will be much easier to produce strokes of more or less equal length.

Conclusion: Other things being equal, an irregular writing will always be more rapid than a regular one.

Speed and Sharpness

If, using a magnifying glass, we now compare the first lines we drew with others traced far more slowly, we will see that the first set contain relatively sharper edges and end in a finer point. The second set will have edges which are more runny or blurred and show slight trembling. They will also end in a slightly enlarged terminal caused by the braking movement. The same is true of circular movements — a lively pace produces a smooth, tight curve and a slow pace a shaky curve.

Conclusion: A sharp writing is quicker than a blurred or trembling one. Sharp pointed endings reflect a more lively movement than those which are blunt.

Form and Position of Dots, Bars and Accents

The speed of movement also tends to alter the formation of the letters. This is particularly noticeable in the diacritics.

Let us attempt to align, at a fairly rapid pace, an acute accent, a grave accent and a dot, an acute accent, a grave accent and a dot etc. etc. These graphic signs, perfectly distinct if we trace them slowly, become unrecognisable and irregular in form and position as we increase the speed of movement.

Imprecision of form and position of dots and diacritics is one of the clearest indicators of rapid writing.

Of course, it is also possible to find writing which is slow, but also contains deformed or poorly placed diacritics. If such writing is heavy, awkward and unorganised we interpret it as a sign of a poorly educated writer who has difficulty in manipulating the pen. If the writing is weak, slack and disorganised, inaccurate diacritics show slovenliness and negligence.

Increased Tendencies to the Right

Although our writing always moves towards the right, some movements, of necessity, go to the left in the formation of circles, loops and ovals. In a rapid writing the writer, carried away by his enthusiasm, tends to amplify the left-right movements, resulting in a more open and expanded script, whereas strokes which should really go to the left in order to complete the letters are neglected and sometimes even omitted (see fig. 87).

Progressive writings are generally more rapid than regressive ones, for any movement which emphasises the pull to the left slows down the act of writing. (See figs. 82, 83).

Increased Connections

It is easy to demonstrate that a fragmented line is slower than a complete one. Indeed every time we lift the pen from the paper we describe in space, before making contact again, a sinuous line which slows the action down. We may therefore deduce that a *connected writing, or one comprised of groups of three or four letters, is more rapid than a disconnected writing*, in which the letters are all separated from each other.

Connecting the dots, accents or t-bars to the following letter favours increased writing speed (fig. 42: the word 'très' 2nd line and fig. 86: 'bois mis à bord de route . . . ' in which each of the first three words contain dots or accents connected to letters).

Beginnings and Ends of Words

The speed of writing also depends on the manner in which letters are begun or finished. The greater the degree of elaboration or emphasis at the beginning or end of letters, the slower the progress of the writing. Simplifications and short cuts in the progress across the page are the greatest indications of speed.

Angles and Curves

Any change of direction which is produced without completely stopping the movement results in a curve. For an angle to appear, the pen must stop for a fraction of a second before recommencing in another direction. This can be demonstrated by tracing a broken line on the paper. If we deliberately stop the pen in order to produce angles at the top and bottom we arrive at a perfect zig-zag. But if we speed up the movement the angles become softer and the line, broken at the beginning, becomes sinuous.

Particular attention should be paid to the letters 'm', 'n' and 'u' which, according to the rules of cursive writing, should present a rhythmic alternation of angles and curves. Any writing in which these alternations are maintained will be, provided other supporting signs are present,

 more rapid than one containing only angles, or an excessively curved writing at the top and bottom. The highest degree of rapidity is seen in ***thready*** (or filiform) writing (fig. 87) in which the small letters resemble nothing more than a wavy line.

Regularity of Speed and Pressure

When the muscles move freely and easily, the movements of the fingers, as they extend and contract, produce a rhythmic succession of upstrokes and downstrokes. But if the fluid movement of the muscles is interrupted for any reason (lack of writing skill, nervous jerkiness, high blood pressure) the pen speed is greatly reduced and at the places where there is actual slowing down, thickening or pastiness appears. (See fig. l5: the 'c' and 'n' of 'cinema', and the 'z' of 'Excusez'). The significance of these irregularities will be dealt in the chapter on pressure. For the time being we should consider them as irregularities of speed.

The principal indicators of speed and slowness in writing are summarised below.

SPEED	SLOWNESS
1 — Irregular writing.	Regular writing.
2 — Smooth edges and flying strokes Sharp pointed endings	Trembling, broken, pasty or blurred strokes. Unorganised or disorganised writing. Blunt end strokes. Inhibited end strokes.
3 — Deformed diacritics. Inaccurately placed diacritics.	Bars and dots etc. carefully formed and positioned.

4 — Progressive or expanded writing. Increasing left margin.	Regressive, more or less squeezed writing. Decreasing left margin.
5 — Connected letters. Dots and bars etc. connected to the following letter (i.e. combined)	Disconnected writing.
6 — Simplified or neglected forms. Decreasing height at the end of words. Absence of starting strokes. Smooth end strokes.	Letters carefully formed. Increased height. Flourishes. Strokes which serve no purpose. Re-touching. Inhibited movements.
7 — Alternating angles and curves. Filiform (thread) connections.	Connective forms with angles top and bottom.
8 — Rhythmic alternation of up-strokes and downstrokes.	Sudden thickening of strokes, appearing at irregular intervals.

Most writings contain signs both of speed and slowness. The overall pace is determined from the proportion in which the respective signs are present. It is a good idea for the student to familiarise himself with the above indicators, but he should get into the habit of assessing the degree of speed at first glance and not working systematically through the lists. Eventually a sample of writing will talk to the student and present evidence of the writing pace in the same way as a photograph will immediately tell us whether someone was walking or running.

Crépieux-Jamin defines the signs of writing speed, in ascending order, as *slow, poised, accelerated, rapid and precipitated*. Their actual speeds range from 100 letters per minute (slow) to 200 plus letters per minute (precipitated). However, these figures are only an approximation and we quote them here as a rough guide.

One may be excused for thinking that the number of letters it is possible to write in a given time diminishes in proportion to the height of the writing, and that it takes longer to write a sentence containing tall letters than one containing short letters. In fact, however, the dimension of writing has only minimal effect on the speed. Retardation is caused more by complicated forms, angles, movements to the left than by increased height. Saudek, who made a particular study of the conditions for graphic speed and conducted many experiments on the theme *(1)*, demonstrated that the speed utilized in producing long strokes (particularly in the letter 'f') is considerably greater than that used by the same writer in tracing smaller lengths. Large writing reveals (except in 'showy' or artificial writing) more spontaneity and greater freedom of movement than small writing in which the limited movements depend on greater constraint.

The student can easily demonstrate to himself the validity of this statement by the following method. He should write the word 'chiffons' several times, as quickly as possible, first of all with his normal style and then using much taller letters. The difference in time will be almost indiscernible. If we compare fig. 69 with fig. 88, we should be able to sense that the movement in the word 'Avenue' is faster than in the sentence 'pour ma documentation personnelle', despite the little curlicue at the beginning of the 'A'. In the word 'Avenue' all the letters are connected, there is a decrease in height at the end of the word, and the final stroke sharpens towards the right. In the small, regular writing of fig. 88 the progressive 'p' and open 'o' suggest a certain rapidity, but overall it is 'accelerated' writing. The 'd' in 'documentation' is formed with two degrees of speed and the writer stops after every 't' stem in order to add the bar. These are movements in time which will never be regained.

For the sake of accuracy we should differentiate, when dealing with graphic speed, between:
— *the progression of the writing* (in letters per minute) and
— *the speed of the stroke.*

---

(1) DR. ROBERT SAUDEK – *Experiments with Handwriting (Allen & Unwin Ltd. London)*

The *rapid* progression of certain writings is principally a result of dexterity and skilful movements as much as it is of actual speed. The writer uses as many short cuts as possible in his connections, simplifications and progress towards the right (see fig. 89). The effort used in writing produces the maximum number of words in a minimum time. Everything is sacrificed for the sake of finishing the job as quickly as possible.

This speed of writing (rapid) signifies: easy adaptability, mental assimilation, intellectual dexterity, quick reflexes, and an aptitude for getting the job done.

When the letter forms disintegrate into imprecise threads (fig. 87) the implications of speed are less favourable. It shows excessive speed at the expense of attentiveness, reflection, depth of thought and feelings. If there is no pressure to counteract the sliding motion of the pen across the page we may deduce superficiality, negligence, instability and evasiveness.

Lively writing, which has *flying strokes*, proceeds by incisive or cross-shaped strokes, often exaggerated in length (figs. 90 & 91). Here speed is not attained so much by easy changes of direction or short-cuts but by the impulsiveness of the gesture.

Vivacity of the stroke corresponds to spontaneity, impulsiveness, quickness of reflexes and reactions, a facility for repartee, excitability and, if the feature is exaggerated, a fiery temper, hot-headedness and violence.

Let us compare figs. 87 and 91: The first shows an extreme speed (precipitation) and reminds us, with its deformations and slight undulations, of a river in full flood. The lower extensions seem not to be able to find a hold in 'terra firma' and the small letters, as if swamped, seem carried along by the current, too far and too fast. The writer does not stop to think or to check. If you were to call on him he would come half way down the garden path to meet you. When talking to you he would not be paying attention because he would already be thinking about what he would be doing in an hour's time or even the next day. He is the type who can deal with half a dozen things at once, but none of them properly. He is the busiest man in town, but his energies are wasted and he accomplishes nothing. Everything he does reveals more dexterity than ability, more diplomacy than profound conviction. He will never say 'no', but he should never be trusted to keep his word because he is quite capable of forgetting anything he promises. He is a man of grand projects which never actually get off the ground.

The writer of fig. 91 is from a different mould altogether. The ardour which emanates from this writing is an expression of passionate zeal and indicates a writer who is firmly convinced that his opinions are the right ones. He is prepared to defend these opinions to the death, if need be. His activity is no less than that of the writer of fig. 87, but here we are dealing with actions firmly rooted in reality. The impetuousness of feelings seen in the flying strokes are put to good use by high intelligence and fed by a powerful dynamism. The writer is the astronomer, Le Verrier, who is feared by those who know him for his irascible nature, but admired for his extraordinary capacity for work.

Slow graphic movements may also take on a variety of meanings depending on the Form Level. With a good Form Level it indicates self-control, thoughtfulness, circumspection, tranquility, patience and application. In less favourable cases: slow reflexes, sluggishness, a dull mind, laziness and indolence. It is always a sign of a lack of spontaneity. It is not possible to say that slow writing is always a sign of lying, but many people who have a capacity for lying (with premeditation) have very slow writing.

In order to demonstrate to the reader just how the Form Level can modify the significance of a graphic indicator, we will have a look at a few examples.

The writing in fig. 92 is slow. Every letter is written (we may say drawn) with great care. The letter 's' is embroidered with a little dot just at the end. All the 'e's', instead of being formed as a continuation of the preceding letter, begin with a concentric movement which slows down the progress considerably. Also, commas as perfectly formed as the one at the end of the first line are very rare. Occasionally the final strokes shoot ahead in what resembles a certain freedom of movement, but always turn back to the left again (que, m'excuse, de). This writer is certainly in no hurry, but as his writing is graceful, harmonious and light we could never accuse him of having a sluggish mind. What we see in these refined formations is taste, care, and a finicalness over every little detail. If he lacks spontaneity it is because he wishes to appear polished, courteous, attentive and moderate in word and deed.

The slowness of fig. 93 is slowness of a different kind. The writing is unorganised, inelegant and awkward. In this case we may talk of ignorance, clumsiness and sluggishness. The reflexes are slow, the writer stumbles and hesitates over his letter formations. He would be suited to work of a coarse nature, but would find it very difficult to adapt to any occupation demanding personal initiative.

Fig. 94 is a good example of *poised* writing. Considered as a whole the writing is progressive on account of the fact that there are no signs of left tendencies. However, the writing is too regular to be considered rapid. Notice the perfectly formed colon at the end of the line. Calm, prudence, wisdom, caution, regular and conscientious activity - these are the conclusions imposed on us by the speed and clarity of this writing.

The writing of fig. 95, which is narrower than the preceding one, is nevertheless more lively. We can see evidence of **acceleration** in the irregularities of the letters, the tapering ends of the words, the upper extensions which seem to lean against each other in an attempt to move faster and faster to the right. But the letters are well formed and the punctuation is precise. This is the writing of an intelligent business man who is conscientious and attentive to details.

Fig. 89 contains nearly all the characteristics of *rapid writing*. There are some leftward movements in the ovals of the words 'besoin', 'dont', 'vous', but these are amply compensated for by the rapid rightward movements of the rest of the writing.

With fig. 96 we come back to the theme of reflection. This is what we call **controlled** writing. The overall movement is quite rhythmic but we can detect occasional signs of inhibition (the small hook at the base of the 't' and the 'p' in 'apportons'). Some words also begin with tiny hooks ('nous' 'le'). Fig. 97 is another good example of controlled writing, but here the overall impression is of a more open, ample and generous style. The control is seen in the small, clubbed endings to the words. The inhibitions in fig. 96 are interpreted as a sign of fainthearted-edness, a fear of action or committing oneself because the writing as a whole contains many signs suggesting narrow-mindedness and pettiness. Unfortunately fig. 97 is rather blotchy because it was written on poor quality paper. However it is still possible to appreciate the firmness and loyalty of the movement. The braking movement which increases the size of the final strokes is here a sign of caution and self-control.

Fig. 98 is **spontaneous** writing. There are no exaggerations and no impetuousness in this writing and the overall impression is of absolute sincerity.

Fig. 90 illustrates what Crépieux-Jamin called **effervescent** or bubbly writing. The movements are very lively, but less progressive than rapid writing, and such writing seems to 'move on the spot' (see the word 'Bastille'), or jump forwards in convulsive and complicated movements. Such is the writing of passionate characters who display excessive zeal and ardour in the pursuit of their goals, but also lack determination and can easily and frequently switch from one goal to another.

The speed of writing is a very important graphological element because it allows us to appreciate the impulsive forces in an individual. We can also assess his reserves of energy, the way in which he uses this energy and whether or not he wastes it, channels it, restrains it, blocks it or controls it.
Associated with **free** graphic movements we have:
   Activity, spontaneity, impulsive character, hotheadedness.
Associated with **inhibition** we have:
   slow or diminished activity, self-control. With reference to feelings: *reserve which can easily lead to dissimulation.*

RECAPITULATION

DESCRIPTION	INDICATION
SLOW (figs. 92, 93). Fewer than 100 letters per minute.	Depending on other signs: Ignorance. Weakness. Passivity. Sluggishness. Awkwardness. Slow and sluggish mind. **With high Form Level:** Self-control. Courtesy. Reserve. Even temper. Deep thinking. Reflection. **With several signs of inhibition:** Effort to combat basic nervousness. Indecisiveness. Timidity. **With very careful writing:** Lack of spontaneity.
POISED (fig. 94) is written without haste, and contains no flying strokes. About 130 letters per minute.	Calm. Circumspection. Caution. Reflection. Wisdom. Stubbornness. **With weak strokes:** Lack of enterprise. Lack-lustre character. Submission to habit.
ACCELERATED (fig. 95) Speed somewhere between POISED and RAPID (about 150 letters per minute).	Good adaptability and intellectual grasp.
RAPID (fig. 89) Economy of movement and adoption of all means to further graphic speed. Simplifications, abbreviations, good connections, combinations etc.	Activity. Skill. Easy adaptability. Lively intelligence. Quick reactions. Enterprising spirit. The 'achiever'. Little inclination to introspection. Superficiality.
PRECIPITATED (fig. 87) combines all the signs of speed in handwriting (200 letters and over per minute).	Ardour. Precipitate action. Excessive haste. Hyperactivity. Lack of care and thought.
CARRIED AWAY (figs. 87, 91) Exaggerated vivacity and fullness of the movements.	Impulsiveness. Rashness. Excitability. Passionate nature. Lack of restraint. Strong ambition. Unmethodical activity.

FLYING STROKES (fig. 91) Results from impulsive movements which lengthen the strokes, particularly the t-bars.

Extraversion. Impulsivity. Spontaneity. Excitability. Impatience. Exaggeration. Zeal (ardent but of short duration).
With firm writing: Combative nature. Will-power. Activity. Initiative. Elan.
Flying strokes covering the word (e.g. two 't's connected with a single bar): Urge to dominate. Feelings of superiority (particularly if the writing is large).
With disorderly writing: Impulsiveness. Lack of caution. Temper. Blind rage.

EFFERVESCENT (fig. 90) Very irregular, more or less angular and seems 'bubbly' and agitated.

Great sensitivity. Impatience. Excessive activity and ardour in the pursuit of short-term goals. Lack of order and method. Instability. Irregular behaviour.

CONTROLLED (figs. 96, 97) Contains movements which are restrained and controlled, particularly in the final strokes.

With good Form Level: Reflection and self-control.
In lifeless writing: Fear of committing oneself. Timidity.

SPONTANEOUS (fig. 98) Simple, natural and devoid of all constraint.

Spontaneity. Straightforwardness. Honesty.

LESSON 9

The Stroke

The term, *stroke*, is applied to the ink-trail left by the pen as it moves across the paper. The course followed by the pen and the relative positioning of curves and straight lines constitute the structure of the handwriting. The stroke, so to speak, is the raw material, the thread with which we weave the writing.

The appearance of the stroke depends on three factors:

> 1 — *The choice of pen*
> 2 — *How the pen is held*
> 3 — *The pressure on the pen.*

The Choice of Pen

The difficulty which many of us experience when writing with anything other than our usual pen (such as the steel-nib pens which used to be provided in banks, post-offices etc.) is a good illustration of how we all need to write with the writing implement which best suits our hand.

It is well known that, except in special circumstances, a writer will always select the pen which adapts best to his individual hand movements, the pressure which he normally exerts on the paper and the thickness or thinness of the stroke he likes to produce.

What are the factors which have the greatest influence on our choice of pen? The answer is: mainly, the *thickness and firmness of the nib or point*.

The Hard or Soft Point

When we write the paper represents an obstacle which acts against us. Paper may be nothing more than insensitive, passive material, but a writer always treats it in the same way that he treats any other substance, whether it be human, animate or inanimate, which offers any kind of resistance. In order to overcome this resistance, the writer must first choose his weapon, i.e. a writing implement.

We have already dealt with the psychological factors involved in the choice of paper and the same factors have a bearing on our choice of pen. Some people like to wage war with their pens and one which disintegrates with the slightest pressure is of no use to such people. They enjoy encountering resistance because of the pleasure derived from eventual conquest.

Writers who fit into this category will therefore select pens which are firm and which allow them to give vent to their aggressive or combative tendencies.

Soft pens, on the other hand, are more suited to indolent or voluptuous personalities. These writers do not seek pens which cut or dig into the paper, but a soft point which glides sensuously and easily across it (fig. 100).

Under normal pressure hard nibs produce a more or less constant width in the downstrokes (see figs. 102, 106, 110, 111), whereas more malleable pens, whose nibs tend to open out under the slightest pressure, easily produce 'bulges' in the middle part of the downstroke. (See figs. 103, 112, 113.)

It is, however, frequently difficult to assess the degree of resistance offered to the pen by the paper since the quality of the pen is not the only consideration. Looking at fig. 115, for example, we could not definitely say if it was written with a soft or rigid pen. All that we can say is that the writing movement is soft. In such cases we must rely for our interpretation on the degree of pressure, which we will deal with later on and which is far more significant than the choice of pen.

Thick or Thin Nibs

With regard to the breadth of the nib, it is no longer the combative or passive inclinations of the writer which govern his choice of pen, but his sense of colour and his emotionality. A broad nib produces a thicker stroke than a fine one. If we compare figs. 100, 101, 105, 108, 118 with figs. 99, 104, 110, 111 our impression of the former will be of the shading, warmth and a feeling of comfort, whereas the second group suggest fragility, delicateness and, depending on the degree of simplification, of coldness (figs. 110, 111).

All that we have seen so far demonstrates that every writer produces, subconsciously, a writing whose form corresponds to his inner nature. Warmth of heart and temperament are expressed by a warm, shaded writing i.e. one containing sharp contrasts between the ink trail and the paper (figs. 101, 105). Delicateness and moderation of instinctual drives, and even their absence, is reflected in light, pale, diaphanous or slender writing (figs. 99, 104). A cold or dry spirit can be seen in dry, spindly or 'stripped' writing (figs. 106, 111).

A broad stroke can be the result of strong pressure or a broad nib. It is interesting, when observing the stroke, to distinguish those features which are due to the pen and those due to the pressure exerted by the writer on the writing implement.

We see genuine pressure where the ovals and curves of the
letters contain 'bulging' only at the base, on the left hand side
of the letter. (See fig. 112, the figure 8 and the letters 'e' and
'l'.) Thickness here only appears on the downstrokes and in
the bottom curves of the letters. In fact, is is very difficult,
when writing with a split pen, to apply pressure on the top
curves. If the upper curves are as broad as the bottom curves
as in fig. 100, it means the writer has used a square nib.

Effect of
broad nib

Effect of
strong pressure

In figs. 101, 105, 118 we find the effects of
both a broad nib and vigorous pressure. The
breadth of the upstrokes show that the
writers used a thick pen, but in general the
downstrokes are thicker than the upstrokes
(see fig. 105, the words 'avec vous', the 'e' of
'avec' and the 'o' of 'vous', fig. 118: the first
'e' in 'sincèrement'). The difference of size
between the left hand downstroke and the
right hand upstroke shows that greater
pressure was applied to the pen when forming the bottom
curve, whereas in fig. 100 there is no sign of pressure at all. *(1)*

The Grip, Pastosity and Precision

When we learn to write we are taught to hold the pen with
the index and middle finger extended along the barrel of the
pen, some distance away from the tip. Children find it difficult
to sustain this hold and because of the effort demanded of
them in writing they grasp the pen with the three fingers kept
as close as possible to the nib and the pen held vertically to the
paper. In the same manner a painter will take a firm grip of his
brush and place his hand close to the canvas when taking
particular care over some detail. When covering a greater

*(1) General Menjaud has made a particular study of the effects of strong and
false pressure in Bulletin de la Société de Graphologie No. 23.*

area, on the contrary, he will take a longer grip of the brush as this allows greater freedom and ease of movement.

Generally speaking the closer to the nib we grip the pen, the greater the tendency for the pen to remain vertical to the paper. *A vertical hold* on the pen results in a ***more precise and incisive stroke*** (figs. 106, 111).

Pen strokes of this type suggest a preference for precision, cleanliness, willpower directed towards achievement, personal discipline and the dominance of reason over instinctual impulses.

An oblique grip results in a *pastose* stroke (fig. 108) a *muddy* stroke (fig. 119) or a *runny* stroke (fig. 120), because the pen, as it touches the paper, offers a greater surface area and therefore the friction is greater than when nothing but the extreme point of the nib moves across the page.

Complete pastosity in writing indicates slovenliness, carelessness, the dominance of instincts over reason, a living for pleasure and sensuality.

Look at fig. 108. The woman who wrote this sample is a gifted Viennese artist. Note how her hand flows freely and generously along the lines. She is a spontaneous personality — open, cordial, carefree and without inhibitions. She is also generous and knows how to take life as it comes without looking for problems. In fig. 119, on the other hand, we find broad garlands filled with ink and which seem to indicate that the writer derives a certain pleasure from pressing down on his pen in an attempt to have the greatest possible area of contact with the paper. Such features indicate brutal sensuality and a liking for coarse pleasures.

In fig. 111, which seems to have been written with the point of a needle, we have, by contrast, the impression that the hand was precariously balanced on the tip of the little finger at the time of writing. Hence the jumpy 'spotted' writing revealing the writer's reluctance to maintain contact with the page. The verticality of the script confirms the writer's aristocratic attitudes and stand-offishness. Here we are far removed from the 'bonhomie' of the preceding sample.

Pressure exerted on the Pen

Even more than the grip on the pen, the type of pressure used by a writer will determine the quality of the stroke and this stroke will be unique to him. One only has to glance at the examples provided to realise that if one were to isolate a single downstroke from the rest, even a novice to graphology would be able to tell which sample it belonged to.

The stroke is one of the most expressive elements of the personality. It is perfectly possible to copy the form and shape of the letters, but it is as difficult to reproduce somebody else's graphic pressure patterns as it is to copy another's voice or facial expressions.

Irrespective of the quality of the pen or the manner in which it is held, the pressure exerted on it can be:

Firm	or	weak
Heavy	or	light
Shaded	or	uniform
Rhythmic	or	irregular

Firmness and Heaviness

We recognise *firm* pressure when the stroke is stretched, well nourished with ink and of regular thickness in the downstrokes (figs. 101, 102).

What can we tell from strong pressure? Basically, it represents energy which has to find an outlet. The writer who presses down firmly on his pen satisfies both the desire to exercise his energy and to experience the pleasurable sensation of overcoming resistance. Behind this energy we find good vitality, good physical equilibrium and strong, if not powerful muscles. More importantly, firm pressure reveals mental energy, combativity and the will to succeed. The writer is demonstrating his love of effort, of struggle and action. By digging into the paper with his pen he leaves his mark which, symbolically, reflects the impression he leaves on his environment. It is a sign of a creative drive which may show up in everyday tasks such as the manner in which he tends his garden, organises his workload, or, in the case of a woman, how she runs her home. Generally speaking, firm pressure writers possess the willpower to put to good effect those ideas formed in their minds. They are decisive, resolute, tenacious and persevering. They know what they must do in order to put their ideas and plans into practice. They are capable of imposing their will on others and they inspire confidence in others with their own self-assurance. When they have gained experience and reached positions of authority they are generally leaders who are admired and obeyed.

Moderate pressure which is also supple and regular and applied with a medium-width pen, produces *nourished writing*. This contains well-inked strokes whose appearance is between the thick strokes of pastose writing and the stretched thread of light writing. It does not have the vigour of firm or heavy writing but it shows good reserves of vital energy, regular activity, good nervous equilibrium and a well-developed sense of reality (fig. 102).

When the pressure is too heavy it produces *heavy* writing (fig. 118) and is a sign of possible brutality. The writer will incline towards materialism because heaviness in the stroke reveals an instinctive nature and a sensual temperament. Heavy writing cannot go with tact and delicacy.

Notched writing (fig. 118) is usually heavy pressure which contains little notches at the top of all the vertical strokes. This effect is produced when the hand pushes the pen in such a manner that the movement increases towards the highest point of the upstroke. Such a movement reflects a tendency to apply force from below and may be an indication of underhand activity. This interpretation only holds good if it is confirmed by other signs. This feature is often caused by a defective pen, or one which is chipped or rusty. If it is a frequently repeated feature in heavy writing it is a sign that the writers wear out their pens more quickly than most.

When the pressure is very great the result is what we call *trenchant* (or sharp) pressure (fig. 109). Here, the energy is not so regularly controlled as in firm writing. The pen now scratches the paper with impulsive and incisive strokes. Trenchant pressure is a sign of a violent, demanding personality and a lack of consideration for others. These writers like to dominate their environment and have their orders obeyed as soon as they are issued. They can be excessive and daring in what they say and do, but their impulsivity means that they seldom bear a grudge and are often capable of abrupt changes of mind.

When the stroke is blurred along its lower edge we have what is termed *runny* writing (fig. 120). This fraying of the lower edge is caused by holding the pen in an almost horizontal position so that the nib sweeps the paper and leaves a trail of ink. In such writing the impulsivity of erratic writing is allied to the brutality of heavy writing, and the implication is of a bad tempered, aggressive and authoritarian personality. For writing to be defined as runny it is essential to make sure that the frayed edge appears on only one side of the stroke and that the other is precise.

Generally speaking, then, strong pressure is an indication of strong instincts, will power, energy which is goal-orientated, an authoritative attitude, a liking for action, personal dynamism and self-assertiveness.

Weakness and Lightness

Weak writing (figs. 103, 104, 115) indicates, on the contrary, a lack of energy and will power, slovenliness, apathy and/or indifference. Weak people may possess a gentleness of spirit which, to a certain extent, makes them more sociable and easier to get on with than the forceful types, but such gentleness is usually the result of passivity, and these people are usually very lazy and unemotive. They easily settle into the rut of routine and can demonstrate a degree of determination against those who try to motivate them. This can be interpreted as strength by those who cannot understand that their stubbornness comes from a fear of straying from their routine.

Light pressure (figs. 99, 111) springs from manual dexterity and delicate movements rather than a lack of energy.

It reveals rather poor reserves of vitality, a delicate nature and weak instincts. With these writers we do not have an impression of drive and energy pushing the pen across the paper. Light pressure suggests sweetness, finesse, respect for others and, in conjunction with roundness and rapid movement, adaptability, suppleness and conciliatory attitudes.

These writers are more idealistic than realistic. The diminished power of the instincts favours spiritual élan by liberating the mind from the demands of the flesh and this in turn leads to a detachment from materialistic considerations. Intuition is present in these writers far more so than in their heavy pressure counterparts. The light pressure writer is receptive, sensitive and subtle. He has antennae which can be far more sensitive than our senses.

As we have already seen, a light pressure stroke does not necessarily mean a lack of moral energy, particularly if the stroke is precise and more or less angular (fig. 99). Such writers can often be surprisingly courageous, wilful and tireless, all of which does not seem to be in keeping with the meagre reserves of energy at their disposal. The reason is that they tend to live on their nerves and the weaker their instinct of self-preservation the less they will pay attention to their physical needs as they are driven along by their idealism. If, however, they look after themselves, they can keep going for a very long time.

Let us compare fig. 99 with fig. 111. The former is progressive, inclined and pulls to the right with passionate zeal, but the latter is restrained, controlled and disciplined. The former, with its enlarged middle zone, wide open letters and concave curves speaks only of feeling, kindness and extraversion. The lack of 'sap' indicated by the slender stroke is compensated for by extreme sensitivity and compassion for others which we cannot detect in fig. 111. In this latter sample the writing is small, dry, extremely simplified, reduced to minimum forms, but containing long antennae projecting into the upper zone. Subtle, sharp-pointed and delicate upper extensions such as these are the mark of cerebral activity and reflect a writer who explores the world with his mind, but at the same time remains detached.

Introversion in this writer makes him disinclined to seek the company of others and careful of how much of himself he gives. His intellectual needs (upper zone greater than middle zone and lower zone) hold sway over his emotional and instinctual drives.

Blurred writing, in which both the stroke edges are frayed, can be included under the heading of weak pressure. Whereas with *runny* writing the stroke has one precise and one frayed edge, in blurred writing both edges are imprecise and remind one of a photograph taken out of focus (fig. 107).

The cause of this phenomenon may be a worn or chipped nib, spongy paper or an oily ink. With a little experience the graphologist can quickly learn to eliminate the accidental causes. In cases of doubt the wisest course of action is to request additional samples.

When it is a regular feature, blurred edges reveal too slack a hold on the pen and a lack of pressure. This muscular relaxation can either be a result of fatigue or a lapse of will power. If the writing is also quick we must infer a degree of impatience which causes the writer to work in a slap-dash manner with little concern for precision (as opposed to precise writing).

With weak pressure, the blurred stroke confirms other signs of fluctuating energy, indecision and slovenliness. Generally it is a sign of the Lympathic temperament.

Irregular Pressure

Irregularities of pressure are revealed in the writing by *spindles* (fig. 112) or sudden thickenings, irregularly spaced, (figs. 114, 116) ink-filled loops and ovals (fig. 115), heavy dots at the beginning or ends of letters (fig. 117) and pastiness (fig. 119).

These irregularities are caused either by sudden bursts of energy (*spasmodic writing*) or inhibitions caused by circulatory problems which interfere with the suppleness of movement (ink-filled loops, heavy dots, unnecessary dots).

Among the spasmodic writings there are several types of spasms which have to be distinguished:

1 — *The soft pressure, produced by sensual writers*, applied fairly regularly on the middle part of the downstrokes and producing *spindle* writing (figs. 112, 113), so called because such downstrokes resemble little spindles.

The novice graphologist can easily confuse spindle writing with writing which is in relief. In order to distinguish between the two it is necessary to examine the bottom of the downstroke very carefully. Writing can only be said to be *in relief* if the pressure is firm. *Firm* pressure is present when the pressure is regular from the top to the bottom of the vertical strokes. Examples of this can be seen in fig. 101, the 'T' of 'Tous' and the 'R' of 'Remerciements'. Compare the squared-off bases of these letters with fig. 112: the fine points of the figure '4' and the 'A' and 'p' of '48, Avenue des Alpes'. In this example the strokes are fuller in the middle but sharp at their extremities because the pressure is not sustained and the pen is lifted before it should be.

We notice also in the latter example that the pressure varies considerably from one downstroke to another: the 'u' of 'Avenue' has the first downstroke twice as thick as the second and the final 'e' of the same word has no pressure at all. The whole sentence resembles a chain in which some links are far stronger than others. In figs. 101 & 105, and even in the slender strokes of fig. 106 we can detect greater firmness and pressure which does not peter out. The quality of a writing depends on the rhythmic application of pressure and not on irregularly spaced bursts of pressure.

Spindle writing indicates sensuality, greed and a love of pleasurable sensations. The writer yields to life's pleasures in the same way that he yields to the sensual pleasure of gently increasing the pressure on his pen. At the same time, however, he relaxes the pressure in sufficient time to avoid having to 'apply the brakes' in order to abort the movement.

2 — *The vigorous strokes of strong minded people* which usually appear in the horizontal movements and produce *clubbed* writing in which the t-bars and final strokes of words or letters spread out into the form of a club (fig. 114).

Clubbed writing is the sign of an emotional and violent character. When the club is short and of only moderate thickness, the writer usually manages to control himself (this feature was dealt with under controlled writing in the Chapter on Speed). But when the club appears at the end of a flying stroke the energy is exploding violently and the writer is likely to do the same, despite any attempts he may make at self-control.

3 — *Sudden pressure on descending strokes, on accents, commas or downstrokes* (fig. 116) also reflects an irritable, violent and explosive character subject to sudden changes of mood and inclined to make a song and dance over trivial matters.

What distinguishes clubbed writing (*final spasm*) from generally spasmodic writing is that the former shows evidence of sudden braking. This is evidence of attempts at self-discipline; attempts which are frequently futile because the writer becomes bad tempered. Nevertheless it does signify a presence of some will power.

A *spasm* which occurs *in the middle of a stroke*, and especially in the downstrokes, is, on the contrary, a sign of renewed pressure after relaxation (fig. 116). The writer makes no attempt at self discipline, but tries to appear stronger than he really is. Frequently, spasmodic pressure is artificial or forced. The writer steels himself, but the effort involved drains him. He is at once impulsive and inhibited and is incapable of co-ordinating his energies, and this produces the jerkiness which makes the stroke resemble a string of rosary beads. He can 'put his back into it' when necessary, but at the same time is incapable of maintaining a steady pace of activity. He is subject to sudden obsessions and fits of activity, gourmandising and sexual over-excitability which he has great difficulty in controlling. The need to be in the right makes him lose control of himself in discussions. He acts instinctively, impulsively and, like an animal, can proceed from total inertia to violent activity in flash.

Ink-filled writing (fig. 115) in which the loops and ovals are filled with ink, can be the result of too soft a pen or thick ink. When not due to these accidental causes it indicates fatigue or sometimes laziness where the writer does not have enough energy to move the pen sufficiently to form the letters properly.

If the writing is precise and light-pressured everywhere else, ink-filled loops are a sign of circulatory problems which interfere with the freedom and agility of the movements.

Sometimes, at the beginnings or ends of letters, the pen comes to rest very briefly, producing unnecessary dots (fig. 117). These unnecessary dots slow down the pace considerably and indicate inactivity, slowness and hesitation. They are character traits typical of a writer who frequently stops what he is doing either to think about it or to rest. When they are very heavy they may indicate feelings of oppression (the writer stops to catch his breath), stemming from heart or lung problems.

Smeary writing is both thick and more or less clogged. It gives us the impression that the writer had too much ink on his pen at the time of writing. If not due to extraneous circumstances (poor quality ink or pen), smeary writing is the result of a certain heaviness of movement which may indicate coarse instinctual drives, sensuality, amorality, heaviness of spirit, lack of tact, negligence or lack of cleanliness.

As with all writing of the congested type, smeary writing can also be a sign of high blood pressure or depression.

It is absolutely vital to take extreme care over the interpretation of clogged writings because of the seriousness of the possible indications. The first thing to do, always, is to eliminate accidental causes. When the graphologist is absolutely certain that the sample he is working from is typical of the writer, he should then observe all the movements contained in the writing structure. If the heaviness or muscular relaxation responsible for the clogging is a feature of the whole text, if the hand seems to move across the page without making an effort, and if the overall impression is of a weak, dirty, vulgar, or neglected writing, then he can begin to suspect materialism, excessive sensuality and moral laxity. If the clogging is only accidental and occurs in an otherwise careful, precise writing, the graphologist should begin to suspect physiological causes.

RECAPITULATION

DESCRIPTION

INDICATION

FIRM (fig. 102) The pressure is strong and regularly applied on all the downstrokes.

Good health. Energy. Will power. Resolution. Virility. Maturity. Stability. Activity. Self-possession.
With large, angular writing: Courage. Assurance. Self-confidence.

NOURISHED (fig. 102) The stroke is precise and well coloured, with a good supply of ink. Pressure is good and the stroke between thin and thick.

Vitality. Physical and intellectual energy. Activity. Will power. Some sensuality. Good equilibrium between delicacy and materialism. Realism.
If there is movement in the stroke: Ardour. Boldness (fig. 21).

HEAVY (fig. 101) Contains heavy pressure.

'Heavy heart'. Sensuality. Materialism. Preponderance of instincts and a life of ease. Lack of sensitivity. Authoritarianism. Brutal opportunism. Realism.

Progressively thickening: Hypertension. Circulatory problems.

IN RELIEF (fig. 105) The harmonious interchange of light and heavy pressure on the up/downstrokes gives the writing an 'embossed' look. A certain firmness must always be present.

Assertive personality. Energy and drive. Good equilibrium. Stability. Will power. Need to get to the bottom of things. Resistance to outside influences. Vitality. **With original forms:** Creative ability. Originality.

TRENCHANT (fig. 109) With strokes which are both impulsive and incisive.

Imperious will power without respect for others. The 'go-getter'. Determination to 'get on' at all costs.

LIGHT (figs. 99, 111) The pressure is feeble.

Refinement. Fragility. Sensitivity. Suggestibility. Lack of the 'achiever' spirit. Fear of reality — the writer avoids conflict. Elasticity. Suppleness of mind. Agility. Adaptability. Receptivity. Intuition. Weakness of instincts. **With feeble lower zone extensions:** Lack of realism. Weak vitality. **Very light:** Extreme sensitivity. Timidity. **If stretched out and rapid:** Superficiality.

WEAK (figs. 103, 104, 115) Contains slack strokes, lacks vigour and the pressure is slight. There may also be drooping lower extensions or ones which return weakly to the left.

Lymphatic temperament. Fatigue. Weak will power. Laziness. Slovenliness. Inactivity. Lack of initiative. Indecision. Apathy. Spinelessness.

PALE (fig. 104) Contains correct formations, but is pale and without relief.

Moral correctness. Good education, but lack of personality. Modesty. Timidity. Frequently the writing of youth, as yet undeveloped.

PRECISE (fig. 106) There are no frayed edges or signs of trembling.

Moderate energy. Concentration. Precision. Personal discipline.

PRECISE *(continued)*

Reason dominant over the instincts and feelings. Firm convictions. **With small writing:** Meticulousness. **With angular writing:** Puritanism. Severity. Coldness. Asceticism.

MEAGRE (fig. 110) Has precise edges and is tall and narrow.

Nervous temperament. Unsociable nature. Grumpiness. Lack of imagination. Inability to enjoy life. Tendency to be virtuous through weakness.

BLURRED (fig. 107) Contains poorly defined, frayed edges and light, unassertive pressure.

Overwork. Fatigue. Weakness. Ardour diminished for health reasons. Imprecision. Negligence. Difficulty in paying attention. Instability.

PASTY (figs. 100, 108) 'Fatty' writing with little or no difference in the up- and down-strokes.

With little or no pressure: Sensory acuity. Aesthetic sensuality. Taste for colour. Love of 'visual' pleasures. Lack of constraint. Sensitivity. Warmth of sentiments. Instincts given free rein. **With good pressure:** See the interpretations of heavy writing.

RUNNY (fig. 120) Has an upper stroke edge that is precise and lower one which is frayed. The writing has flying strokes (pay particular attention to the t-bars and signature underlining. Watch out also for signs of a faulty pen.

Quick tempered. Aggressive and violent character.

SPINDLES (figs. 112, 113) In which the pressure increases in the middle of the downstrokes, resulting in 'spindle' forms.

Greed. Sensuality (manifested or repressed). Love of pleasurable sensations. Love of life. **In copybook writing a few muted spindles simply indicate:** Adherence to habit. Lack of agility. Slow adaptability. Routine.

CLUBBED (fig. 114) Contains strokes which have club-shaped endings.

Ardent character. Passion. Tendency to violent reactions. Brutality. Constraint applied in order to impose a certain equilibrium in one's behaviour.

SPASMODIC (fig. 116) Contains irregularly spaced sudden thickening of the stroke, particularly in the downstrokes.

Emotivity. Impulsivity. Unconscious reflexes. Dominance of instinctual drives. Over-excitability. Irritability. Nervous twitches. Lack of self-control. Irregular activity.
If the spasm is brief: Impatience. Writer 'flies off the handle' but not in a spiteful way.

INK-FILLED (fig. 115) Loops and ovals flooded with ink (Care with the quality of ink and pen).

With muddy, heavy or blurred writing: Reinforces the significance of these types of writing.
With light or precise writing: Possible circulatory troubles.

UNNECESSARY DOTS (fig. 117) Where there are punctuation marks within the letters or between the letters.

Dots at the beginning of words: Slow intellectual grasp. Hesitation. Worry.
Pressure points appearing at random throughout the writing: May be a sign of depression.

SMEARY (fig. 119) Appears to have been written with an overloaded pen.

With excessive pressure: Materialism. Sensuality. Vulgarity. Amorality. Heaviness of spirit.
When occasional: Circulation troubles. Depression.

NOTCHED (fig. 118) When there is a splitting at the top of the vertical strokes. If the writing elsewhere contains light strokes, the chances are that this splitting is the result of a faulty pen (fountain pen).

With heavy pressure: This phenomenon confirms the indications of heavy writing.

LESSON 10

CONNECTIONS

Connections

The up and down movements of the pen on the paper correspond to two different phases of activity. Movements from top to bottom, which form the downstrokes, are gestures of affirmation expressing the degree of the writer's grip on the exterior world. It is a gesture of efficiency and the ability to get things done.

It is possible, in theory at least, to decipher a writing which is comprised of nothing more than downstrokes, but it would be totally impossible to make anything of one consisting only of upstrokes.

The manner in which a downstroke is connected to the following one, or one letter is connected to the next, signals the continuity and co-ordination between successive events in our lives, the progression from the past to the future and the bond which connects the 'I' to the 'You'. The brief journey taken between two adjacent strokes is the clearest indicator of

how a writer adapts to the world, whether it be on the plane of
activity, intellect or emotions.

We shall now consider:

— *The forms of connection*
— *The degree of connection between letters*

The Forms of Connection

There are four basic ways in which letters may be joined to
each other:

angular	
garland	
arcade	
thread	

Those which contain a mixture of the above are termed
'mixed connections', 'semi-angular' or 'semi-rounded'. *(1)*

Angular Connections

We saw, when we were dealing with Speed, that the angle
depends for its formation on a sudden stopping of the pen at
those points where a change in direction is needed. Instead of
proceeding from one letter to the next with a supple
movement of the fingers and hand, the writer employs precise,
rigid and abrupt movements. The writing no longer appears
with that flowing continuity so beloved of teachers of cursive
styles, but on the contrary, looks full of broken lines, darts and
aggressive sharp points.

---

*(1) See the interesting studies by M. DELAMAIN in the Bulletins de la Société de
la Graphologie.*

The angular writer is, in fact, a fighter. He does not compromise: he sets himself up in opposition or enjoys being provocative. He is unyielding, intransigent, contrary, stubborn and firmly entrenched in attitudes and opinions which he is extremely reluctant to abandon.

With firm pressure and regular rhythm, angular writing indicates will power which dominates oversensitivity. In the realm of activity the writer can be combative, aggressive and energetic, and his personal morality will make him loyal, uncompromising, and if the writing is rigid, with inflexible principles.

Once he has made a decision he sticks to it. He is authoritarian and will be as severe on himself as he is on others. He is a tireless worker who needs to find suitable outlets for his energy. If, on account of external circumstances beyond his control (physical disability, retirement etc.) his need for activity can no longer be satisfied, the invalid or old man will continue to wage war by tyrannising over the people around him.

Angular writing is always an indication of a latent ability to engage in conflict. If the writer is also strong he externalises his aggression. If he is weak, which is often the case with writing which contains both angles and weak signs, or angles and signs of inhibition (fig. 122), his aggression will remain on the inside. He is then torn between conflicting tendencies: love and hate, desire and scruples, ambition and impotence. Tortured by doubt and obsession, he cannot experience inner peace.

It is therefore important, when dealing with angular writing, to assess the degree of vitality released into the writing.

Garland Connection

Garland writing is that in which the letters 'm' and 'n' resemble a letter 'u', or, to express it another way, the writer produces concave curves in place of the convex arcs prescribed by the school model.

The effect of this is that the angle connection between two elements of the writing
appears at the top, whereas the arc which
should be at the top appears at the bottom
of the letter, producing a cup-like formation.

The movement involved in the writing of garlands requires
less effort than that needed to produce an angle or arcade. It is
quite natural, therefore, for a more conciliatory attitude to be
associated with this kind of formation than with angles or
arcades. The garland is not a gesture which suggests opposition or inflexibility. It is a graphic movement which binds
together the various elements of a letter or word in an
agreeable, gentle manner.

Within the context of the symbolism of forms the garland is
a gesture of openness towards the top and the outside. The
wide open garland (fig. 123), forming a basket or basin,
symbolises expansiveness, receptivity and giving. We extend
our arms both to receive and to offer, hence the double
significance attached to this form: on the one hand, receptivity, an eagerness of spirit, sensitivity to both joy and anguish;
on the other, kindness, altruism, self-sacrifice, sociability and
hospitality.

With this kind of connection we have none of the indications
of intransigence of the angle, nor the affectation of the arcade,
such as we see in fig. 124 in the word 'Merci'. Garland writing
corresponds to benevolence, sweetness, leniency, generosity
of feelings and, if the pressure is light, an amiable, charming
and easy-going nature.

However, if the writing is also weak and lacking in
structure, we are dealing with weakness rather than charm,
slovenliness rather than nonchalance. When
the garland loses its distinctness of form it
also loses the favourable interpretations of
depth and rhythm which we have spoken of above and
illustrated in figs. 123, 125. In figure 127, for example, there is
no question of depth of feeling. The writer has adopted the

garland simply in order to speed up his writing. He yields because he cannot be bothered to waste time on useless discussion.

Occasionally we come across garlands which contain little loops between the calix walls (fig. 128). In a writing which lacks vitality, or in which there are signs of disorganisation (this is not the case in the example shown) the *sham* or *ringed* garland may be a sign of fatigue. With signs of inhibition it shows timidity and a fear of expressing one's feelings. But in all cases the sham garland, because of its regressive movement (loops formed with left tendencies), is an expression of egoism.

When the rings of this type of garland appear crushed together and proceed along the baseline with pasty pressure, the slovenliness indicated by the sunken garlands and the sensuality indicated by pastosity, indicate amorality.

All features of writing must always be interpreted in conjunction with the other features present. If we look at fig. 126, for example, we will see that there are two distinct characteristics of this writing. There are the wide, open garlands which are also deep and regularly formed and may indicate great richness of feelings. At the same time the pastosity and heaviness of the stroke reveal a sensual and materialistic temperament. The Sensation and Feeling functions are therefore well developed, but they express themselves in a rather passive way. The writing is slow and heavy, reflecting the writer's restrained activity. If we compare this example with figs. 123, 125 we can detect a degree of vigour in the cruciform strokes and lively angle of the 'f' in fig. 123 and in the right slant and the constant squeezed movement of fig. 125. In both cases activity produces great sympathy in the writers for their fellow men and this in turn leads to altruism and a readiness to lend a helping hand. In figure 126 the 'a' of 'affecteusement', the regressive 'f's, the discontinued letters terminating in mid-air all indicate a pronounced egoism in the writer's make up. The writer of this example is, broadly speaking, very understanding, but she would not interrupt her life style in order to help somebody else. She is far too settled in her own comfort to be prepared to sacrifice it merely to help another. She is not mean and would not protect her belongings too fiercely, but neither would she be profuse with her offers of them to others. Rather, her motto would be 'take what you want, as long as it does not cost me anything'. The looped connection we can see on the 't' and 'u' in the middle of the word confirm the egoism which we can deduce from the other regressive movements.

Arcade Connections

In our cursive system of writing the constituent parts of the letters 'm' and 'n' are bound together by a convex curve in the form of an arcade.

The arcade formation is more difficult to produce than the garland because it demands more effort on the part of the extensor muscles. Also, most writers abandon this form of connection and adopt either the garland or a mixture of connective forms which allows the muscles to rest in-between the different types of movement.

Some people, rather than adopt easier forms of connection, prefer to keep to the forms they were taught at school and this should be considered, first and foremost, as an indication of respect for established principles, or, at the very least, respect for external appearances and, in particular, social conventions.

But we also come across writers who, not content merely to reproduce arcades in the letters 'm' and 'n', as per the school model, go a stage further and produce arcade formations all over the place, linking letters with them and using arcade-form t-bars to connect with the following letter. In such cases it is not simply a question of adhering to the school model: we now see a preference for a particular form which corresponds to a definite character trait or inner need.

The graphic gesture involved in describing an arcade (figs. 124, 129) reveals a deliberate choice, conscious design, refinement and an attempt at emphasis. With this concentric movement of the pen the writer is attempting to construct a monument for both his own glorification and his protection.

It therefore seems appropriate to attribute *two interpretations* to the arcade:

— On the one hand there is a *striving for external effect*, pride and/or pretension. This concern with external effect leads to an urge to build, to erect, to compose, often in combination with artistic or aesthetic talents.

There are many forms which this creative urge can take and it may reveal itself in activities as diverse as architecture and founding a religious or philosophical system. Both of these activities can evolve from a desire to give form to one's ideas.

— On the other hand, the arcade indicates *a degree of resistence to outside influences*. The writer, sheltered in his crypt, intends to remain faithful to his true personality. Whereas the garland writer is open to the floods of impressions from without, on an intellectual as well as emotional level, the writer who constructs arcades is enclosed within himself and allows no incursions into his intimate inner world. He hides his real feelings under a veil of conventional politeness. If his writing is elegant, noble and neatly presented it is the result of the somewhat stilted courtesy of the urbane gentleman or 'grand seigneur' (fig. 124). In a vulgar writing containing vulgar arcades such courtesy can easily become obsequiousness, the sign of the servile courtier who glibly dispenses flattering compliments. In slow or discordant writing the arcade is an indication of hypocrisy and the shallowness of those frequently assessed as being 'too good to be true'.

The form level, and particularly the spontaneity, will help us decide which interpretation we should apply to any given writing.

In fig. 124 we see a writing which is both arcaded and superelevated, but clear and harmonious in its proportions.

The writer is somewhat haughty, but he can be flexible, as we can see from the 'm' of 'amie' which suddenly changes into a garland.

Fig. 130 is taken from a much more vulgar sample. We are no longer dealing with the proud but artistic arcade, but with a creeping arcade, lacking in confidence, and proceeding along with a movement which suggests dissimulation rather than elevation (look at the word 'm'annonçant'). Does it not resemble the tortuous, soft trail of a caterpillar?. The twisted and ambiguous letter formations elsewhere in the sample confirm this assessment of a tendency to cheating. The word 'envoi', line 2, has to be guessed at rather than read, and as speed cannot be used as an explanation for the deformity, we must conclude that it reveals falsehood and hypocrisy.

In fig. 129 we come back again to spontaneity. There is something a touch too ostentatious about these tall, spectacular arcades, but no sign of dishonesty. Rather, what we have here is the flamboyant gesture of an artist who draws the images of his imagination in space.

The Thread Connection

In thready writing the pen, instead of moving towards the upper zone to produce the normal height of letters and then coming down again as the downstrokes are formed, stays close to the baseline and only produces the upstrokes. In this way letters such as 'm', 'n' and 'u' are expanded in a rightward direction so that the writing comes to resemble a piece of thread (figs. 131, 132).

Of all forms of connection, the thread is the quickest and requires least effort and it shows that the writer can control his energies. He does not meet obstacles head-on, but circumvents them. This can either be on account of realising how to cope with a situation in the most economical way or because of a tendency to avoid responsibilities.

The thread connection has always been associated with suppleness, ruse, diplomacy and evasiveness.

We recognise the writer who is true to himself, or consistent in his behaviour, by the purity and consistency of the forms of connection in his writing (angles, garlands etc.). But the thread connections, devoid of precise form, reveal an ability to change demeanour at the drop of a hat. This facility may be due to an absence of personality. The writer can play many roles because he does not feel particularly at home in any one of them. Here we have the inconsistent, changeable, versatile, malleable or amorphous types.

When excessive, i.e. when the writing is both exaggerated and formless and the connections are all threads, we must deduce hysteria, instability and an inability to maintain consistent mental attitudes (fig. 132).

If, however, the writing also contains signs of will power and backbone and is more or less homogeneous overall (fig. 133), thready connections reveal a rich fund of talents. This type of writer will have many strings to his bow and be able to use any of his abilities as and when the occasion arises.

Thready connections can be found in the writing of creative people of all ages. This feature reveals a refusal to submit to established principles, a refusal to accept the ideas of others and, at the same time, a degree of impatience in getting rid of obstacles so that he can get to the end of the job in hand.

The simplification involved in opting for thready connections nearly always indicates a concern for speed. If the pressure is good we interpret this concern with speed as a sign of a forceful personality striving to express itself, and strong instincts. With light pressure, thready connections are more of an indication of a Lymphatic or Nervous Temperament.

Mixed Form of Connections

The different forms of connection we have been studying can frequently all be found in one sample of writing. A mixture of forms will generally indicate good adaptability and supple intelligence which has little difficulty in adapting to circumstances.

The graphologist has to learn to distinguish the most frequently used type or types of connections in any writing submitted to him for analysis. If the dominant form is the angle (as in figs. 134, 135) we should immediately begin to think in terms of will power and backbone with reference to the writer. If the curve is dominant (fig. 134 'b', the word 'ci-joint') we can suspect a 'softer' personality. A combination of arcades and garlands (fig. 129, the word 'tendrement'), in an original writing, will suggest a certain creative ability which takes account of exterior influences.

If we come across a writing in which many different forms of connection are used and the writing is generally irregular, we may assume that the writer, although not so evasive as the thready writer, can assume whatever mask the situation requires so that different people will have very different opinions of him.

There are two further types of connection in writing which are relatively rare: the *double curve* and the *supported letter.*

The *double curve* (fig. 137) accentuates, with an unfavourable significance, the indications of weakness, carelessness and lack of backbone associated with rounded forms. The example shown was written by an inoffensive type totally lacking in will power. In an otherwise mediocre, discordant writing this is a sign of an almost total inability to make a decision or face up to obligations and a lack of moral fibre and principles.

The *deviated* or *supported* connection (fig. 138) is that which begins by moving back up the downstroke and then deviates to the right. This is the form of connection prescribed by the Sacré-Coeur calligraphy, and in such a style indicates nothing more than conformism, as it is merely an adherence to the rules. But if this form is found in a fluid writing it cannot have the same meaning because it is no longer the result of a habit inculcated

in the writer by a particular system of education. This type of
connection is a good illustration of a deviated movement
which, spontaneously, makes as if to go in one direction then
suddenly switches over to another. Hence we consider it a sign
of hypocrisy.

The Degree of Connectedness

Letters within words may either be connected, indicating a
single, continuous movement of the pen, or they may be
disconnected. Connected and disconnected writing reveal two
different attitudes.

The movement which binds together all the letters of one
word establishes a continuity between all the elements of the
whole. The fact that the writer maintains uninterrupted
contact with the paper reveals an instinctive need not to 'lose
the thread', to proceed from one idea to another, or one
action to another at the same time as keeping as close as
possible to the logical connections between them.

The method of instruction which teaches us to write words
in a single, uninterrupted movement invites us, at the same
time, to consider these words as indivisible entities. The writer
who conforms to this practice comes to accept traditional
values and fashionable ideas uncritically.

Connected writing, on the one hand, expresses good
co-ordination of ideas, an aptitude for reasoned argument,
deductive thinking, consistency of thought and perseverance
of effort. On the other hand it shows good adaptation to
accepted principles and the established order.

What are the implications of this continuous movement to
the right concerning the writer's emotional life? Can the
constant urge to join each letter to the following one reveal
anything other than a desire for contact with one's fellow
men? Connected writing reveals a sociable nature, solidarity,
a feeling of dependence on others and a need to belong to a
social, professional or family group.

Excessive connectedness gives us what we call *overconnected* writing (fig. 135).

In this type of writing logic leads to strait-jacket thinking and consistency of thought to dogmatism. In his determination to have his ideas accepted and to 'stick to his guns', the writer sees connections which do not really exist. If writing which is slightly more connected than average is a mark of attachment to tradition, overconnected writing reveals a narrow-minded writer who gets on his high horse over matters of principle and is incapable of shedding his opinions and prejudices. Team spirit and 'esprit de corps' in these people degenerates into chauvinism, sectarianism and cliquishness.

The writer, who, on the other hand, refuses to write words as a single entity and prefers to produce letters one at a time, isolating them from each other, as is the case with *disconnected* writing (fig. 136) reveals a determination to preserve his independence on both the intellectual and emotional level. The connected writer is more inclined towards synthesis, the disconnected writer is more inclined towards an analytical approach. The tendency to complete one letter before moving on to the next reveals a need to analyse every detail even if it means losing sight of the whole.

By detaching himself from the traditional ideas or concepts which most of his fellow men adopt 'en bloc', this writer can come up with new and original ones. He feels no need to bind himself to logic with Ariadne's cord in order to find his way out of the labyrinth of reasoned thinking. His thought processes progress in leaps and bounds. He senses things through his intuition, on account of his particular sensitivity. He can also be contemptuous of well trodden paths when making his way in life.

The path this type of writer chooses very often leads inwards rather than outwards. The absence of connecting links comes from a restriction in the movement from left to right, or from the Self to others and the world. Disconnected writing is almost always a sign of an inability to adapt, and writers of this style tend to be people who are unsure of themselves when

faced with problems of a practical nature. In such circumstances they will usually be awkward, timid and hypersensitive.
They are self-centred and lead a life characterised by isolation
and independence from their fellow men. They give little, but
ask for nothing, professing great respect for others but
frequently totally indifferent to them.

This aptitude for introspection and a meditative life can
favour literary or artistic talent. It is no coincidence that
disconnected writing is common among intellectuals —
particularly if they are also hypersensitive — rather than
among men of action.

Between the two extremes of overconnected and disconnected there is the intermediate stage known as **grouped**
writing, in which letters are connected in small groups (figs.
124, 133, 140).

Grouped writers know how to combine logic and intuition
and can adapt to what *is*, at the same time as leaving the door
open to new ideas. The greater the suppleness and originality
of combinations within the groups of letters the more likely
the writer is to be highly intelligent.

For instance, if we follow the ink-trail of fig. 124 with the
point of a needle, we will be able to sense the continuity of
direction between the end of one letter and the movement
which begins the next. We will not have this impression if we
do the same with fig. 137. There is no connection in space
between the second 'n' and the 'e', or between the 'm' and 'e'
of 'personnellement'. In fig. 124 we have an underlying
continuity of movement. In fig. 137 there are sudden ruptures
of direction.

This observation may also be applied to disconnected
writings. There is more continuity, and therefore adaptation,
in the word 'pigeonnier' (fig. 139), containing two groups of
combined letters, than in the jerky letters of fig. 136.

Grouped writing is a good sign of quick thinking, independence and originality of mind, but only if the grouping is
intelligently done and in a manner which favours the elasticity
of the stroke. The different parts of the words in fig. 207, for

example, are like static slices of writing, rather than ingenious groupings. This writing has nothing in common with the rigid writing of a totally unadaptable person or the small, simplified, vivacious writing which shoots off in all directions in fig. 133. In a cleverly grouped writing each little packet of letters must resemble a complete monograph and look like the writer's own shorthand, spontaneously invented for his own usage.

The interpretations we have given above only apply to organised writing, in which the writer is in full command of his physical powers. Some health problems have a considerable effect on the suppleness of movement and, consequently, on the connecting links between letters.

Disconnected writing, for example, is frequently found among the writings of old people. In this case it is a sign of fatigue and diminished faculties.

In *broken* writing (fig. 141) the letters contain fractures in the downstrokes. This feature is frequently observed when certain respiratory or circulatory problems, and their accompanying breathing difficulties, and anxiety are present. These should not be interpreted as functions of the personality.

The same is true of *stick writing* (fig. 142) in which the downstrokes within the letters are isolated. This is often a sign of inhibition and hypersensitivity, but it may also reveal circulatory problems. The graphologist should never make medical diagnoses, and when, confronted with obviously disorganised writing, he should seek clarification on any possible medical problems before drawing conclusions concerning the writer's personality.

Consistent disconnectedness within or between letters is always a sign of inadaptability and limited activity.

RECAPITULATION

DESCRIPTION	INDICATION

ANGULAR (figs. 121, 122, 138) Curves replaced by angles.

With strong pressure: Firmness. Decisiveness. Strong resistance. 'Sang-froid'. Aggression. Positive character. Intransigence. Concern for rules and principles outweigh other needs. Reason. Logic. Correctness. Austerity. Severity. Inflexibility. Intolerance. Susceptibility. Professional conscience. Discipline. Consistency. Perseverence.
With rhythmic writing: Untiring energy
With squeezed writing: (figs. 122. 153) Emotivity. Inhibition. Avarice. Sophism. Narrow-mindedness. Pedantry. Obstinacy. Excessive susceptibility. Distrust. Inhibition. Obsessiveness. Contradictory feelings. Interior division of the personality. Egocentricity.

JERKY (fig. 143). Contains irregularly spaced angles in what should be curved strokes. Jerky writing is due to sudden changes of direction in irregular writing.

Irritability. Excitability. Grumpiness. Inner conflicts. Suspicious mind.

GARLAND (fig. 123) Rounded at the base and 'm' and 'n' resemble letter 'u'.

General indication: Receptivity. Amiability. Benevolence. Gentleness. Easy-going nature. Complacent. Open-heartedness. Naturalness. Aptitude for both joy and suffering. Sympathy. Kindness. Self-sacrifice. Altruism. Hospitality. Femininity. Strong feelings. Desire. Eagerness of spirit.
With right slant: (fig. 125) Devotion.

DEEP, rather weak garlands (fig. 126).	Calm. Tranquillity. Melancholy. Contemplative temperament. Passive sympathy. Indolence.
RAPID, inexpressive garlands (fig. 127).	Superficiality. Adaptability. Tendency to prefer conciliation to useless conflict.
RINGED OR SHAM garlands.	Egocentricity. **With weak pressure:** Fatigue. Overwork. Timidity. Inhibition in expression of feelings. **With normal pressure:** Calculated amiability.
RINGED 'FLABBY' garlands with PASTY PRESSURE (fig. 128).	Amorality.
SQUARE garlands (fig. 126).	Personality which is both materialist and conventional.
ARCADE (figs. 124, 129, 130) 'm' and 'n' and connections in convex arch forms.	May express need to (a) be seen (b) build (c) protect oneself Hence the following meanings according to accompanying signs. (a) Formalism. Good manners. Good social behaviour. Pride. Nobility. Snobbery. Pose. Ceremonious politeness or, with an inferior level, servility, obsequiousness. **Tall, superelevated arcades:** Pretentiousness. Self-importance. Vanity. Arrogance. Disdain. Standoffishness. (b) **With good combinations or artistic forms:** Sense of beauty. Talent. Creative originality. Sense of form and composition (plastic arts or literature). Constructive ability. (c) Prudence. Reserve. Lack of spontaneity. Secretiveness. Resistance to external influences. Individualism. Impenetrability.

ARCADE *(continued)*

With high form level: Taste for the mysterious. Tendency to meditation and introspection.
Flattened, creeping arcades and those curved inwards at the bottom: Hypocrisy. Falseness. Insincerity.
In banal writing: Application. Conformism. The writer is content to reproduce the model.

THREAD (figs. 131, 132, 133)
Resembling an unwinding coil.

The excessive progression symbolises flight from the Self into an indeterminate, external ideal. The writer flees from the world while fleeing from himself.
The rapidity satisfies impatient writers and active people who are always in a hurry and whose ambitions frequently outstrip their ability. There may be a certain brutality in the way they pursue their aims.
The suppleness of their movements and the variability of the forms express the variability of the writers' gifts, the ability to adapt, ingenuity, a creative mind, cleverness, diplomacy, ruse, independence regarding established principles, aptitude for metamorphosis and playing different roles.
If the writing lacks firmness (fig. 132): instability, agonising indecision, suggestibility, versatility, opportunism, inconsistency, lack of moral fibre, avoidance of responsibilities, lack of scruples.
With discordant writing: Predisposition to mental illness.
With soft, light pressure: Lymphatic temperament.
With descending writing: Fatigue, exhaustion.
Thread ends to words are only a sign of speed and impatience and do not

THREAD *(continued)*

carry the interpretations associated with threads in the middle of words. The same applies to softened angles (fig. 144 and to some degree, fig. 131) which are frequently means of simplification. The overall pressure is the vital indicator of thready writing.

SEMI-ANGULAR (fig. 134)
SEMI-ROUNDED (fig. 140)
Contains a mixture of angles and curves.

With good form level: Intelligence. Suppleness of mind. Useful activity. Adaptability. A predominance of curves shows greater gentleness: angles greater firmness. The attitudes can vary according to the environment and circumstances.

DOUBLE CURVE connections (fig. 137)

Weakness. Gentleness. Inconsistency. Difficulty in adopting a firm stance over issues.

DEVIATED OR SUPPORTED connections (fig. 138)

With Sacré-Coeur writing: Conformism.
With fluid writing: Hypocrisy.

CONNECTED (fig. 144) More than 4-6 letters written without taking the pen off the paper.

Logical mind. Deductive thinking. Systematic thinking. Reason. Realism. Foresight. Flow of ideas.
With a mediocre form level: Lack of initiative. Routine activity.

OVERCONNECTED (fig. 135) in which the words are connected.

Excessive association of ideas. Determination to have one's opinions accepted. Sophistry. Sectarianism. Cliquishness. Writers who get on their high horse over principles.
Writing continuously connected: Mania. Obsession.

GROUPED (figs. 133, 140) Letters in unequal groups of 2 or 3 letters.

Critical observation. Good co-ordination of ideas and actions. Initiative. Inventive mind. Personal ideas. Independence of judgement. Adaptability.

DISCONNECTED (fig. 136) All the letters stand apart from each other.

Moral isolation. Refusal or inability to establish relationships. Lack of adaptability. Lack of practical sense. Tendency to analyse the details rather than consider the whole. **If there is continuity of movement despite the disconnections:** Original thoughts. Intuition. Original ideas. **If there are changes of direction between the end of one word and the beginning of the next:** Sluggish activity. Fickle, unco-ordinated behaviour. Lack of sociability. **In all cases:** Egoism. Egocentricity. Avarice. **In disorganised writing:** Sign of exhaustion and diminution of activity through age or illness.

BROKEN (fig. 141) There are breaks in the stroke itself.

An indication of respiratory or circulatory problems.

STICKS (fig. 142) All the vertical strokes are disconnected from each other.

Hypersensitivity. **With other signs of disorganisation:** Circulatory troubles. Anxiety. Anguish.

GAPS in the middle of words.

Psychological troubles.

LESSON 11

The Varieties of Form

The form of handwriting is a synthesis of all the graphic elements. Writing is enriched by in-relief pressure, ease of movement, harmony and proportional balance.

Whereas pressure, slant, direction, the speed or slowness of movement are the main indicators of an individual's temperament, the forms used depend largely on his intellect.

When an adolescent escapes from the constraints of the school model and begins to develop his own style, most of his attention is focused on the form of the letters. Some young people prefer sober forms, simplified and almost typographic, whereas others expand their writing with graceful ornamentation or complications.

With some people the writing effortlessly and spontaneously acquires a personal style, an almost definitive appearance which alters only with age or health. Others, who are more impressionable, pass through several stages of imitation, each year copying the writing of a different friend or teacher on whom they have a 'crush'. Later on they grow out of this mimicry and gradually abandon the stylish quirks which temporarily seem so attractive to burgeoning youth. As these writers approach maturity their writing preserves those features which correspond to their real tastes and personality.

Form, therefore, more than any other feature of writing, reflects the ability to judge, select, imitate, conceive, create, imagine, regulate or organise and, to a certain degree, it also reflects the level of intellectual development.

Certain technical means are available for measuring pressure, dimension, slant and speed. Form can only be appreciated with the eye and by comparison with the model on which it is based.

Some writers are content to reproduce the school model (we will see samples of this later on when dealing with copybook or conventional writing). The majority, however, modify the copybook forms.

We are not about to study every little deformation or variation of each individual letter of the alphabet. This would be a return to the days of interpreting the 'little signs' which, happily, modern graphology has now discarded. *The observation of individual letters, as we shall see in the next lesson, is only important in so far as it allows us to grasp the overall movement of the writing and helps us to understand the reasons for any general deformations.*

The variations of form, depending on the general characteristics, can be summarised as follows:

Original	or	Banal forms
Simplified	or	Amplified/Complicated forms
Rich	or	Poor forms
Open curves	or	Closed curves/Lassos
Natural	or	Artificial/Conventional forms
Clear	or	Confused forms
Elegant	or	Vulgar forms

Originality — Banality

The terms, original and banal, are self-explanatory. The writer who is content to reproduce the style he was taught at school, without any attempt at innovation, expresses his docility, his submission to established principles and his acceptance of others' ideas. Such is the significance of copybook writing (fig. 145).

The writer, however, who rejects the well-trodden path, creates his own model in accordance with his personal needs. If we compare figs. 145 and 146 we notice immediately that the latter reveals a vivid imagination and originality which is totally lacking in the sober minded writer of fig. 145.

It would be a mistake, however, to assume that the highest degree of originality is expressed by extreme eccentricity. The value of writing lies in the spontaneity of the graphic gestures. A bizarre or ornamental writing which is at the same time rigid and systematic (fig. 147), makes us deduce that the writer possesses a certain gift for design work, but lacks a genuinely original mind. *(1)*

Simplification or Amplification

Simplification

The most efficient means of simplifying writing involves suppression of the secondary strokes of the letters and a retention of the essential ones. Generally speaking, any thought which demands to be put into action the moment it is conceived, forces the hand to shoot ahead and shorten the distance covered by the pen, simultaneously choosing between the strokes which must be preserved and those which can be omitted.

---

(1) See Lesson 4: Originality, Rhythm and Harmony

Writing which is simplified in the manner of fig. 149 indicates intelligence, a facility for distinguishing between what is essential and what is not, rapidity of thought and culture. It is a characteristic which raises the Form Level.

In some writing, however, the body of the letters is neglected and degraded by a lack of control of the graphic movement (fig. 132). When this happens the movement is no longer propelled by the desire for speed, but is the result of insufficient effort. We interpret *neglected* writing as a sign of carelessness and laziness in a clear writing (fig. 148) and of negligence, indecision, imprecision and general laxity if it is a marked characteristic (fig. 132).

Amplification

In the amplification of movements we see the opposite tendency, that is to say, no longer an economy of movement, but over-activity. The writer has abundant reserves of energy and he expends his excess energy in graphic expansion, ballooning, and general embellishment of the letter formations.

Intelligence, taste, culture and an aesthetic sense in the writer's make-up will ensure that such exuberance has an harmonious effect on the letter formations, and will animate the movement and flow of the writing (fig. 146). *Animated* writing, which comes from an enrichment of the writing as a whole, denotes, as does writing containing *full* loops, imagination, fantasy, and a certain tendency to embellish reality which goes with a happy personality, a love of life and an attractive light-heartedness.

However, when the amplification of movement affects the secondary parts of the letters (*spirals*, *arabesques* and all the over-ornamentation of *ornate* writing, (figs. 150, 151) while the small letters are pale and lifeless, we may deduce that in the writer's mind, as in his writing, the supplementary is more important than the essential. 'Padded-out' writing, generally speaking, reveals a lack of taste, low intelligence, vanity, pretentiousness and bragging.

Full and Lean Forms

We talk of rich or full forms *(1)* when the curves of the writing, by natural but not excessive movement, tend to encircle an appreciable area of white space. Poor, lean or dry forms occur when the loops and ovals are squashed flat (fig. 152 contains full forms; figs. 153, 154 more meagre forms). The thickness of the stroke reinforces the impression of richness which comes from rounded forms, whereas leanness is accentuated by a predominance of straight lines (figs. 105, 110).

Fullness of letter formation has always been associated with a rich imagination, fantasy, and creative ability, whereas leanness suggests reason, critical powers and a tendency to consider principles more important than the demands of life.

In fact, imagination is the ability to evoke images, to bring to mind objects in minute detail and to recreate them by thought processes in terms of their size, shape, colour and/or emotional content. Creative intuition is born of the association of ideas.

Reason, in its pure form, does not stem from an ability to reconstruct images or states of mind, but rather an ability to separate and classify. It is satisfied with abstract, linear representation. The aim of reason is not to bring to life objects in their real, tangible forms, but to create from deduction or theory.

Too much of one quality implies a lessening of the other. An over-active imagination interferes with the powers of judgement and critical ability. Thought processes which can only theorise and criticise lose touch with life and this leads to a withering of the soul and poverty of feelings and imagination.

---

(1) L. KLAGES – L'expression du Caractère dans l'Ecriture p.151. (Niestlé Delachaux, Ed.)

Fullness or leanness can affect one zone more than the others.

Fullness in the middle zone (the zone of the emotions) shows warmth of heart, enthusiasm for day-to-day living, emotional needs, sentimental dreams (fig. 152, 155).

Fullness in the upper zone (curved upstrokes on the 'd', connections between dots, dashes and the letters etc., fig. 156) shows imagination and lively intellectual interests.

Fullness in the lower zone reveals an intensive instinctual life which manifests itself in strong activity, strong sexual urges and a sense of values based on a materialistic outlook. It is also an indication, depending on the form level, of good practical sense, an aptitude for mechanical work or, if the curves are harmoniously integrated, a rich unconscious nurtured by artistic gifts. Poets and romantic novelists frequently have dish-shaped lower extensions which are an indication of great instinctive receptivity. An example of such lower curves is seen in fig. 157 : the 'f' of 'faisait' and the last 's' of 'passionnés'.

When evaluating the form it is essential to distinguish between true richness and ostentation. Excessive prolongments, inflated forms, ballooning, distended loops which destroy the graphic equilibrium and proportion with the neighbouring letters, must make us suspect illusions and the vanity of a frog who wishes he could be as tall as an ox (fig. 158). *(1)*

Dryness in writing expresses:

In the upper zone — a mind lacking in imagination, but nevertheless lucid.

In the middle zone — a 'cold' character, a withdrawn nature.

In the lower zone — detachment from materialism and the world of sensation.

---

(1) Re-read in the lesson on Dimension, 'inflated forms, expanded forms, upper and lower extensions'.

Open Curves, Closed Curves, Lassos

The curve is a form which abounds in symbols. It represents equally, grace, femininity, opulence and fecundity. Directly opposite to the dryness of the angle or single stroke, the curve is a gesture of tenderness, receptivity and warmth. It is a symbolic gesture of protection or containment and sometimes of encirclement, dissimulation or monopolising.

We have already examined the significance of the open curve in our dealing with the garland and the arcade. Now we will see what happens when we examine loops and, particularly, the ovals. For example, let us compare fig. 159 with figs. 152, 155, and 160.

In the first example the ovals are wide open at the top (see the 'o' of 'Monsieur', the 'a' of 'fais' the 'd' and 'g' of the last word). First and foremost, the indication of not finishing off the curve movement is one of carelessness. It is the door left open without fear of burglars. It may also signify a tendency to share one's all with others. People who have *open* writing (the usual description for this type of writing) are generally spontaneous, generous and more than frank and can be inconsiderate in their remarks. A great openness of heart. mind and thought governs their conduct which is often imprudent and impulsive.

Double joined (closed) writing (figs. 152, 155, 160) shows just the opposite personality traits. In this type of writing the ovals, instead of being closed with a simple rightward movement at the top of the letter, as recommended by the copybook, are hermetically sealed with a regressive movement which doubles back on itself. Openings in this type of writing, where they exist, are usually to the left i.e. facing the writer. (See example on the left.)

The door is no longer open to all comers. The writer keeps vigil over everything: his possessions, his emotions, his thoughts, his secrets. In the most favourable cases, when the writing is clear and spontaneous, a moderate degree of 'closing up' in the ovals, as in fig. 161, is simply an indication of prudence and discretion. When the feature is pronounced (figs. 152, 155) or found with a slow speed, (fig. 160) the interpretation will usually be dissimulation.

Sealing is always produced by a regressive movement and indicates, therefore, a certain degree of egoism. It may happen, however, as in fig. 155, that such a movement is compensated for by very open garlands. This leads to the conclusion that the writer's first impulse is to be kind, sympathetic, generous and receptive, but that this generosity is soon exhausted and the Self quickly insists on its due.

The most unfavourable interpretation must be reserved for the sealing which takes place at the base of the letter or forming the letter in two distinct parts. In a mediocre form level such features are almost invariably a sign of dishonesty.

Lasso movements are like superfluous loops or knots frequently found in t-bars (fig. 162) or other letters. The final 'd' of 'demande' (fig. 155), the 'b' of 'aimable' (fig. 146), the second 's' of 'passionné' (fig. 157).

Sometimes the loops of 'e', 'l' and 'b' may start with a slightly concentric movement. See the examples on this page and (fig. 163) the 'e' of 'heureux'.

Any circular movement which is superfluous to the normal formation of the letter reveals the intention to envelop, capture, draw towards oneself, and a certain facility for captivation (as Michon said of young girls who form their 't's with a lasso formation at the base). One also detects with closed lassos, a certain skill at 'getting round' people, as in the word 'Paris' (fig. 164). The form level and combinations of other signs will allow us to decide which of the interpretations, ranging from amiable seduction to downright deceit, apply in any given case.

Spontaneous or Artificial Writing

The person who cannot appear to be anything other than he really is writes in a simple and spontaneous manner without any attempt at affectation. Naturalness and simplicity express themselves instinctively in *simple* writing (fig. 165). Such writing does not contain the deliberate sobriety of *simplified* writing (fig. 149). It is less constrained than school model writing from which it deviates little (fig. 145) and only makes such changes that reveal spontaneity and honesty. When such writing contains no unfavourable signs, the interpretation is quite straightforward: purity, simplicity, sincerity, correctness.

On the other hand we frequently meet people who hide their true natures behind a mask, either because they wish to hide certain weaknesses or because they wish to shock the world with their excesses. These are the people who present us with the variety of *artificial*, or bizarre, styles.

An artificial writing can be recognised by the degree of constraint present, a certain 'stilted quality', a stereotyped appearance, slow speed and systematic regularity in the deformations or exaggerations (figs. 147, 158, 166).

Fig. 166, derived from a printed style, was written by a sixty year old man who, with this copybook style, was attempting to regain co-ordination of graphic movements as his writing had become illegible through illness. The clarity, grace and simplicity of some forms (see the curves on the letters 'g' and 's'), indicate good taste, aesthetic sense and intellectual superiority. However, the strokes lack confidence and the letters, formed with several movements of the pen, reveal extreme impressionability. The complete absence of connections, as we have seen in the preceding lesson, reveal great difficulties in adapting to the practical side of life, and a profound emotional isolation.

It is difficult to penetrate what Pulver called 'the wall of impenetrable typographic style'. The famous Swiss grapholog-

ist considered such writing a 'façade of hypersensitive intellectuals'. When faced with the problem posed by most artificial
writing, it is nevertheless interesting to distinguish between
genuine sensitivity, hidden behind a mask of disconnected
writing (fig. 166), and the cynical deception revealed by other
types of artificial writing.

People who use the latter style show a desire to be original
at all costs. They cover up their lack of personality to such an
extent that they become prisoners of their own deception and
lying.

In inflated forms, exaggerations and attempts at 'fashionable' writing (fig. 158) we have good examples of distorted
illusions, snobbery and vanity.

Generally speaking, artificial writing reveals, to varying
degrees and for different reasons, the very opposite of
sincerity.

Conventional Writing

This is the style of writing which used to be taught in
convents and 'high-society' ladies' finishing schools. The
majority of conventional styles in France derive from the
copybook style termed 'Sacré Coeur'.

This school model, perfected by M. Carré, aimed at
teaching children to produce absolute regularity in their
writing. At the beginning, he forced the children to regulate
their hand movements with a metronome, which accounts for
the rigidity, angularity and triangular ovals which are features
of this style. Nowadays the metronome has been discarded,
but the rigidity, angularity and obligatory full connectedness
has remained. Fig. 161 is a good example of this.

Conventional styles, because of the degree of inhibition
associated with them, have long been considered a sign of
insincerity and a lack of spontaneity. One does not learn how
to behave in society without self-discipline and the inhibitions
which this implies are recorded in the writing. Dishonesty,

however, is no more prevalent among strictly brought up people than among others, even if the former are sometimes, by virtue of their education and environment, inclined to put on a show of superficial feelings which they do not really experience. Behind the mask of convenience it is possible for the heart to remain pure and the soul loyal and steadfast.

Conventional writing is analysed in the same way as any other. The closer such writing is to the school model, the more submissive the writer is to established rules, conforming to the impersonal tone of his upbringing. However, even among a dozen scripts written in the Sacré-Coeur style, a graphologist of relatively little experience will notice the differences in dimension, pressure, slant, direction, speed etc. and these features will allow an assessment of the degree of submission on the part of the writer to rules and regulations.

Let us compare figs. 2 and 3. In fig. 2 the writing is monotonous, automatic, lifeless and displays limited intelligence. There is no sign of any spark of interest in anything beyond the material preoccupations of everyday existence (note the heavy stroke, following the baseline as if 'glued to the earth'). By contrast, fig. 3 shows a sensitivity and intelligence which are far more lively. The lower extensions have lost their angularity and we can detect simplified movements, a certain deftness and a far more nuancée stroke than in the preceding example. There is no doubt that the writer (female) would have revealed her true personality earlier on if she had not been subjected to a conventional style. Nevertheless, we can still ascertain a good deal from the writing concerning her personality, even though an in-depth analysis may be impossible.

Clarity or Confusion

In his *A.B.C. de la Graphologie* Crépieux-Jamin states that 'A handwriting is clear when it is legible, the formation of letters is regular and there are no unnecessary complications.'

Clear writing is an indication of a clear mind. If the writer is an intellectual he will be a good stylist, a good orator and teacher with a flair for communicating his knowledge in a way which will make others understand easily (fig. 166). If he is a man of action he will be good at organisation and the type who gets things done (fig. 149).

With meagre or banal forms (fig. 145), clarity is mainly a sign of an ordered and methodical mind.

Whatever the form level, a clear writing, if it is also spontaneous, is a sign of frankness and moral integrity: the writer has nothing to hide.

Clarity is also a sign of good manners. The purpose of writing is to produce something which can be read by someone else and not to set undecipherable enigmas. But as an excess of anything is treated as a negative sign, we must be very wary of any writing which is 'affectedly designed'. Forgers frequently write with a slow, copybook style which can often mislead the inexperienced graphologist. The 'give-away' is their extreme precision and restrained movement.

At the opposite end of the scale we have *confused* writing (figs. 163, 167). This term is generally applied to illegible, muddled or tangled writings.

When examining a confused writing it is essential to decide whether or not the writing is also incoherent. The odd sentence or word which is repeated, capital letters in the middle of words, or baroque forms, may reveal mental disorder (fig. 168, the writing of an idiot).

We must also pay attention to the dynamism and speed. When deformed letters are the result of haste we must suspect a certain impetuosity in the writer's make-up. (Re-read the chapter on Speed.) The writer forgets that what he is writing has to be read. Everything has to yield before his driving will power which tolerates neither resistance nor slowness. Illegibility reveals not only the haste of a man in a hurry, but also the haughty distrust of one who heads straight for his goal without any consideration for the rights of others. The greater the firmness and power the more it reveals rudeness on the part of the writer.

When the lack of legibility is due neither to negligence nor haste, it can be a sign of a devious mind. We all know people who seem to dislike anything which is straightforward. They seem to prefer 'muddy waters', convoluted solutions, complications and vague projects. Their attitude is never frank. They give presents apparently reluctantly, they say 'yes' when they mean 'no', they slip ambiguous clauses into their contracts in the hope of being able to use them to their advantage later on. All these character traits are shown by false or evasive gestures and, in writing, by equally equivocal forms.

In fig. 167 ('vous faire la commission dont' . . .) the writing is not deformed by speed, the pace is relatively calm, and yet there is some ambiguity in the letter formations: the 'v' could be an 'n', the 'o' could be a 'u'. In fact there is something generally evasive and elusive about it, as if the writer were refusing to commit himself unequivocally on paper.

There are also people of a hypersensitive nature, who although not dishonest, do like to surround themselves with an air of mystery in their attempt to camouflage their weaknesses. Their hesitant movements, detours and 'retreats' come together in such a way as to make the writing look like a deeply rooted bush. We can recognise in fig. 163 a writer of timid, indecisive, spineless, anxious and inhibited character who is always ready to seek refuge behind a lie or to take advantage of evasion and deceit rather than admit his mistakes.

Distinction or Vulgarity

Although these features involve what is largely a personal, subjective opinion, they are still too important to be discounted. Distinction or vulgarity, in writing as in an individual, depends on nuances which cannot be measured. They have to be felt and they become part and parcel of an individual's personality to such an extent that they can be detected, even by children, with unfailing accuracy. Distinction or vulgarity has an effect on every aspect of the way in which a person conducts himself in his environment, including his voice and his gestures.

Noble writing can be found among people from humble backgrounds, just as common or vulgar forms can be found among people whose upbringing should have protected them from the influence of coarse behaviour. Apart from one or two exceptions a writer's family background and the appearance of handwritings he comes into contact with will, from quite a young age, have a profound influence on him. For this reason it is often possible for graphologists to accurately place a writer in his social milieu and to judge his degree of refinement or otherwise.

Elegance or vulgarity are qualities which the graphologist has to learn to appreciate intuitively, but which are also valuable aids when it comes to building up a character portrait.

RECAPITULATION

ORIGINAL OR BANAL HANDWRITING
(Re-read Lesson Four)

SIMPLIFICATION — AMPLIFICATION

DESCRIPTION	INDICATION
SIMPLIFIED (fig. 149) The letters are reduced to their essential structure. Loops, curls etc. are suppressed. Capitals are typographic.	Intelligence. Culture. Adaptability. Ability to distinguish between the essential and non-essential. Loftiness of ideas and clarity of judgement.
NEGLECTED or INCOMPLETE (fig. 132) Letters are poorly formed or suppressed in a generally weak, tensionless writing with missing t-bars and punctuation marks.	Laziness. 'Couldn't care-less' attitude. Negligence. Slapdash working habits. Superficiality. Lack of method. Unpunctuality. **If these features are temporary:** Fatigue.

ANIMATED (fig. 146) Lively and more or less AMPLE overall. Also a certain originality of movements.

Extraversion. Vivacity. Grace. Imagination. Gaity. Love of life. Exuberance. Activity.

With extended movements: Need for exteriorisation. Sanguine temperament. Exuberance. Search for outward effect. Vanity. Poor taste. Boasting. Inferiority complex overcompensated by excessive pride.
With moderate dimensions: Importance of non-essentials exaggerated. Poor judgement.

ORNATE, EMBELLISHED (fig. 150) Writing with exaggerated capitals.

COMPLICATED (figs. 151, 163) There are strokes that are totally superfluous to the formation of the letters.

Hesitation. Inhibition. 'Finicky' character. Meticulousness. Indecision. Lack of openness and simplicity. Dissimulation. Insincerity.

FULLNESS AND LEANNESS

FULL (fig. 152) Without being inflated, the loops and ovals cover a noticeable amount of area on the page.

Imagination. Creative mind. Aesthetic sense. 'The art of living'.

SOBER (fig. 149) All the movements are contained within moderate dimensions.

Introversion. Self-control. Reflective mind. Modesty. Wisdom. Prudence. Good sense. 'Thinking' Function.

NARROW (figs. 153, 154) The ovals are flattened and the downstrokes are very close to each other.

Lack of imagination. Inner poverty. Critical mind. Dogmatic tendencies. 'Planning' mentality. Little aesthetic sense. Timidity. Modesty. Lack of self-confidence. Distrust. Repression.
With superelevations and angularity: Inferiority complex. Vulnerability. Egocentricity.

CIRCULAR MOVEMENTS — OVALS AND LOOPS

ROUND (figs. 152, 155) Ovals in circular form.

Adaptability. Sociability. Egoism (very rounded forms are always somewhat regressive).
With nourished strokes: Cordiality.

OPEN (fig. 159) Ovals are open to the top and right.

Spontaneity. Trust. Sincerity. Easygoing nature. Altruism. Generosity. Devotion.
With flying strokes or weak writing: Thoughtlessness. Talkativeness. Inability to keep things to oneself. Lack of self-control. 'Putting one's foot in it'.

DOUBLE JOINED (figs. 152, 155) Ovals are closed with a large regressive loop, or the ovals are open to the left.

In clear, simple and spontaneous writing: Discretion. Prudence. Self-containment.
With a mediocre Form Level: Dissimulation. Distrust.
With noticeable regressive movements: Egoism. Captivating skills.

CLOSED AT BASE or FORMED WITH TWO SEMI-CIRCLES.

Dishonesty. Deceit.

LASSO (figs. 155, 157, 162, 169) There are superfluous loops.

Cleverness. Captivating attitudes.
Depending on Form Level and other features: Skilful and inventive imagination. Or: Grasping egoism.
Lassos at the base of a 't': Stubbornness. Tenacity.
Lassos placed high, like a whip lash at the top of a 't' stem: Dynamism. Authoritative nature.
Lasso paraph: Commercial skill.

SPONTANEOUS OR ARTIFICIAL

SIMPLE (fig. 165) Contains no attempts at effect.

Simplicity. Modesty. Sincerity.

AFFECTED (fig. 157) There are some individual pretentious eccentricities.

Affected manners. Ceremonious politeness. Narcissism. Self-admiration.

CONVENTIONAL (fig. 161) Derived from Sacré-Coeur style. Quite tall, angular, very connected and with ovals in the shape of triangles.

Conformism. Attachment to principles. Lack of personality. Repression. Sometimes snobbery. Hypocrisy.

ARTIFICIAL (figs. 166, 147, 158) Constrained writing. Affected writing. More or less stereotyped. Systematic exaggerations.

Almost always conceals some weakness.
Constrained: Tension. Fear. Anxiety. Hidden inferiority complex.
Exaggerated and inflated: Snobbery. Pretentiousness. Lack of taste and spontaneity. Superficiality.
With regressive movements: Egoism.
Bizarre forms: Desire to stand out. Strange tastes.

CLARITY OR CONFUSION

CLEAR (figs. 149, 170) Legible with limpid shapes.

Order. Simplicity. Clarity of mind.
With spontaneous writing: Sincerity.

IMPRECISE (figs. 87, 91) Letters are poorly formed and often illegible.

If imprecision is due to speed: Over-riding desire to get the job done.
With firm or trenchant pressure: Rudeness. Brutal activity.
Imprecise through lack of firmness or ambiguity of forms: Insincerity. Ambitiousness. Elusive character. Avoiding responsibilities.

CONFUSED (fig. 163) Illegible through agitation, complication, confusion. Disordered incoherent forms.

In children's writing: Instability. Nervousness.
In adults' writing: Confused mind. Lack of judgement. (Inner conflicts, disorder, laziness)

DISTINGUISHED (fig. 170) The forms are simple and pleasing to the eye and harmoniously proportioned.

Courtesy. Good manners. Good education. Refined tastes.

VULGAR (figs. 150, 164) Contains inharmonious disproportions and ungraceful forms.

Bad taste. Lack of education. Awkwardness.

PROTEIFORM (fig. 168) One letter has many forms (see the letters 'q', 't', and 'd' in this example).

Depending on the Form Level and other signs: Instability. Inconstancy. Dissipated character. Hypocrisy. Insincerity. Ability to play several roles.
With a good Form Level: Improvisation skills. Inventive mind. The value of the writing as a whole will tell us if we are dealing with an inventive skill accompanied by good or bad intentions.

RETOUCHED (fig. 25) Parts of the letters added after a break. The tops of 'r', 'e' etc. or the upper extensions.

Finicky nature or simple scruples. The odd retouching may make the writing easier to read and therefore indicate a desire for clarity and precision. However, many retouches show anxiety, nervous troubles and fatigue.

LESSON 12

Free Movements

In the previous lessons we have attempted a methodical examination of the deviations and changes which character can produce in personal movements and, consequently, in the handwriting.

These deviations are particularly evident in the initial and final movements of letters, the t-bars, accents and paraphs, all of which should be considered as the free movements of writing.

When we write anything, it is essential, if the finished product is to be legible, that the form we give to the letters should resemble the standard form, to some degree at least.

However, the pen is not guided by expediency before we begin each letter or after we have completed it. Unfettered by any sort of constraint, the pen will move in accordance with our natural impulses. The graphologist will frequently be obliged to pay great attention to these free movements in order to ascertain the spontaneous direction of the graphic movements with greater accuracy. Movements begun or freely expressed in the initial or final strokes of a word, syllable or letter (depending on whether the writing is connected, grouped or disconnected), the accents, t-bars or paraphs, emanate from the same causes as those which govern the overall appearance of the writing. Therefore there is no need for us to re-examine the theoretical explanation for such movements or the symbolism of the features we are about to discuss here.

Initial Movements (starting strokes)

Absence of initial stroke : The writer makes a direct attack on the structure of the letter (simplified writing) showing: Decision. A quick mind. Conciseness of thought. Immediate grasp of the essentials.

Initial stroke in curved garland, or slightly rounded and enlarged (animated writing): Grace. Playfulness. Gaiety. Talkativeness. Sanguine temperament.

Centrifugal initial stroke: Letters beginning with a rigid, ascending stroke : Spirit of opposition. Systematic objection.

Complicated initial stroke: Verbosity. Vanity. Bad taste.

Initial resting dot: Slow thinking. Reflection. Meticulousness.

Initial stroke superelevated in comparison to the rest of the letter: Conceit. Pride.

Final Movements (finishing strokes)

Short final movements: Self control. Reserve. Introversion.

Final open curves : Friendliness. Generosity. Kindness. Willingness to help. Extraversion.

Regressive, thrown final movements : Calculated amiability. Need to be rewarded or repaid. Need to be noticed. Impulsivity.

Final movements in regressive hooks : Egoism. Grasping nature. Greed.

Centrifugal final strokes, thrown to the right and ascending : Physical courage. Elan. Rebellious mind. Protest. Argumentative nature.

Suspended final strokes : Due to a certain type of inhibition which causes the letters to be prematurely finished. Noticeable particularly in the letters 'l', 't' and 'e' when they do not reach the line : Inhibition. Scruples. Sense of propriety. Fatigue. Tendency to over-react and worry unduly.

In a low Form Level : Dissimulation (the writer refrains from saying what he thinks or knows in order to deceive).

Final strokes extended horizontally : Extraversion. Talkativeness.

Centripetal or plunging final strokes (A centripetal stroke moves in the direction of the writer and the base): If the stroke stops abruptly : Decision. Need for material achievement. If the pressure is more or less spasmodic : Tension. Irritability. Over-excitability. Impatience.

Centripetal and regressive final movements : Egoism. The born beggar. Grasping mentality. Avoidance of responsibilities.

National

toute

Sharp-pointed final movements: Critical mind. Spirit of contradiction.
Final movements clubbed: Intensity of will. Violent temperament which is ardent and passionate, but which makes some effort towards self-restraint.

T-Bars

t

f toit

obstiné

ete

t

t

t

Totalitaire

volonté

t

toi et

toile

Sharp-pointed, centrifugal or clubbed: Same significance as the final strokes.
Thrown: Vivacity. Impulsiveness. Hot temper.
Cruciform (Crossing the stem at right angles and with a gesture of decisiveness and firmness): Combativity. Fighting spirit. The same feature can be seen in the letters 'f' and 'z'.
Descending: Tenacity. Opinionated nature.
Long and fine: Weak will.
Imprecise, wavy: Hesitation. Indecision.
Convex: Seriousness. Inhibition of aggressive instincts.
Concave: Frivolousness. Caprice. Inconsistency. Superficiality.
Above the stem: Desire to dominate. Independence. Authoritarianism. Despotism. Desire to 'get on'.
Strong and regular: Will power. Resolution. Energy. Confidence.
Feeble: Lack of will power (if confirmed by other signs).
Placed low on stem: Timidity. Lack of self-confidence.
Absent: Laziness. Weakness. Carelessness.

Tenace

entêté

fouet

adaptah

With hooks : Tenacity. Determined pursuit of goals.
In lasso form : Stubbornness. Cleverness. Taste for practical work.
In 'whip' form : Indomitable character.
Forming a link with the following letter : Adaptability. Efficiency. Rapidity.

Some Typical Strokes

plus fort

faiblesse

trait

hésitant

t y

M f

δ f lors

Precise, firm downstrokes : Self-confidence. Decisiveness. Assertive will. Dominance of others. Ability to 'get things done'.
Wavy or weak downstrokes : Lack of assertiveness. Self-effacing personality. Weak will. Impressionable character. Lack of powers of persuasion.
Firm, elongated horizontal strokes : Physical courage. Confidence. Determination in action.
Fine, light horizontal strokes : Hesitation and lack of will power. If the bars are long: Impulsivity, but feeble emotional energy.
Regressive angles at the base of 't's or lower zone extensions : Stubbornness. Resistance. Restive nature.
Discontinuous forms (Letters made up of several strokes or in separate parts): Instability. Irregularity. Caprice. Sense of fun.
Reverse movement forms : Movements made in the opposite direction to that stipulated by the copybook (right tending stem on a 'd', lower extension on 'f'

tending towards the left, clockwise movement used to form letter 'o'): Independent mind. Restive character. Obstinacy.

Capitals

Wide: Self confidence. Vanity.
Squeezed: Timidity. If angular and superelevated: Narrow-mindedness. Vulnerability.
Superelevated: Pride. Conceit.
Low: Modesty. Simplicity.
Connected to the following letter: Adaptability. Sympathy. Altruism.
Underlining the word: Vanity. Need to
feel appreciated.
Roofing the word (like a plume or
umbrella): 'Grand seigneur'. Need to be
protective.
Final stroke in lower zone: Search for
material success. Positive character. (The
same interpretation applies to the small
letters).
Printed form: Aesthetic sense. Intelligence. Culture.
**Capitals in place of small letters in the
middle of words:** Short-lived enthusiasm.
Tendency to embellish reality. Lack of
judgement. Tendency to 'fly off the
handle'.

Lower Zone Extensions

**Lower zone extensions plunging, right tend-
ing and animated:** Talkativeness. Enthusiasm in words rather than action.

voyez

wagon

portou

pays

Lower zone extensions open, with a loop which is unfinished: Playfulness. Imagination.

Lower zone extensions in triangular forms: Obstinacy. Domestic/material authoritarianism.

Lower zone extensions finished off with a regressive, spasmodic, sharp-pointed spike: Malicious deceit.

Lower zone extensions weakly turned to the left: Weakness. Indecision.

Punctuation

i

cité

été

lisibilité

l'oiseau

i brève

même

reço

néglige

Dots and/or accents light and high: Idealism. Lofty aspirations. Ambition. Illusions.

Dots heavy and placed very close to the letter: Materialism. Positive mind, 'Feet on the ground'. Pessimism. Lack of élan. Neurasthenia.

Dots and accents deformed, thrown haphazardly onto the paper: Impatience. Carelessness. Thoughtlessness.

Precisely placed: Reflection. Attention to detail. Reserve.

Spasmodic and sharp-pointed: Over-excitability. Aggressive impulses.

Dots and accents regressive or circular: Egoism. (Similar interpretation to double joined)

Animated accents: Imagination. Sense of fun.

Dragging accents in unsteady writing: Fatigue. Weakness.

Dots and accents omitted: Lack of attention or impulsiveness.

Signature

The signature is a reflection of the attitude adopted by the individual in the face of the collective. It is, to use Jacoby's phrase, 'the psychological visiting card', the expression of the official side of the personality and the face he shows to the world.

For this reason we should not always expect to see the whole character of the writer expressed in his signature, because a man can be very different in his private life from his social and professional life.

If the signature is written in a style which is similar to that of the text, it is safe to assume that there is no difference between the writer's intimate self and the 'front' he shows to society. But when there is a marked difference between signature and text it is a sign of a two-sided personality, of behaviour in public which does not correspond to the writer's inner nature. The former is reflected in the signature and the latter in the text.

These differences are often revealed in the angle of slant: a right-slanted text with a left-slanted signature, or a vertical text with a slanted signature. Sometimes the differences will be revealed in the letter formations: a cursive text with block letters in the signature or some other variation of style.

We should always be wary of illegible signatures, particularly when they are weak or complicated with coiling paraphs suggesting dissimulation. These signatures reveal a writer who is evasive and lacks the courage of his convictions.

It sometimes happens that the signature, for one reason or another, does not evolve in tandem with the writing. In a child or adolescent all playfulness is tolerated and variations in the signature are not considered important. However, as soon as the man becomes responsible for his actions and has to honour his commitments with his signature, signing important documents in connection with financial transactions, his signature must remain constant. Hence it is not unknown for people to be stuck with a ridiculous signature all their lives, simply because necessity forced them, in spite of themselves, to preserve the one they developed during their youth.

The signature and the writing may not always evolve simultaneously. A medical student, accustomed to taking notes down as fast as he can, will soon develop a rapid, fluent, simplified and uncluttered writing whereas his signature may remain awkward and childish. Later on, as he gains experience in his profession and signs more and more certificates and prescriptions, his signature will acquire a certain firmness, but his writing will remain unchanged.

As the repetition of the graphic gestures leads to automatic movement, the writer eventually acquires that lightness of touch which accompanies greater professional confidence and self-assurance which only time can bring out in those whose outer timidity conceals genuine substance.

The young executive who is obliged, because of his position, to sign a great many letters every day will have a signature which will frequently become simpler and firmer before his writing. The habit of thinking, supervising and making decisions quickly, in order to direct the work of his subordinates, is reflected in a signature which becomes progressively less of a gesture of command or acquiescence. The end result is not an individual's name, but merely a stamp. In such cases we must judge the firmness, degree of simplification, harmony and composition rather than the legibility because what we are dealing with is a kind of shorthand monogramme which never varies. For an example of a signature which is more developed than the text, look at fig. 182: it reveals far more authority and character than the writing of the P.S. which follows and yet both come from the same person.

Simple signature without
paraph

Straightforwardness. This type of signature is also found among uneducated people who have difficulty in using a pen as well as among the famous who are confident of the force of their personality and feel that their name should be enough. (see fig. 190: this fragile and sensitive signature belongs to Chopin. Fig. 191 is the less individual signature of Ampère, the mathematician and fig. 192 is the precise, clear yet very emotive signature of the psychologist, Le Senne).

Signature taller than text

Conceit. The writer is conscious of his own worth.
If there is considerable disproportion: pride and presumptuousness.

Smaller than text (fig. 171)

Timidity. Modesty. Lack of self confidence.

Wide signature (fig. 179)

Extraversion. Self confidence.

Illegible and evasive (fig. 188)

Tendency to avoid one's responsibilities.

Christian name more
developed than surname

Narcissism. The 'spoiled child' character.

Christian name more developed than surname (continued)	According to Pulver, a married woman who neglects the surname of her signature reveals hostility towards her husband.
Signature followed by full stop	Inhibition. Caution and/or distrust.
Rising signature (fig. 176)	Drive. Elan. Ambition. The desire to 'get on'.
Falling signature	Fatigue. Exhaustion, or sheer obstinacy.
Horizontal (fig. 175)	Even temper. Lymphatic temperament.
Placed to right of text	Extraversion. Activity.
Placed to left of text (fig. 171)	Introversion. Fear of life.
Covered by a horizontal stroke or between two parallel lines (fig. 180)	Determination to 'get on', will to dominate.
Firmly underlined (fig. 175)	Will power.

The Paraph

In an age when art and fashion are dominated by simplicity, the paraph, a superfluous piece of adornment, should disappear, or, at the very least, remain discreet. When archives reveal documents dating from the last century with the complicated flourishes our ancestors thought necessary as an

addition to their signatures, we cannot but regard the custom
as rather amusing.

Despite the modern concern for simplicity, the paraph is
still very revealing of tendencies, frequently subconscious, in
the individual. The symbolism of form and direction which we
apply to the writing is just as applicable to the paraph.

The centrifugal stroke, preceding or following the signature
(directed towards the right and high), as in fig. 184, reveals
élan, physical courage and a generally aggressive attitude.

The paraph written in zig-zag form, angular and resembling a
streak of lightning, suggests a cold, vindictive and brusque
nature.

The paraph which encircles the name may be considered as
an attempt at protection or dissimulation. In fig. 172, written
by a young girl who had developed agoraphobia, the overall
weakness and inhibited nature of the stroke reveal fear and
unhealthy anxiety. In fig. 174 the vigour of the writing cancels
out such an interpretation — this writer wants to create a false
impression rather than conceal a weakness.

The paraph in lasso form at the end of the name or
underlining it is usually a sign of a supple, adroit, diplomatic
or commercially adept mind (fig. 177).

When the lasso is complicated in form and appears in the
body of the name itself, as in fig. 189 (the signature of Dr.
Petiot), the graphologist knows he is dealing with a dangerous
and devious writer who can be difficult to 'shake off'. A
further example is seen in fig. 176.

The centripetal stroke which moves in a downwards direction
and stops abruptly (fig. 182) indicates the will to be successful
in material terms.

The following examples are shown for the sake of interest
and comparison.

Fig. 173 — The presumptuous and sprawling signature of
Mussolini.

Fig. 185 — Hitler's tiny, tense signature which remains
obstinate right up to its sudden 'droop' at the last moment.

Fig. 186 — The supple, intelligent, but rather weak signature of Aristide Briand.

Fig. 178 — The actress Madeleine Sologne's artificial and evasive signature.

Fig. 181 — A much more dynamic signature belonging to Josephine Baker. Note the vitality and need for physical movement in the first over-extended lower extension, and the ardent will power in the hooked underlining of the surname.

Fig. 193 — A fragment of a signature which heads off in all directions, but retains an aesthetic appearance. The writer is a 'man of the world' who is somewhat eccentric, but extremely gifted in many fields.

LESSON 13

1. Examination, Definition, Interpretation and Character Sketch

A graphological analysis involves two basic stages:

1 — Examination of the document and a recording of the the signs in the handwriting which will help us to compose a 'definition'.

2 — The psychological interpretation of these signs and drafting the portrait.

Examination and Definition

In order to make a proper examination of a sample of writing it is essential first of all to put the mind into a receptive mood and to banish thoughts of everything except the writing and its graphic elements. As we have seen in the preceding lessons, the measurable elements in writing are of very little importance; everything should be assessed 'by sight' and this is where the graphologist's sensitivity and training have a vital role to play.

The truth is that the graphologist should not 'observe' handwriting, he should 'feel' it. He must be able to sense the hardness or softness, tension or slackness, harmony or discordance, warmth or coldness, richness or poverty etc. The first contact between a graphologist and a sample of writing should evoke an 'emotional' reaction.

The beginner is advised to take note of the first impressions a writing makes on him and to describe them using the first words which enter his head. In time he will learn to isolate the particular features of the writing which produced the initial impression on him. This is when he will learn to apply scientific descriptions to writing, using the 150–200 terms which make up the graphologist's terminology.

The definition of the writing is its description based on those terms which apply only to graphology, and these terms were laid down, mainly, by Crépieux-Jamin and Abbé Michon. Modern graphology retains most of their terminology to avoid the confusion there would be if every practioner decided to invent and employ his own descriptive phrases. At some time in the future it is quite possible that new terms will be invented, but, for the time being, all students are advised to restrict themselves to the terminological descriptions used in the recapitulations of each lesson.

For the graphologist, a knowledge of basic graphological signs is as essential as the knowledge of basic symptoms for a physician: both are a repertoire of indicators which allow a diagnosis to be made.

The graphologist, however, has to use the information assembled in this manner to the best possible advantage i.e. by giving each feature its relative value. Crépieux-Jamin's advice was to structure the definition of the writing on three levels, and his method is still valid:

1st	—	the dominant signs
2nd	—	the secondary signs
3rd	—	the particular signs

When dealing with the 'dominant signs' we make a note of the general features and those elements which make it individual, because it is at this stage that we acquire an insight into the basic structure of the writer's character. The information gained at the second stage will reinforce, complete or, occasionally, modify what we find out in the first stage.

A common fault among beginners is to latch onto the details of the writing without appreciating the expressive quality of the whole. Handwriting should be seen as a continuously flowing and evolving process rather than a mere juxtaposition of unconnected images or letters.

Thus the first stage of the definition will be to describe the writing in terms of the following generalities:

Dynamism	or	Inhibition
Harmony	or	Inharmony
Order	or	Disorder
Extension	or	Contraction
Clarity	or	Confusion
Firmness	or	Weakness
Lightness	or	Heaviness
Vivacity	or	Slowness
Vulgarity	or	Elegance
Simplification	or	Complication
Regularity	or	Irregularity
Angularity	or	Roundness
Originality	or	Banality etc.

Only when we have noted the overall features of the script should we then proceed to examine the secondary and particular signs in greater detail.

As an example of how Classical French Graphology (founded by Crépieux-Jamin) works we will make a definition of the first handwriting sample given.

Mr. A's Handwriting
(Business man — 50 years old)

This ordered and homogeneous writing gives an impression of harmony, clarity and distinction. We are dealing with a noble writing of a higher than average Form Level.

The lightness of stroke reveals a general lack of dynamism, but the layout is aerated, the forms simplified, quite original and the pen progresses in a supple movement across the page with no sudden discordances.

We note immediately that the writer is distinguished for his moderation rather than his vigour, and for qualities of intellect and savoir-faire. The signs which we note in the first stage of the definition, therefore, are those which create a climate of moral serenity and intellectual superiority.

The writing is:

Harmonious	Aerated
Distinguished	Clear
Ordered	Simplified
Homogeneous	Nuancée
Light	Original

We may also take note of the general calmness, suppleness, elasticity and the ease with which the pen glides over to the right with a slightly ascending baseline. There are also ingenious shortcuts and advantageously utilised forms of connection and yet absolutely no forms which suggest any kind of aggressiveness.

This fluency and calmness may be accounted for by writing which is:

Semi-rounded	Combined
Progressive	Slightly ascending
Accelerated	Mixed connections
	(arcades and garlands)

Let us now have a closer look at the proportion and specific features of the letters themselves. The middle zone could never be described as being enlarged, because it never exceeds its own well defined limits. The upper and lower zone extensions deserve mention, however, because they are rather short in comparison with the height of the middle zone. This means that we are dealing with *low* writing. Also, the letters have a tendency to decrease in size towards the word ends : this is *diminishing* writing.

In the longest words of the text, letters always appear in groups of two, three, or at the most, four. Thus we have *grouped* writing.

There are no starting strokes on the initial letters. Each letter is reduced to its basic form and there are no signs of hesitation or superfluous flourishes. The final strokes are short and sometimes even slightly *suspended* (see the word 'cuisine' line 6, 'candidature' last line).

There are, in addition, many printed or typographical letters, particularly the 'd', the 'j', and certain letters 'a' are written like the Greek alpha.

Also present are clockwise movements. Not only is this to be seen in the letters 'd' and 'a' but also in other letters where the pen movement runs counter to the direction of the school model. Some 'o's and 'a's are also open at the top : this feature is called *open* writing.

For the second stage of the definition, therefore, we use the terms :

Fairly low	Diminishing
Grouped	Sober (no starting strokes,
Printed letters 'o' & 'a'	short finishing strokes, occa-
Sometimes open	sionally suspended)
Some clockwise movements	

If we run our eyes over the text for any small features which may have escaped our notice, we see that several t-bars are missing, an accent has been left off the word 'ménage', as has the dot of the last 'i' in 'désirerait'. Generally speaking the diacritics are very light, placed rather high and sometimes ahead of the letter (a sign of progressiveness).

The signature (not reproduced here for the sake of preserving the writer's anonymity) was similar to the text, ascending slightly and not underlined.

Thus, in the third stage, we include:
— Some t-bars and i-dots omitted.
— Dots and bars light, quite high, ahead of the letters.
— Rising signature, similar to the text.

Interpretation of Signs

When we have completed the list of characteristics, we write the corresponding interpretations alongside each one. As we do this, of course, we must consider the accompanying signs and the Form Level.

Harmonious	Courtesy. Refined manners.
Ordered	Order. Method.
Homogeneous	Assertiveness and constancy
Light	Delicacy and suppleness of mind. Adaptability.
Aerated	Nobility of mind. Logical thinking.
Clear	Loyalty and clarity of mind.
Simplified	Intelligence. Ability to grasp essentials.
Nuancée	Suppleness of mind. Intellectual sensitivity. Broadmindedness. Tolerance.
Originality	Individuality of concepts and ideas.
Semi-rounded	Mild and conciliatory nature.
Combined	Ingenious mind. Lively intellect. Ready, effortless adaptability.

Progressive	Activity. Altruism. Interest in the future and surroundings. Self confidence.
Slightly rising	Optimism
Accelerated	Adaptability
Mixed connections	Lack of rigidity. A mind which can adapt depending on the circumstances. Receptive and constructive mind.
Quite low	Modesty. Peace of mind. Concern only with day-to-day matters.
Diminishing	Susceptible to fatigue. Activity interspersed with frequent rest periods.
Grouped	Good co-ordination of ideas and actions. Initiative. Independence of mind.
Sober	No starting strokes — Gets down to the essentials. Short finishing strokes — self control. Some suspended — scruples. Inhibition of Feelings.
Printed letters	Culture. Aesthetic sense. Taste for beauty.
Reverse letters	Independence. Need to be different. 'Whims'.
Some ovals open	Confidence. Openness. Generosity.
Some t-bars and i-dots missing	Some lack of attention to detail.
Diacritics light and placed high	Idealism
Rising signature	Ambition.

We have now accumulated those character traits indicated by the writing and we must now synthesise them and put them into order so that a portrait may be constructed.

As with any construction, we have to begin with a 'plan' and this plan will be provided by the elements detected in the writing.

The writing in question shows a certain ease of movement, but little expansion and the starting point for our analysis can be the writer's outward discretion and courtesy. We should then examine his everyday activity and assess his ability to adapt to his surroundings. Finally, we must delve into the more intimate side of his personality and try to understand the needs, aspirations and ideals which comprise his real nature.

The plan for the portrait will resemble the following:

    (1)   Outer presentation of Self

    (2)   Adaptability to the world
         — Intellectual abilities
         — Activity
         — Ability to make social contacts

    (3)   Intimate life
         — Emotionality
         — Sensitivity
         — Intimate needs

    (4)   Aspirations — ethical code.

Such an approach will encompass all the information provided by the writing.

Character Portrait of Mr. A.

This harmonious, contained, graceful and sober writing is that of a man who is courteous and refined and whose byword is moderation in everything he does.

Mr. A. is very intelligent, cultivated and gifted with clear judgement, high ideals and great independence of mind. He is ambitious in those areas where he is confident of his ability to achieve success and is generally optimistic. This latter quality is not due to a susceptibility to illusion, but rather a confidence in his own abilities and his gift for adapting to his surroundings and circumstances.

His working habits are characterised by intelligence rather than dynamism and he is good at using his talents in such a way that he will always gain maximum benefit from minimum effort. Both his professional and social life are ruled by orderliness, method and foresight. He is adroit, diplomatic and his will power is best described as sustained but discreet; he always prefers conciliation to intransigence, gentleness to brutality.

He can be authoritative, but never imperious. When face to face with a stronger will than his own, this writer will not engage in combat. He much prefers to use his talent for skilful manoeuvring and if this fails he will retreat in order to cut his losses.

He is also very respectful of the law and has a deep sense of honour. He would consider it very bad form if he were to break a promise.

Although he can be somewhat standoffish, he can be kind, understanding and generous. He considers it his duty to help others and will do so out of genuine altruism, with as much devotion as discretion.

The more intimate side of his life will be characterised by finesse, delicateness and sensitivity, but little passion. His attachments tend to be based on intellectual attraction. He knows why he loves and will only be attracted to what deserves to be loved. In all things he will be selectively discriminating.

However, there are times when he needs to come out of his shell and express his feelings freely. He enjoys recreation and is very receptive to aesthetic impressions. At such moments he can break free of all constraints. He is a serious man with a subliminal sense of fun.

The secret of his balanced personality lies in his ability to alternate between work and pleasure, intellectual intensity and relaxation, activity and dreams and an ability to enjoy things in moderation without succumbing to obsessions. He is a wise man who always regulates his action with the power of reason and not passion.

The definition and portrait which we have just seen illustrates how Crépieux-Jamin's method works. It is a method which involves the extraction from the writing of those character traits which the graphologist will then assemble into a portrait which should be as accurate as possible. But a portrait arrived at in this manner is not dependent on any typology.

It has to be understood that, in order to gather together all the graphic signs at each of three stages of the definition and then present a portrait of the writer which is accurate and in perspective, a great deal of experience is necessary.

It frequently happens that the student, guided by his teacher, can appreciate all the dominant features without any difficulty as they are pointed out to him. But, as soon as he is left to his own devices and is confronted by an unfamiliar writing, it means absolutely nothing to him.

It is precisely here that the graphic similarities of the character types discussed in the first two chapters will be a great help because it will enable him to spot the dominant features immediately and construct an analysis around them.

It will not always be necessary to use the technical terms in order to describe the characteristic features of each temperament, as we advised when discussing the layout of the definition. Often we will use comparisons which speak to the imagination. To say of a writing that it reveals will power, aggressiveness, laziness, playful or inane frivolity, is not to put the cart before the horse, by interpreting a sign before even labelling it. Rather it is to unleash our intuition and let it extract what reason and method will then control. It is not a question of attributing a meaning to each individual sign: groups of them should be compared, the graphologist should learn to feel what lies behind them and to appreciate the rhythm which has produced each one.

2. The Temperaments and their Graphic Signs

The graphic signs for the **Bilious, Nervous, Sanguine** and **Lymphatic** temperaments *(1)* were studied by Doctor Carton and Madame Saint-Morand. *(2)*

We have reproduced a typical writing for each of the temperaments and three samples for the binary types.

Fig. 194	Bilious
Fig. 195	Nervous
Fig. 197	Sanguine
Fig. 198	Lymphatic
Fig. 196	Bilious — Nervous
Fig. 199	Sanguine — Lymphatic
Fig. 200	Lymphatic — Bilious

Bilious writing is firm, more or less angular, quite nourished, trenchant or sharp-pointed, with an abundance of cross shapes in the 't's or underlinings. (fig. 194).

As we saw in Lesson One, the Bilious type is characterised by motion, i.e. he is active, energetic, entrepreneurial and decisive. Bilious types are brave, built for fighting, authoritarian and capable of leadership.

Their writing contains vigorous horizontal downstrokes which end abruptly at the base. Starting strokes are absent and

---

(1) Reread the first lesson

(2) DR. CARTON – Diagnostic et Conduite des Tempéraments (Brevannes [Set-O]).

   H. SAINT MORAND – Les Bases de l'Analyse de l'Ecriture (Vigot, Ed.)

the end strokes are abruptly terminated (in clubs) or, if the writer is a more impulsive type, projected ahead aggressively in sharp points or sword strokes. The writing may be regularly cadenced (fig. 194) or chopped up by movements shooting off in all directions (fig. 196).

The Lymphatic (fig. 198) is the character directly opposed to the Bilious and his writing is lazy, round, weak and rather flabby. The pressure may be light, blurred or pasty, sometimes with large loops or spindled, but never very firm. The letter formations are generally enlarged at their base, at baseline level, when the writing is vertical or squeezed with a regular slant (fig. 103). Connections are rounded, continuous and sometimes thready. The pace of the writing is calm or poised.

The light pressure of such writing will incline our interpretation towards the concepts of contemplation, dreaminess, impressionability and spinelessness which are associated with the Lymphatic temperament. Heavy pressure is indicative of sensuality, practical sense and an aptitude for manual work. Regularity suggests ponderation, a reflective mind, submission to habit, constancy and fidelity.

Nervous writing (fig. 195) contains many irregularities of height, pressure and slant. The movement is lively and rapid, the words fragmented and 'cut into pieces'. Agitated and jerky movements frequently make the text confused and difficult to read. Nervous writing may be tall, dry and angular or small, hard and pointed. It may also be thready on account of excess speed.

Whatever the height, Nervous writing will always be cramped in some way, either in the layout or in the width of the letters. The writing always looks agitated in some way: a reflection of the state of perpetual dissatisfaction in which such writers live.

The Sanguine (fig. 197) type is recognised by ample and generous movements. His expansive nature, his imagination and his love of life are reflected in rounded forms, broad, inflated and animated letters. These are often embellished with long ascending strokes or spirals in ordinary writing and graceful, ample curves in the more evolved kinds. Natural vitality endows the writing with warm pressure and generous layout.

When the Sanguine type's natural extravagance is not released into broad gestures which occupy as much space as possible, the need for exteriorisation will increase the pressure or cause superfluous bars to appear, such as at the top of the letter 'b' in fig. 199.

* * *

Pure types, or even people in whom an extremely marked predominance of the Bilious, Nervous, Sanguine or Lymphatic temperament can be detected, are very rare. Most of the time we will find traces of two or even three temperament elements. It is important to assess the degree of each element.

When it is difficult to decide which temperaments are dominant, the best thing to do is to proceed by a process of elimination by deciding which temperaments are not dominant.

For example the writing in fig. 196 is full of broken lines, hard angles and 'sparks'. There are no rounded letter bases and none of the softness or lightness of Lymphatic writing. Nor are there any of the inflations of the Sanguine type. However we do detect the lightning strokes of the Bilious and the irregularities, jerkiness and fragmentation of the Nervous type. As the pressure is firm and suggestive of vitality we deduce that the Bilious temperament is dominant and therefore we describe the writing as Bilious/Nervous.

The writing of fig. 200 is too calm to belong to a Nervous type and of too moderate dimensions to be Sanguine. The rounded forms of connection with a slight tendency to threadiness and the overall steadiness suggest a Lymphatic temperament. The finishing strokes and t-bars in crosses or sharp points reflect the Bilious element, and we may therefore deduce that the writer is Lymphatic/Bilious.

It is at this point that the graphologist's feeling for psychology should intervene to explain just what it is that produces these combinations.

In fig. 196 (Bilious/Nervous) both types of temperament are restless, demanding and dissatisfied. Such a combination will, without the slightest doubt, result in a hyperactive temperament. Such a writer will be an achiever, but at the same time violent, aggressive and difficult to get on with.

On the other hand, fig. 200 (Lymphatic/Bilious) combines calmness with activity and the overall effect is beneficial. The Bilious element will motivate the Lymphatic and stimulate ambition in a writer who otherwise might slide into the comfortable routine of daily existence.

The ideal man would combine the determination of the Bilious, the lively intelligence of the Nervous, the vitality and cordiality of the Sanguine and the 'sang-froid' of the Lymphatic.

Any over-development of one temperament to the detriment of the others can lead to psychological imbalance. The Bilious needs an element of the Lymphatic to temper his impatience, just as the Lymphatic can benefit from something of the Bilious to shake him out of his passivity.

The Sanguine needs some of the cold judgement of the Nervous to control his exuberance and make his judgement more objective. As for the Nervous, he can become far too preoccupied with dry, abstract speculation if there is nothing of the Lymphatic or Sanguine in him to remind him of the joys of living.

3. The Psychological Types of Heymans-Le Senne and their Graphic Indicators

The Franco-Dutch typology has not, as yet, been applied to graphology on a sufficiently rigorous statistical basis to allow an accurate table of graphic signs for each character to be drawn up. *(1)*

René Le Senne, in his work *Traité de Caractérologie*, made lists of famous personalities and categorised them under the various typology headings — Choleric, Passionate, Sanguine, Phlegmatic, Nervous, Apathetic, Amorphous and Sentimental — and, by comparing our knowledge of these people with their writing we have managed to compile many of the graphic features for each type. However, much more methodical research needs to be done.

Choleric (EAP) *(2)*
Figs. 133, 204

The writing of the Choleric types combine the characteristics of the Hippocratic Bilious and Sanguine temperaments. The similarity to the Bilious can be seen in the firm, warm pressure (activity and cordiality), cross formations (combativity) and the lance or club strokes (impulsivity of will). As with

---

(1) The recently published 'Caractères et Ecritures', by EMILE CAILLE has now corrected the situation.

(2) See first lesson again.

Sanguine writing, this kind will contain large movements, bouncy curves (vanity, exhibitionism). Emotivity, however, makes the writing more intense. E.A.P. writing shows lively or fierce projection and seems to explode, seethe or crackle.

It is a more robust writing than its neighbouring Emotive-nonActive type (Nervous). It is never controlled, never artificial but is natural and spontaneous, even if it does sometimes look rather ordinary, reflecting a simple, straightforward and companionable writer.

There is less tension here than in the writing of the EAS types (Passionate). The pressure, which is often spasmodic, reveals energy, often violently discharged. Nourished or thick pressure shows the writer's warm feelings and sensuality.

The sinuous lines and variations of slant show a variability of aims and interests, opportunism and inconstancy.

The overall impression is of overflowing vitality which refuses to be disciplined.

Apathetic (nEnAS)
Figs. 23, 54, 208

The characterological formula for this type is diametrically opposed to the Choleric and his writing contrasts sharply with the latter's because of its placidity.

The writing of the Apathetic type is heavy, stagnant, regular, sometimes even rigid and contains no surprise movements. It is the most monotonous of all writings.

The unbroken regularity is indicative of the submission to habit which is characteristic of people who fall into this category. The heaviness and prolongments into the lower zone reflect the great importance the writer affords to primitive bodily needs. In the rigidity we can see the writer's attachment to principles and self-discipline.

Certain types of Passionate writers also have rather rigid writing. However, this rigidity is accompanied by tension, a sign of ardent Emotivity and constantly controlled energy, quite unlike Apathetic writing. The latter has no need to control his emotions because they are never very strong. As far as activity is concerned, it is usually kept to an absolute minimum.

Passionate (EAS)
Figs. 91, 109, 203.

Passionate writing is always tense. The forms are sober, simplified (sometimes to the point of austerity) and angular. The pressure is firm and regular. The pace is constant and rapid. Direction is progressive, frequently with a right slant and with some rigidity. The baseline is horizontal or ascending, rarely sinuous. Letters are grouped or connected, sometimes unrelentingly over-connected (the writer does not want to lose contact with the page), but connections are always made with tension in the stroke. There are never signs of slackness.

Overall this is a strong writing which seems to charge to the right in an effort to overcome obstacles. The impression given is of fierce, constant, obstinate energy which will not be deflected from its purpose.

When excessive Emotivity or impatient over-Activity bursts through the barrier of Secondarity, as sometimes happens with certain impetuous EAS types, the writer loses control of the movements and it may be difficult to distinguish the writing from the Choleric type. In such cases the tension and contortions due to the squeezing of some letters will be sufficient to identify the writing as being Passionate.

Amorphous (nEnAP)
Figs. 103, 115, 155

The characterological opposite of the Passionate writing is the Amorphous type, recognised by its slovenliness.

The pressure is weak, blurred, light or pasty, never firm and incisive. Forms are distended, stretched in height, or they hug the baseline. The ovals are frequently deformed and inelegant. Finishing strokes are frequently impulsive, but of uncertain direction. The t-bars are fine, a shade too long and slightly curved, and unsystematically positioned — but never aggressive (Amorphous types are not malicious). There is an absence of firmness of direction and the baseline is often sinuous.

The pace tends to be slow and, although there may be the odd sign of vivacity, there is never any sustained speed. The capitals are generally large and rather sprawling and wide.

There is an overall disorderliness and invading quality which is more noticeable than in Apathetic writing. In the latter case the impression of the present is always kept under control by the Secondarity. The Amorphous type, on the other hand, lives for the present and submits to it, either from boredom or fascination. This is why this type of writing often looks uncontrolled, and amongst the most Primary of the type, there appear impulsive adornments in a writing which otherwise lacks structure and relief (fig. 150).

Very seldom are there writings of a high Form Level among the Amorphous types. From an early age they have a deep-rooted aversion to effort. The Apathetic type, when directed, can succeed by qualities of constancy and loyalty, but the lazy Amorphous type is undisciplined and desires nothing but pleasure out of life. He is usually a disappointment to his teachers and parents.

Phlegmatic (nEAS)
Figs. 35, 205

Phlegmatic writing is so unspectacular and varies so much from person to person that it would be much easier to define what it is not than what it is.

This type of writing contains neither the strong pressure nor the exaggerations, explosions or effervescence of the Choleric. Nor does it have any of the tension found in the Passionate writing.

It is more alert, more lively and nuancée than Apathetic writing, and never slovenly like the Amorphous type. It lacks the fullness and assurance of the Sanguine, but has more continuity, sobriety and discipline than is found in Nervous writing. Finally, it is more supple; the letters are more intelligently grouped and it shows more slant variation than Sentimental writing.

Phlegmatic writing is contained, controlled, yet with signs of sensitivity beneath the outward moderation. It is generally homogeneous with little variation from page to page.

The pressure is light or nourished, connections semi-rounded or semi-angular, and usually quite smooth. Letters are connected or grouped and frequently combined.

The size of the letters is moderate. There is a balanced proportion between the zones and the pace is accelerated with an equal distance between the slow and speeded up strokes.

If the term 'phlegmatic', because of its use in everyday language, evokes a calm, cold personality, it should be remembered that in Heymans-Le Senne's classification the Phlegmatic type is Active. It is natural therefore that his writing should be more animated than that of the Apathetic or even than that of certain Sentimentals.

Nervous (EnAP)
Figs. 163, 201.

The most Primary of all the Primary Characters cannot but have a writing which reflects 'fantaisie', mobility of feelings and instability which characterise their type.

In Nervous writing the pen 'plays truant'. Lively and agile, it covers the ground very rapidly and yet it may also be so confident of its own speed that it can also dawdle along, or frolic in useless but amusing flourishes, unnecessary prolongments or flashes of artistic inspiration. The gaps from one word to another can be wide and unequal, so that the whole text acquires an appearance of both clarity and disorderliness (this writing should not be confused with the spaced out writing of certain 'distant' Characters). The irregular spacing here symbolises the time wasted or spent in aimless wanderings.

The pressure tends to be light, blurred or slightly nourished, sometimes spasmodic, but never very firm or regular.

Nervous writing contains all sorts of irregularities (of dimension, direction, slant, speed and even form : Primarity is a factor of inconsistency).

Letter formations may be graceful, original or mannered (we should always remember that the Nervous types were favoured by the Muses). There may also be superelevated or inflated capitals, indicative of the vanity which hides the feelings of inferiority so prevalent in the character. Certain artificial writings serve as examples here (fig. 147). The Nervous type, hypersensitive and inactive, but very proud, may use this type of writing to conceal his impotence behind an affected manner or to throw people off the scent with ostentatious eccentricities.

Sentimental (EnAS)
Figs. 27, 153, 202

The Sentimental writings which we have observed have been characterised by :
(1) Great regularity of slant, (2) Inhibitions : numerous retouchings which slow down the pace, (3) Squeezed forms or forms which are stretched upwards.

The overall impression given by the writing is of idealism, dignity or pathological hypersensitivity.

The ambition to 'get on' which is so typical of the Sentimental type is revealed by the impulsive or upwardly directed movements. The important middle zone reflects the strong self-awareness and dominance of the emotions.

The inhibitions reflect the emotional vulnerability, timidity and fear of contact with the outside world, contact which is nevertheless sought after, because the writing is nearly always slanted to the right.

Inactivity is seen in the slowness, lack of ease, numerous retouches within words and also in the wide, empty and irregular spaces, which, as with the Nervous, reveal time spent in dreaming, meditation and melancholy rumination.

Sanguine (nEAP)
Figs. 206, 210

Directly opposing the Sentimentals, the Sanguine types have writing which is characterised by ease, roundness, fullness and generosity of movement.

The need for expansion which is typical of all the Primary types reveals itself here in animated movements throughout, or by capital letters embellished with curves and spirals or large, rhythmic writing or prolonged loops, especially in the lower zone.

The Sanguine knows how to achieve success and enjoy life more than any of the other Characters. He is both sensual and diplomatic, and we find in his writing the signs of a man of good sense, realism and occasional cynicism. There are none of the signs of inhibition which paralyse the Sentimentals.

Sanguine writing is less violent than that of Choleric types and far less austere or tormented than that of the Passionates. There is more fullness than in Phlegmatic writing, more stability than in the Nervous, more tenseness than in the Amorphous and more playfulness than in the Apathetic.

In order to help the student to memorise the general features of each type, we can say that:

Choleric writing   is warm, dynamic, explosive
Passionate writing is tense and often austere
Sanguine writing   is supple, expansive and relaxed
Phlegmatic writing is moderate, and of balanced
proportion
Apathetic writing   is regular and monotonous
Amorphous writing is weak and without tension

Sentimental writing is inhibited and often with rigid
                              slant
Nervous writing   is unstable, frivolous or artificial

Frequently it is difficult to say definitely to which Character group a writing belongs, because it seems to straddle two neighbouring types, either because there are detectable signs of both Primary and Secondarity, Emotivity and non-Emotivity or Activity and non-Activity. All living things are subject to change, and the graphologist's skill consists in explaining between which extremes the personality swings and the extent of the movement.

It cannot be repeated often enough that the main traits of each of the Characters, as outlined here, are merely landmarks and the graphologist must never automatically attribute all the features of one character type to any writer. *The typological indicators must always be interpreted in the light of the definition of the writing as a whole and, after all, the signs listed in the definition are the important ones.* It is only by virtue of the definition that we discover the particular character traits which make any individual entirely unique.

LESSON 14

1. The Jungian Types and their Handwriting

The graphological features corresponding to Jung's typology were first explained by Ania Teillard in her book 'L'Ame et l'Ecriture', which we have drawn on for the following descriptions.

Extravert

The Extravert's attitude is expansive, adaptable, sociable and open to the external world. Such individuals' writings are ample and generous (fig. 210). Their considerable ability to adapt to the environment is seen in the ease of movement, which can be large, tall, rhythmic and resolute (fig. 64) or small, lively rapid and spontaneous (fig. 133).

Impulsive strokes, ballooning, amplified movements, ascending baselines, incorrectly placed capitals, underlining, and exclamation marks are also to be found to a greater or lesser extent, depending on the degree of extraversion.

Writing which is both dense and animated (fig. 90) in which the words seem to flow from the pen in a scramble of intense, nourished strokes is also the result of a need for expansion which is common among Extraverts.

We should also include in this category, writing which is very progressive, expanded, released, formless or thready (fig. 215) as it reflects an unchecked flight from the Self and a need to lose oneself in the external world.

Introvert

The Introvert is much more concerned with the inner world. He is hypersensitive, vulnerable and circumspect and his writing is more constrained and controlled than that of the Extravert. There is a certain economy of movement and layout.

The dimensions in Introvert writing are reduced, the forms sober and simplified and the finishing strokes short. It is more likely to be vertical or left slanted rather than right slanted, the letters are frequently disjointed and the words spaced out. The pressure is often 'colder' than is the case in Extravert writing. The overall appearance of the text, the address and the signature all have a tendency to move over to the left, producing a margin on the right-hand side of the page.

In cases of extreme introversion the writing conveys an impression of sterility.

The writers of figs. 209, 211, 213 are all Introverts and those of figs. 210, 212, 215 are Extraverts.

A good balance between the two attitudes can be detected by a comfortable co-ordination between movements of contraction and relaxation, between the progressive and regressive strokes which give form to the writing (fig. 214).

The Psychic Functions
(Thinking, Feeling, Sensation, Intuition)

Thinking

The writing of the Thinking type is generally sober, small, well ordered and aerated and the paragraphs clearly defined.

It is usually simplified, sometimes combined, supple, rounded or semi-rounded, slightly irregular or nuancée, rapid and alert. If the writer is Thinking extravert it will be progressive (fig. 214) but the Thinking introvert will produce a more constrained or concentrated style (fig. 209). The stroke is often dry, with sharp-pointed finishing strokes. The slant may vary between vertical and a slight inclination to the right. The letter formations, even when full, are denuded of all ornamentation. For the Thinking type, writing is a means of expression and not of creating an effect.

Feeling

The writing of the Feeling type is large with a dominant middle zone (the zone of the emotions). The formations are generally simple or conventional. The writing is frequently constant, broad, connected, expanded when the slant is vertical, or tall if it slants to the right, particularly with Feeling extraverts (fig. 210). The pressure is nourished and quite warm. Frequently there is an invading layout, and upper and lower zone loops often mingle because of lack of interlinear space.

The Feeling introvert's writing lacks ease of movement; the strokes are more inhibited and contained and frequently there are false connections (fig. 211).

Feeling types can be prone to narrow-mindedness and the resulting intolerance can be seen in the great rigidity of slant (fig. 207).

Sensation

The Sensation type has a writing which is heavy, more or less rich, stable along the baseline, with well developed lower loops (fig. 212) and finishing strokes descending into the lower zone. Starting strokes are absent and there is vigour in the way each letter is begun, with firm downstrokes resembling stakes planted in the ground.

Other features of Sensation writing are the roundness of forms, the graceful curves and the soft pressure which is also slightly pasty and 'velvety', to use Ania Teillard's expression (fig. 100). Sensation types frequently produce spindles in their writing (figs. 103, 113).

Sensation writing is large or medium-sized, both in introverts and extraverts, but in the case of the former the writing is more ordered and stylised, sometimes a little artificial, embellished or mannered (fig. 213).

Intuition

Intuition type writing is light and ethereal with supple, 'bouncy' movements. There are daring combinations, connective forms which seem to 'jump' from one letter to the next (fig. 215, next to last line: 'je compte sur vous'). The connecting stroke covers the required distance without crystallising into any definite form. Connections are of variable form and are often interrupted, particularly among the introverts of this type (fig. 216).

Intuition writing frequently lacks the orderly layout associated with Thinking types and the regular rhythm of Feeling types. Nor does it have the stable appearance of Sensation writing. Rather it creates an impression of precarious equilibrium, with letters sitting uncomfortably on the baseline and seeming to dance along it. Energy, when it is present, is seen in irregularly spaced bursts of trenchant, lightning pressure (fig. 109). This is just the opposite of Sensation writing in which the pressure is heavy but quite rhythmic.

* * *

When we have applied the above criteria and ascertained the *main function* of a handwriting, we know automatically which is the *inferior function*.

This function plays the role of a mischievous little goblin residing in our unconscious. It is a primitive, infantile, poorly directed function which is not amenable to our will power and which, according to Jung, we can never control because, on the contrary, it controls us and makes us do stupid things.

The Thinking type is as blind and awkward in the domain of feelings as the Feeling type is ill-at-ease when it comes to logic and abstract thought. This does not mean, however, that the former is immune to 'falling in love at first sight' and nobody is more likely to quibble and split hairs than the Feeling type. Equally, we often see Intuition types who fling themselves into the grocery business and Sensation types, who, convinced they have 'flair', suffer financial ruin through speculating. Man always yearns for the talents he does not possess!

The individual has to take account of his weaknesses and he should also attempt to control his instinctive inferior function. However he must guard against being too concerned with such a capricious part of his make-up and thus harming his psychic constitution. The most useful advice the graphologist can give his clients is to suggest they listen to what their dominant function tells them, as this is their main instrument of adaptation to the environment. It is also the function on which the complete development of their personality depends.

The opposing psychic functions are arranged as follows:

If the *main function* is: The *inferior function* will be:

Thinking	Feeling
Feeling	Thinking
Sensation	Intuition
Intuition	Sensation

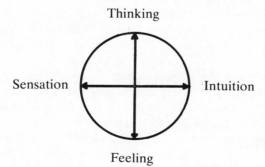

Once the main and inferior functions have been assessed the graphologist has then to determine which *auxiliary function* acts most frequently in combination with the main one. Let us have a look at some examples.

In fig. 209 (male, aged 45, *Thinking introvert*) the stability of the writing tells us that the auxiliary function is Sensation.

In the same way fig. 210 (female, aged 60, *Feeling extravert*) the firm downstrokes reveal a developed sense of reality. Once again we may deduce that the auxiliary function is Sensation.

In fig. 211 (male, aged 50, *Feeling introvert*) the handwriting is a little pasty and far less stable than in the previous example. Note how the downstrokes contain an uncertainty of direction. This tells us that the auxiliary function is Intuition. Sensation is not totally deficient, but it is far less influential in the writer's make-up than the other two functions.

The beginner might easily be misled by the thickness of the stroke into thinking that this is a Sensation writing. However, on close inspection we should be able to detect that the thickness is not the result of strong pressure, but is caused by a broad nib with somewhat worn edges. The upstrokes and downstrokes are of the same width and the 'f' of 'faire' (2nd line) hardly shows any pressure at all. (Compare this rather unsteady writing with the steady variety of fig. 212.)

Fig. 212 (female, aged 50, *Sensation extravert*) combines the signs of the Feeling type (garlands, warm pressure, expanded bow ties or loops) with those of Sensation.

In fig. 213, on the contrary *(Sensation introvert)* the order, sobriety and good layout come from a Thinking which is fairly well-developed and which serves as an auxiliary to the Sensation.

Fig. 214 (male, aged 40, *Thinking extravert*), quoted above as an example of the good equilibrium between introversion and extraversion, we have a writing in which all functions appear to be harmoniously developed. The Thinking function governs without too much rigour with either Intuition or Sensation as the auxiliary function. As regards Feeling, it seems more accessible here than is usual in this type of writing. Of course Thinking, as the dominant function, orientates the writer towards a more objective view of the world than would be the case in a Feeling type writing, but nevertheless Feeling is not repressed into the unconscious as happens when Thinking invades and consumes the whole of an individual's psychic life.

The writer in Fig. 215 (*Intuition extravert*) could only have Thinking or Feeling as the auxiliary function as the inferior function is Sensation. Now, as there is plainly no indication of Feeling in the writing, Thinking is the sole auxiliary function.

In fig. 216 (female, aged 35, *Intuition introvert*) we arrive at Intuition as the dominant function on account of the delicateness of the writing, absence of stability, and the disconnected letters. In addition, the sobriety and extreme simplification shows that the Thinking function can unite with Intuition as the auxiliary when, at certain moments, the Feeling is inactive.

At this point it should be stressed that care should be taken not to confuse the extreme mobility of movement associated with Intuition writing with the species *unstable*, which was dealt with in the chapter on Regularity. Unstable writing contains changes of direction or marked differences of appearance from one text to another. If we confuse the two types of writing we are led to believe that all unstable people are intuitive and this, obviously, is not the case. The sensitivity to imponderables which make the movements of the Intuition type pulsate rapidly, is perfectly compatible with an overall homogeneity in the script.

* * *

In the first chapter we used writing as a starting point to approach character. In the last two chapters we proceeded from character to writing. However, we must realise that in practice graphological analyses do not always follow the same strict pattern in a step-by-step procedure. In fact, the preceding chapters are interlinked and the graphologist should learn to move from writing to character and character to writing, depending on the circumstances.

In order to help the beginner keep control of his interpretations the principal signs of character traits are listed below as are those of the personality features which will most often be required.

2. The Graphic Signs of the Main Character Tendencies

A

Activity	Rapid. Firm. Constant. More or less angular. Letters 'm', 'n', and 'u' (within words) with all the downstrokes complete. Ovals ('a' and 'o') more elongated than rounded. Right slant. Progressive.
Adaptability	Supple and rapid strokes. Ingenious combinations. Good co-ordination of movement. More or less connected. Semi-angular or semi-rounded. Slightly thready.
Adaptability (lack of)	Automatic. Rigid. Very angular or disconnected. Irrational grouping. Unaccountable breaks in words.
Aesthetic sense	Harmonious layout. Margins which frame the text. Graceful curves. Well proportioned capitals. Printed letters.
Affectation	Artificial. Constrained. Superelevated with large arcades.
Aggression	Flying strokes. Sharp-pointed. Angularity. Progressive. Trenchant pressure.
Altruism	Right-slanted. Progressive. Spontaneous. Constant. Garland connections or semi-rounded.
Ambition	Rising baseline. Centrifugal strokes. Ample and superelevated capitals. Rising signature. Horizontal strokes sharp and decisive.

244   LESSON FOURTEEN

Amiability	Soft. Rounded. Quite progressive. Garlands. End strokes in open curves. (With arcades: conventional amiability)
Anxiety, apprehension	Inhibited. Squeezed. Suspended letters. Hesitant movement.
Aspiration (excessive)	Initial upward movement. Developed more in height than width, particularly in the upper zone.
Authoritarian	Rigid. Angular.
Authority	Firm. Resolute or homogeneous. Clear. Aerated layout. Combination of signs for will power, intelligence and an ability to synthesise information.

C

Calmness	Poised. Regularity. Contained. Supple. Rounded. Regular pressure. Precise punctuation.
Clarity of mind	Clear. Sober. Aerated.
Cleverness	Supple. Rounded. Lasso formations. Clever grouping. Sinuous ends to words. Thready connections. Slightly undulating baseline.
Coarseness	Heavy pressure. Muddy. Heavy pressure on dots and diacritics. Spasmodic pressure in messy writing.
Combative nature	Firm. Impulsive strokes. Sharp-pointed. Clubs. Progressive. Cruciform.
Concentration	Small or more or less condensed. In relief pressure. Dots very close to the stem. Weak upper and lower extensions.
Constancy	Homogeneous. Firm. Cadenced. Regular slant and line direction.
Constancy (lack of)	Unstable writing which varies from one document to another or within the same document. Light pressure. Thready connections. Sinuous baseline. Variations of slant, direction and spacing.

Control (self-)	Sober. Constrained. Vertical or left slant. Moderation in size and pace.
Conventional	Regular. Automatic or conventional. Similar to school model.
Co-ordination	Good co-ordination of energies and inclinations is reflected in a harmony of movements which are economical without being impoverished. Supple and yet firm.
Courage	Firm. Progressive. Rising baseline. Resolute strokes. Centrifugal movements. Rising, prolonged paraphs with progressive increase of pressure.
Courtesy	Legible. Poised. Ordered. Clean. Adequate margins.
Critical mind	Sober. Some dryness. Sharp-pointed.
Culture	Simplified. Combined. Original. Typographic style. Layout which is pleasing to the eye.

D

Decisiveness	Resolute. Firm. Progressive. Rapid. Angular or semi-angular. Horizontal or vertical strokes ending abruptly.
Decisiveness (lack of)	Weak. Inhibited. Hesitant. Suspended. Unstable. Slowed down.
Delicacy	Light. Soft pressure. Diminishing size.
Depression	Shaky. Descending lines. Ends of words drooping below lines.
Despotism	Angular. Trenchant. Tall capitals. Heavy pressure. Superelevated t-bars or placed high on the stem.
Detached attitude	Light pressure. Strokes thrown upwards. Sober and 'stripped' forms.

Diplomacy	Supple. Light pressure. Nuancée. Sinuous baseline. A greater or lesser degree of threadiness.
Dishonesty	(See the end of this list)
Disorder	Disorderly. Lax. Neglected. Unstable. Discordant.
Dissimulation	Constrained. Artificial. Slowed down. Double joined. Regressive forms. Left slant. Confused. Complicated. Sinuous baseline.
Distrust	Squeezed. Double joined. Inhibited. Hesitant. Suspended. Arcade.
Doubt (self-)	Low. Inhibited forms. Narrowness. Small size. Retouched strokes. Feeble t-bars or bars which are placed very low.
Dryness	Small. Vertical. Sharp. Dry. Angular or thready connections. Narrow. Simplified. 'Stripped' forms. T-bars and finishing strokes short or sharp-pointed.
Duty (sense of)	Firm. More or less angular. Tense. Cadenced.
Dynamism	Energetic. Large. Firm. Resolute. Rising baseline. Thrown. Progressive.

E

Egoism	Regressive. Angular. Cramped. Condensed. Hooked end strokes. Vertical or left slant. Ringed (or sham) garlands.
Emotional	Large. Nourished or pasty pressure. Inclined or expanded. Connections in deep or semi-angular garlands. Variations in the height of letters.
Emotive	Small constantly repeated irregularities. Jerky movements. Tension in the strokes. More or less angular connections. Frequent interruptions in the flow. Heavy pressure in small concentrated writing. Lively and impulsive movements in large writing.

Endurance	Firm. Cadenced. Homogeneous. Nourished and regular pressure.
Energy	Firm. Resolute. Cadenced. Progressive. Angular or semi-angular. Rising baseline.
Energy dissipated	Unstable. Prolongments in upper and lower zones. Excessively progressive. Irregularity of direction. Irregularities of rhythm and layout.
Enthusiasm	Rising baseline. Flying strokes. Progressive. Spread out. Effervescent. Dynamic. Incorrectly placed capitals and punctuation marks.
Extraversion (expansion)	Large. Ample. Spread out. Full. Fluid. Stretched. Rapid or precipitated. Broadening at the base of letters. Enlarged with extended movements.

F

Faithful	(See 'constancy')
Fatigue	Diminishing or faltering.
Fear	Inhibited. Compressed. Narrow. Disconnected. Suspended. Trembling and hesitant.
Feebleness	Very light or blurred. Unsteady. Broken. Fragmented. Disorganised.

G

Gaiety	Effervescent. Graceful, playful starting strokes. More or less rounded forms.
Generosity	Ample. Progressive. Expanded with few words on the page.

H

Honesty	Clear. Spontaneous. Firmness of direction. Harmonious. Balanced.

Hypocrisy	Variety of forms for the ovals ('a' and 'o'). Ovals closed at the bottom in a slow writing. Indecisive strokes. Lack of firmness. Sinuous baselines. Equivocal forms. Soft arcades. Supported connections.

I

Idealism	Flying strokes. Loops extending into upper zone. Rising stem of the 'd'. Light pressure. General tendency for movements to the top of the page. Delicate dots and punctuation (placed high).
Imagination, creative	Full and original forms. In relief. Effervescent. Well developed loops and ovals. Playful movements. Abundance of curves.
Imbalance of tendencies	Inharmonious. Discordant. Shocking irregularities of height and pressure. Lack of unity in the letter formations, spacing and stroke direction.
Impatience	Rapid or precipitated. Formless. Threads. Illegibility due to speed. Stretched strokes. Abrupt finishing strokes. Final of the letter 's' ending below the baseline. 'Pincer' lower zone extensions ('p' and 'q' connected to the right to the following letter).
Impressionability	Round or very rounded. Weak garlands. Double curve connections. Sinuous baselines. Variable slant.
Impulsive	Lively. Spontaneous. Progressive. Centrifugal. Large 'thrown' strokes. Spasmodic pressure.
Inactivity	Slow, soft, very round with frequent false connections. Complicated. Artificial. Marked arcades and large, unequal spaces between words or syllables.
Inconsiderate	Invading layout. Broad with large movements. Lack of restraint.
Independence	Reverse movements. Centrifugal t-bars. Spaced out. Vertical or left slanted.

Initiative

Lively. Rapid. Progressive. More or less 'thrown'. Right slanted. Sharp-pointed. Letters combined and/or grouped. Hastily written diacritics running ahead of the stems.

Instincts dominate

Heavy pressure. Nourished. Thick strokes. Spasmodic or spindled pressure. Fairly large. Lower zone well developed.

Intelligence

Clear. Simplified. Aerated. Nuancée. Combined. Progressive. Supple. Rapid.

Intuition

Light. Nuancée. Rounded. Combined. Grouped or disconnected. Ethereal movements lacking 'ballast'.

Irritability

Very irregular writing which is also dry and jerky. Spasmodic. Centripetal finishing strokes. Abruptly terminated strokes. Angular or semi-angular connections. Pointed or cramped forms.

K

Kindness

Broad. Open. Rounded forms. Curved finishing strokes. Warm pressure which is also pasty or nourished.

L

Logical

Clear. Sober. Regular and fairly connected.

Laziness

Slow. Weak. Very round and lacking in pressure.

Lying and dishonesty

(See end of the list)

M

Melancholy

Descending baseline or writing which contains deep garlands. Some monotony.

Memory

There is no point looking for signs of memory because it has nothing to do with character. All well

Memory *(continued)*   organised intelligence depends on memory. The latter develops with use and depends on our particular interests. Research into how visual and auditory memory is revealed has failed to produce conclusive results. Experimental psychology has far more reliable tests for assessment.

Meticulous   Very careful writing. Frequent retouching. Accurately placed punctuation marks.

Moral sense   Clear. Legible. Spontaneous. Firm. Harmonious. Well proportioned.

N

Naïvety   Enlarging. Unorganised. Heavy, with ungainly formations.

Narcissism   Round. Calm. Affected. Regressive with concentric movements. An important middle zone. Ostentatious capitals.

Narrow minded   Rigid. Angular. Squeezed. Invariable direction. Connected words.

Nervousness   Very irregular and jerky. Dry pressure (or spasmodic). Sharp-pointed. Frequent retouching.

O

Objectivity   Clear. Aerated. Sober. Rather small. Simplified. Nuancée. Well proportioned. Semi-angular or semi-rounded.

Obsession   Too regular. Rigid. Automatic. Monotonous. Very cramped. Over-connected. Lifeless.

Obstinacy   Angular. T-bars and finishing strokes pointing downwards. Steps 'galloping' downwards.

Orderliness   Well ordered. Fairly regular in form and spacing. Moderate pace.

P

Parsimony

Condensed. Narrow. Short, abrupt end strokes. Squeezed layout.

Practical sense

Nourished. Stable. Fairly connected. Well developed lower zone loops.

Pride

Superelevated. Large. T-bars above stem. Broad or inflated capitals.

Primarity

Lively. Lurch or flying strokes. Signs of impulsivity either in the intensity of the pressure or in the exaggerations of size.

Prudence

Poised. Constrained. Suspended. Double joined. Dashes filling in the ends of lines. T-bars and diacritics placed accurately. Signature followed by a dot.

R

Receptivity

Round or rounded. Open garlands. Expanded. Progressive.

Refinement

Harmonious. Elegant. Poised. Sharp. Well ordered.

Reflection

Poised. In relief. Moderate dimensions and pace. Well formed letters. Precise punctuation.

Reserve

Sober. Vertical. Restrained. Spaced out. Double joined.

S

Secondarity

Sober. Ordered. Contained. Fairly constant. Moderate size.

Self-possession

Sober. Restrained. No excesses of dimension or pressure.

Sensuality

Nourished. Pasty. Thick. Spindled. Muddy. Inflated lower loops. If the pressure is heavy: strong sex drive.

Sincerity	Clear and spontaneous without any discordances.
Sociability	Right slant. Progressive. Garland or semi-rounded. Open finishing strokes.
Stability	Homogeneous. Nourished. Regular. Well developed lower extensions. Horizontal or parallel lines.
Stubbornness	Angles formed by a movement to the left at the base of the letter 't' or in the lower zone extensions. Rigid. Left slanted.
Stupidity	Slow. Banal. Copybook. Awkward and vulgar forms.
Submissive nature	Small. Light. Rounded. Regular. Monotonous. Weak t-bars placed low on stem.
Suppleness of mind	Combined. Grouped. Nuancée. Alert. Thready. Sinuous.
Subjectivity	Large. Rigid slant. Important middle zone.

T

Tenacity	Firm. More or less angular. Good stroke tension. Hooks on end strokes.
Timidity	Small. Vertical. Inhibited. Light pressure. Narrow. Hesitant forms.
Tolerance (broadminded)	Aerated. Nuancée. Grouped or disconnected. Open garlands. Rounded or semi-rounded forms. Lack of rigidity.

V

| *Vanity* | Inflated. Broad. Superelevated. Embellished. |
| *Verbosity* | Broad. Loose. Open. Large. Effervescent. Inflated. Invading. |

Violence	Flying strokes. Clubbed. Heavy pressure. Runny. Trenchant or spasmodic.
Vivacity	Rapid. Light. Supple. Aerated. Flying strokes.

W

Will power	Firm. Sharp. In relief. Resolute. More or less angular. Strong and regular t-bars. Signature underlined with a sharp stroke showing progressively increasing pressure.

Signs of Dishonesty and Lying

Honesty is not, strictly speaking, a character trait. It is a rather complex manner of behaviour which results from an emotional agreement between our principles, our convictions and our will power.

None of these factors, in themselves, is sufficient to determine our actions. We cannot say that honesty is a question of ideals, nor of discernment between good and evil because an individual may have high ideals and not put them into practice. Another individual may deep down adhere to excellent moral principles and yet, through weakness of character, be unable to act in accordance with them. Will power is not enough by itself to make us move in the direction of what is good. There are energetic men who use their will power for evil intentions.

Hence the best indication of honesty is the combination of signs for equilibrium, altruism, clarity of mind and will power.

A writing which is spontaneous, clear, sharp or of regular pressure, progressive, harmonious and well proportioned is a fairly sure indication of moral probity.

On the other hand, we should be on our guard against writing which is constrained, disorderly, confused, very disorganised with striking irregularities of pressure, form, size or direction.

The inexperienced graphologist runs little risk of confusing the writing of a person of integrity with that of an out-and-out rogue. Outside these two extremes, however, the diagnosis can be very difficult, and we would advise the beginner to exercise extreme caution in this matter. If such a graphologist is asked to comment on the degree of trust which should be afforded to a certain writer and he cannot be absolutely definite, he should decline to express an opinion. Otherwise he should say that the writing sample contains insufficient graphological evidence for him to make a categorical reply.

Listed below are the most frequently found signs, according to Saudek, of dishonesty and lying. Before stating that a writer is capable of dishonest acts, it is essential to find the signs of group one and those of at least three other groups. In the absence of signs of group one, that is to say if the writing is lively and spontaneous, Saudek advises against drawing any conclusions.

1 — *Abnormally slow writing.* (We are not talking here of slowness due to illness or ignorance.) A deliberate slowing down of the writing on the part of the writer may be an indication of a bad conscience or a fear of giving himself away.

2 — *Lack of stability.* Disjointed, malformed formations, lack of pressure, lack of firmness and relief, threads, weak strokes, sinuosity. These signs may be an indication of passive complicity rather than active dishonesty.

3 — *Numerous retouches,* which make the text more confused rather than clearer.

4 — *Letters which can be read as other letters.* 'a' for 'd' etc.

5 — *Pasty and muddy writing.*

6 — *Writing containing false connections.* The pen is frequently lifted from the paper. (This should not be confused with disconnected writing in which letters are deliberately separated.)

7 — *Omission of letters or parts of letters in slow writing.* (Suspended writing.) Of no significance when the writing is rapid.

8 — *Heavy pressure on starting strokes.* (Discordances of size and thickness in comparison with the rest of the writing.) Sign of vanity and the desire to impress.

9 — *Ovals written in two parts.* (see examples) A very significant symptom, as are arcades forming semi-ovals curved towards the left.

To the above may be added two other signs:

10 — *Covering strokes.* (the pen travels several times over the same strokes as in double joined writing and supported connections (Sacré-Coeur).

11 — *Marked difference between the text and the signature.*

LESSON 15

General Advice

After two years of serious study any graphologist of at least average ability should be able to produce a portrait based on a handwriting of average difficulty. However, an in-depth analysis, as most experts agree, should only be attempted by graphologists with several years' experience.

One may be forgiven for thinking that the only difference between a portrait and an in-depth analysis is that the latter is based on the observation of less obvious graphic signs which are discounted in the former. But this is not the case. In fact, the information on which the graphologist bases an in-depth analysis is the same information gathered before a portrait can be produced. The full analysis and the brief portrait both require a full inventory and interpretation of all graphic signs.

However, whereas in a brief portrait it is possible to rely confidently on graphological evidence for a broad outline assessment of the writer, in an in-depth analysis one is looking for the effects different tendencies have on each other. One is also attempting, by a system of cross-checking and psychological deduction, to understand the effect of their antagonism or harmonious co-operation. Success in such a delicate operation depends on sensitive intuition, a good knowledge of psychology and wide experience of life.

Many graphologists never get beyond the stage of the character portrait but, it must be said, do acquire with time, considerable skill and confidence in this area.

For those who wish to make a living out of graphology we should point out that there is more money to be made in character portraits than there is in in-depth anlaysis. This is mainly because a portrait can be produced in a matter of hours whereas an in-depth analysis can take days of synthesis and compilation.

The character portrait is sufficient in most cases of personnel selection where, generally speaking, the qualities sought by an employer are: orderliness, a methodical mind, intelligence, will power, energy, moral conscience, and not an explanation of an individual's inner conflicts.

Anyone likely to be put off by the difficulties involved in an in-depth analysis would be well advised to limit himself to brief portraits. An intelligent client would always prefer a portrait of a few telling and succinctly written lines than sixteen pages of needless repetition and padding.

Young graphologists should be warned against looking for signs of physical illness, or even for fashionable complexes.

Medical graphology should be left to the doctors and psychoanalytical graphology to psychoanalysts. Anybody who is not experienced and well versed in these fields should confine himself to character portraits.

We have to admit that, as things stand at present, we cannot see everything in the writing. Certain personality quirks escape us, either because we do not yet know their graphological signs, or because the writer does not always reveal his true self even in his writing. We can state, however, that good graphologists will be right 90% of the time, which is a high score rate, considering the complexity and evasiveness of the human personality.

Handwriting reveals what is durable and permanent in human personality and frequently what is subconscious, but certain aspects of outward behaviour can escape the graphologist. Indeed, some people can repress or disguise their true selves to such an extent that their behaviour in public is no reflection of their true nature. In such cases the graphological portrait, revealing what they are really like, will be considered inaccurate by their friends.

To love a science implies first of all a desire to understand it, and once a degree of understanding has been achieved, a willingness to accept the limitations while trying, in good faith and without presumption, to push these ever further back.

Moreover, the graphologist should also be capable of placing limits on himself. A report, if it is sincere, should avoid being senselessly cruel or indiscreet. What good does it do, for example, to tell a mother that her son is unintelligent and will never make anything of himself, or a young man of humble background that there is nothing special about his fiancée. There is no reason to tell an employer who consults a graphologist regarding a secretary whom he is thinking of employing that she is 'highly sexed'.

The same considerations apply to graphology as to medicine or any of those professions in which one human being is required to reveal his darkest secrets to another. *We must exercise discretion and tact, listen to our conscience and deal with people humanely as we try to help and enlighten them.*

Graphology, considered as a branch of psychology, has a constructive role to play. It is not up to the graphologist to criticise, moralise or correct the faults of Nature. Rather he should guide people towards creating a virtue out of a vice, towards converting a sterile rut into a fertile furrow which will allow their personalities to develop and evolve. This is the art of individual orientation.

This is not the same as professional orientation which demands from the consultant not only the ability to apply a whole battery of tests, but also a very detailed knowledge of various professions and the aptitudes required for each one. The graphologist can be of great assistance to the consultant by assessing the subject's moral and intellectual qualities as these are not determined by other tests. But it is not advisable to offer professional guidance on the strength of a graphological report alone.

Character is not the only factor to be taken into consideration when advising a young person on what career to follow. It is necessary to take into account his state of health and his mental and physical abilities which are far better revealed by tests other than graphological analysis. Also, the preferences of the adolescent or employee who is thinking of a change of career have to be considered as well as his social background, family situation and the strains and stresses of different occupations.

The graphologist should therefore avoid being dogmatic or offering advice within too narrow a framework or impinging on areas in which he is unversed.

He should also strive for the greatest degree of objectivity when expressing an opinion. All too frequently we come across graphologists who concentrate on the negative aspects of a writing and ignore or underplay the positive ones. Nobody is all bad or all good. Everybody has his dark as well as his light side and honesty should compel us to give credit where it is due, however much we may dislike the writing.

At the end of this lesson there is a bibliography of the main text books on the subject which graphologists should read. Anyone who intends to study the subject seriously should also realise that graphology is not an end but a beginning, a door which opens on to the infinitely rich and varied world of human nature.

In order to help the beginner there is also an aide-memoire of graphic signs and a list of characteristics, all of which should help his investigations.

When the beginner has examined all those traits which a sample spontaneously reveals he will be able, with the help of these lists, to discover those features which he had overlooked, or become aware of questions he had not asked himself and to which the writing requires an answer.

However, he should not feel obliged to answer all the questions on the questionnaire. This would make the portrait pedantic and probably inaccurate. What is interesting in any analysis is to see those traits which distinguish the writer from his fellow human beings. One should never mention any trait which one does not see in the writing, and, when dealing with those writings which are genuinely insignificant, we should remember what Crépieux-Jamin said, 'Rich handwriting is defined thus because of its richness, poor writing because of its poverty'.

Signs detected in the Handwriting

(Numbers indicated refer to page numbers)

GENERAL LEVEL

Degree of Organisation, 77
Degree of Dynamism, 78
Degree of Harmony, 80
Degree of Rhythm, 80
Degree of Originality, 80

SLANT

Vertical, 108
Left slant, 109
Right slant, 109
Rigid, 109
Slack, 109
Irregular slant, 109

LAYOUT

Harmonious, 80
Ordered, 90
Disordered, 90
Invading, 90
Confused (or tangled lines), 91
Aerated, 91
Compact, 91
Spaced out, 91
Typographic, 90
Appearance of the margins, 91

DIMENSION

Large, 120
Exaggerated, 120
Small, 120
Very small, 121
Prolonged (into upper zone
    and lower zone), 121
Low, 121
Superelevated, 121
Soaring, 121
Tapering, 122
Increasing, 122
Dilated, 122
Squeezed, 122
Expanded, 122
Inflated, 122

REGULARITY

Automatic, 101
Monotonous, 101
Regular, 102
Cadenced, 102
Homogeneous, 102
Nuancée, 102
Irregular, 102, 109
Agitated, 103
Jerky, 103, 175
Unstable, 103
Discordant, 103

DIRECTION

Progressive, 127
Regressive, 127
Centrifugal, 200, 201
Centripetal, 201
Baselines rising, 127
Baselines falling, 127
Baselines galloping, 127
Baselines concave, 128
Baselines convex, 128
Baselines horizontal, 128
Baselines sinuous, 128

SPEED

Slow, 140
Poised, 140
Accelerated, 140
Rapid, 140
Precipitated, 140
Carried away, 140
Flying Strokes, 141, 158
Effervescent, 141
Controlled, 141
Spontaneous, 141

PRESSURE

Firm, 79, 156
Nourished, 156
Heavy, 156
In relief, 157
Trenchant, 157
Light, 157
Weak, 157
Pale, 157
Precise, 157
Meagre, 158
Blurred, 158
Pasty, 158
Runny, 158
Spindles, 158
Clubbed, 159
Spasmodic, 159
Ink-filled ovals and loops, 159
Unnecessary dots, 159
Smeary, 159
Notched, 159

CONNECTIONS

Angular, 175
Jerky, 175
Garland, 175
Arcade, 176
Thread, 177
Semi-angular, 178
Semi-rounded, 178
Connected, 178
Over-connected, 178
Grouped, 178
Disconnected, 179
Broken, 179
Sticks, 179

FORM

Simple, 196
Simplified, 194
Affected, 197
Conventional, 197
Artificial, 197
Neglected, 194
Animated, 195
Ornate or embellished, 195
Sober, 195
Full, 195
Narrow, 122, 195
Round, 196
Open, 196
Double joined, 196
Clear, 197
Imprecise, 197
Confused, 91, 197
Distinguished, 198
Vulgar, 198
Proteiform, 198
Retouched, 198

ASPECTS OF FREE MOVEMENTS

Starting strokes, 200
Finishing strokes, 200
Signature, 206
Paraphs, 209

T-bars, 202
Capitals, 204
Lower loops, 204
Punctuation, 205

Characterological Investigation

Ask yourself the following questions:

TEMPERAMENT

— Are there signs of vital reserves, weakness, strength or a good balance? .....
— Is the writer active, enterprising, phlegmatic, indolent or apathetic? ....
— Is he impulsive or reflective? ....
— Is he even-tempered, unstable or changeable? ....
— Is he emotive, agitated or thoughtful, calm and placid? ....
— Is he hot tempered and impulsive, or even-tempered with good self-
  control? ....
— Is he patient or impatient? ....
— Is he generally enthusiastic, optimistic or pessimistic, depressed and
  melancholic? ....
— Is he cautious or reckless? ....
— Does he show 'joie de vivre' or is he 'grumpy' and permanently
  dissatisfied? ....
— Does he have a keen sense of fun or are his tastes ascetic? ....
— Is he trusting or suspicious? ....
— Is he courageous or cowardly? ....
— Is he decisive or hesitant? ....
— Is he wilful and energetic or passive and 'soft'? ....
— Is he virile or effeminate? ....
— Is he of mature or childish nature? ....

INTELLECTUAL AND MENTAL APTITUDES

— Is he open-minded or dull-witted or of average intellect? ....
— Does he think in a reasoned, logical and deductive manner or is he
  intuitive, inventive, impulsive and adaptable? ....
— Does he work in an ordered, methodical and careful way or is he untidy,
  negligent and unmethodical? ....
— Is he of regular working habits or does he work in fits and starts, depending
  on his mood? ....
— Is he more interested in practicalities or abstract theories? Are facts,
  people or ideas more important to him? ....
— Is he able to see more than one side of an argument or does he have a
  narrow-minded, one-sided view of things? ....
— Can he distinguish between what is important and what is not or does he
  get 'bogged down' in the details? ....

— Is he a born realist or has he an imagination? ....

— Is his imagination fertile, creative and constructive or is he given to fantasy, romanticism, and utopian day dreaming? ....

— Does he possess artistic sense, good or bad taste? ....

— Is he conventional in outlook or original and versatile? ....

— Is his judgement clear and objective or does his imagination cloud the issues? Is he too subjective? ....

— Does he display any degree of critical ability? ....

— Can he express himself in a clear and concise manner or is he confused, verbose? ....

— Does he make instant decisions or does he vacillate? ....

— Is he far-sighted and punctual and can he organise his time and money or does he tend to leave things to the last minute? ....

— Is he adaptable or does he easily 'lose his bearings'? ....

— Is he resourceful and good at improvisation or is he slow on the uptake? ....

— Is he credulous or not? ....

— Is he open-minded or given to prejudices? ....

'— Is he tolerant or intolerant and sectarian? ....

— Can he formulate his own opinions or does he merely repeat other people's? ....

— Does he impose his ideas on others or just agree with the last speaker? ......

— Is he assertive or conciliatory? ....

— Does he commit himself on impulse or is he diplomatic, prudent and capable of planning for the future? ....

— Does he listen to his head or his heart? ....

SELF-AWARENESS

— Does he have faith in his own abilities or is he afflicted with an inferiority complex? ....

— Does he have too much or too little self-confidence? ....

— Is he guided solely by self-interest or does he take account of other people's points of view? ....

— Does he adapt to the wishes of others or does he impose his will on them? ..

— Is he suited to positions of authority or does he need supervision? ....

— Is he good or bad at carrying out orders? ....

— Is he self-disciplined or not? ....

— Does he listen to the advice given by others? Will he respond to guidance or is he rebellious? Is he headstrong or simply independent? ....

— Is he vain and conceited or modest and self-effacing? ....

— Is he proud or humble? ....

— Is he ambitious and determined to 'get on' or is he content with his lot? .....

SOCIABILITY AND MORALITY

— Is he sociable and cordial or cold, distant, reserved or totally unsociable?...
— Is he selfish and egocentric or altruistic? ....
— Is he witty and jolly, or taciturn and withdrawn, or quiet, calm and phlegmatic, or monotonous and boring? ....
— Is he talkative and inconsiderate, liking to make his presence felt, or is he discreet and respectful? ....
— Is he very correct and ceremonious, or friendly, informal and casual? ....
— Is he snobbish, haughty and disdainful, or artificial and affected, or straightforward, natural and spontaneous? ....
— Is he sensitive, polite and affable, or rude, awkward, or vulgar and lacking in social graces? ....
— Is he tender or cold? ....
— Is he sincere, direct, or diplomatic, clever, dissimulating and hypocritical? .
— Is he open and communicative, or reserved, enigmatic and inscrutable?.....
— Does he possess team spirit? Is he co-operative, or an individualist who keeps his distance? ....
— Is he wilful, rebellious, or easily led or capricious? ....
— Is he difficult to please, materially demanding, or easily satisfied? ....
— Is he extravagant or avaricious, generous, economical, or parsimonious? ...
— Is he dogmatic, given to moralising, strong on principles and unable to tolerate opinions which differ from his own? Or is he respectful of others' ideas, their interests and pleasures? ....
— Is he instransigent and inflexible, or broad-minded? ....
— Is he virtuous and tolerant, or clearly amoral? ....
— Is he an idealist, or materialist? ....
— Does he show integrity and respect for the law, or is he deceitful, sly and dishonest? ....
— Does he possess a strong sense of duty or is he incapable of resisting temptation? ....

Preparation of an Analysis

The writing of fig. 217 is that of a man of sixty and we will now attempt to apply the information contained in the previous lessons in order to produce an analysis. (The signature which is normally found on the right hand side of the page, is here in the top left corner. This is for reasons connected with printing.) *(1)*

The first thing we notice is the inhibition of the movement and the vibrant quality of the stroke. Taken together these two features reveal the writer's hypersensitivity. In the Hippocratic classification he is, therefore, of the *Nervous* type.

How should we classify this writer according to Le Senne? *Emotive* — undoubtedly, because the writing is jerky, inhibited and contains trembling movements.

Non-active— the rhythm is constantly interrupted and the continuity is faulty. The writer does not enjoy the benefit of an inner drive which pushes the Active type from one activity to another.

Secondary— because the writing is careful, contained and orderly. Primary writing progresses, dashes across the page or glides easily over the paper. Nothing of the sort can be said about this writing.

We are dealing, therefore, with a writer who is EnAS or *Sentimental* in Le Senne's characterology.

If we now move on to apply Jung's theories we see that the dominant attitude is *Introversion* because the writing is retracted, hesitant, inhibited and somewhat squeezed. This is

---

(1) Translator's note: No signature is given in the French edition.

seen in the letter formations which are more contracted than expanded.

The main function is *Feeling*. In fact, the middle zone (the zone of the emotions) is rather important here, considering it is a man's writing. The form is close to the school model; the capitals very close to those taught in school, which is rare in Thinking function writing which is normally simplified. The vibrant and blurred stroke confirms the intensity of the emotions here. The over-extended upstrokes reveal the repressed aspirations of the feeling introvert type. The slant and the starting strokes moving from left to right (see the letters 'p', 'l' and 't') reveal the writer's dependence on others, his seeking of human contact, even if this contact is selective as is generally the case with introverts.

The Feeling function here has *Intuition* as its auxiliary, as can be ascertained from the fragile stroke which lacks confidence. The writing is unstable on the line, indicating a feeble grasp of reality, but at the same time great impressionability, good perception and subtlety in the writer's judgement of others. As a counter-balance to the emotional vulnerability, typical of the Sentimental, the writer knows at the outset if the person he is talking to is favourably disposed to him and what to expect from him.

These basic points of information will direct the interpretation of the graphological indications as we work systematically through the definition.

General Level

Average	Personality of modest scope
because of:	
Inhibited writing.........................	Fear. Inhibition.
Broken rhythm...........................	Shortness of breath and lack of co-ordination in actions.
Forms in accordance with school model...................................	Conformism.

Layout

Ordered................................... Courtesy. Respect.

Decreasing left margin .... Search for security

Regularity

Irregular height .... Emotionality.

Irregular width .... Variable self-confidence.

Irregular pressure .... Variable patterns of activity.

Irregular speed.......................... Lack of adaptability.

Pressure

Light pressure with darker, pasty
stroke................................... Irregularities of energy discharge.
Variable tension. Lack of assertion.
Sensuality.

Direction

Superelevated starting strokes........ Arrogance.

Lurch strokes .... High aspirations.

Final strokes inhibited or regressive. Fear of taking risks, but determination to hold on to what he already has. Bitterness.

Slant

Average slant with verticality at end
of words............................... Desire for contact coupled with lack of trust.

Right slant with gentle pressure ...... Tenderness.

Dimension

Prolonged upwards and downwards. With squeezed writing: Need to escape from 'status quo'. Search for improvement. (Klages)

Capitals tall and squeezed .... Susceptible. Touchy.

Words sometimes tapering .... Finesse. Susceptibility to fatigue.

Connection

Semi-angular .... Moral strength (despite the hesitancy, the writing remains upright).

Letters occasionally fragmented ..... Hypersensitivity. Reduced activity.

Speed

Accelerated, but with irregular
rhythm .... Good assimilation, but lack of adaptability.

Form

School model in a nuancée milieu ...	Respect for established principles, conformism, but a certain delicacy of mind and feelings.
Occasionally open	Clumsiness.
Absent t-bars	Work not always completed.
Clear.......................................	Clarity of mind.
Some retouching........................	Honesty. Scruples.

Signature

Rising	Ambition.
Centripetal paraph	Self interest.

'Particular Signs'

Some doubling of t-bars or formed with regressive angle at base.	Stubbornness.
Regressive hooks at end of words....	Striving for gain. Determination.

The experienced graphologist will normally pass from the above inventory of signs straight to a *structured definition* which would be as follows:

1st Level: The Dominants.

Average Form Level, very inhibited writing, hesitant, squeezed, irregular and jerky, nuancée, quite ordered, school model, irregular pressure, slightly pasty.

2nd Level:

Prolonged upwards and downwards, soaring, some neglected formations, some retouching, regressive finishing strokes. Rising signature, centripetal paraph, regressive left margin.

This definition, together with the earlier psychological definition, will form the basis of the analysis. However, it is to the beginner's advantage to restrict himself to the detailed, methodical process already described until he can categorise writers into their psychological types with confidence.

Having listed all the information needed for the analysis we can now proceed to a detailed plan :

Temperament:

Weak vitality. Profound emotivity which has an inhibiting effect. Difficulty in expressing his feelings. Aspirations exceeding the ability to realise them.

Intellectual Tendencies:

Clear mind. Little intellectual power, but a capacity for grasping subtle nuances. No attempt to see beyond what is obvious and penetrate to the deeper levels of a problem. Subjective judgement. Intuitive judgement of others.

Emotional Tendencies:

Very great sensitivity. Deep attachment to people and things. Emotional vulnerability. Little self-confidence. Haughtiness and a need to be admired.

Instinctual Life and Concept of Reality:

Moderate impulses. Great impressionability. Passive sensuality. Low self-assertiveness. Clumsiness. Fear.

Will Power and Activity:

Little imperious will power, but this is compensated for by determination (hooked finishing strokes). Activity sustained by pride and conceit. Poor adaptability, but scrupulous conscience.

The Self and Others:

Inferiority feelings. Susceptibility. Need to be admired and loved. Delicacy and tact. Finesse. Fear of social contact. Selectivity. Vindictive mind.

Morality:

Honesty. Professional conscience.

From the above we can now proceed to a more refined portrait by imagining the writer in the various situations he is likely to encounter in life. This can be done in two ways: either we can develop each of the paragraphs by including the finer details revealed in the writing, or we can rely on inspiration, abandoning certain details so that the dominant character traits stand out in greater relief. The latter method produces a more true-to-life portrait, but every graphologist will choose whichever method best suits his own personality.

The following is the author's suggested version. It should not be considered as a model, rather as one of several ways of dealing with a portrait.

The Portrait

This vibrant, fragile and restrained writing reveals a writer of a gentle nature whose vulnerability generates an attitude of defensiveness rather than assertion.

He is rather timid and he hesitates for a considerable time before making a decision. This does not imply that he is incapable of reasonable control over his deeds and actions (he has a clear mind and can be critical in a constructive way) but he does fear the consequences of his actions and strives to guard himself against problems which he is ill-equipped to cope with.

The writer is of average intellectual capacity. He is able to make clear judgements when dealing with problems encountered in everyday life. His approach to these problems involves the application of those ideals etc., which he inherited from the preceding generation. He is therefore governed by a certain conformity, respect for tradition and the manners of his social milieu.

However, his judgement of people is on a more personal level and he is inclined to sound people out with his particularly acute defensive instinct. Sensitive to the slightest nuance he displays remarkably keen intuition and knows exactly what he can expect from everyone else. He will select his friends from among those who will indulge or protect him and avoid all who outshine him.

His extreme emotional selectivity leads to great fidelity. But it would be a mistake to expect unquestioning devotion from this man because he lacks the spirit which makes a man suited to the service of others. His relationships with others must be based on respect, compassion, gentleness and tact.

If this writer is ever deceived, long-suppressed wrath can bring him to commit belated acts of vengeance. He is not big-hearted enough to forgive and his sense of fidelity, which normally acts for the good, can also be used for the not-so-good.

He has a very great need to be loved. He does not derive great pleasure from dominating others and finds his pleasure in the solicitude he receives from others. He is not indifferent to the pleasures and indulgences life has to offer, but his appreciation of them is passive and he does not go out of his way to look for them.

There is little likelihood that he will 'make his fortune', but what he has he holds on to ferociously. This he does out of both sentiment and a need for security and he 'hangs on to it' as a miser clings to his money.

In his professional life he will carry out his daily tasks scrupulously, without feeling the need to introduce innovations, but with a conscientiousness imposed by pride, because he values the respect given to him by others.

This need for respect is a powerful lever which helps him to overcome his weakness and timidity. Under certain circumstances it allows him to rise above himself.

He is not always open with everybody, particularly when frankness would demand courage, but he does appear to be honest.

To summarise, the writer is a man of modest talents, cautious, circumspect and a frequent victim of anxiety. However, his dignity sets him apart and his sensitivity is enriched by subtle emotional experiences which will always prevent him from being banal.

* * *

Students cannot be warned too often against becoming discouraged by the problems encountered in the early stages of their studies. They must, before 'turning pro', examine a great many writings, enlist the services of their relations and allow themselves to be questioned by friends or parents about mutual acquaintances as this will allow independent opinions to be expressed about their deductions and interpretations.

All beginners make mistakes. But the most serious mistake is to speak in irrelevancies in order to cover up one's incompetence. It is far better to admit one's limitations than to discredit graphology by indulging in hasty or 'hit and miss' diagnoses.

The preceding lessons are not sufficient to exempt candidates for the Diploma in Graphology from improving their knowledge of psychology or from examining in depth the great masters such as Crépieux-Jamin, Klages and Pulver. Every good graphologist must have a thorough understanding of their works.

The present manual is not intended as anything other than an introduction to graphololgy. Anyone with a sense of vocation will find the desire and the courage to take his studies further.

The Rights and Responsibilities of a Graphologist

The question has often been asked whether or not an individual has the right to have somebody else's writing analysed without that person's knowledge. The problem has been discussed at length and the 'Groupement des Graphologues — Conseils de France' (French Association of Consultant Graphololgists) has issued a policy statement to its members, from which the following extract is taken.

'A letter belongs to the recipient from the moment he has received it, except when the sender has had a change of mind and asks him to destroy it. The recipient therefore can use the letter as he sees fit: he may keep it or burn it; sell it to a collector; reproduce it in a court of law in evidence against the writer; analyse it graphologically or have it analysed by a third party.

But the recipient does not have the right to publish the letter in a journal or book without the writer's permission since thoughts are non-transferable and the contents remain the property of the writer.

Analyses carried out under third-party arrangements are the responsibility of the person who requested the analysis. They may not, under any circumstances, use the documents they have had analysed against the writer, either to harm him or to bring about or support legal proceedings against him (Act 1382 of the Civil Code). But anyone who commissions an analysis does have the right, while not divulging the results, to refuse to employ the writer of the document as he is free to make such a decision'.

'The graphologist is sworn to observe professional confidentiality' (Act 378 of the Penal Code).

As a matter of prudence, the graphologist should never mention by name the person whose writing he is analysing in the portrait. The usual practice is to refer to the subject by an initial or even by a reference number. Documents should be returned to their owners without any marks or annotations of any sort.

ALPHABETICAL INDEX OF SIGNS

BIBLIOGRAPHY

Dr A. ADLER — *Le Tempérament Nerveux* (Payot éd.)
Dr. CORMAN — *Manuel de Morpho-Psychologie* (Stock)
ANDRÉE COURTHIAL — *Introduction à l'étude de l'Orientation Professionelle* (Bloud et Gay)
DALBIEZ — *La Doctrine Freudienne*
C. G. JUNG — *Types Psychologiques* (George et Cie, Genève) — *L'Homme à la Recherche de son Ame* (Ed. du Mont Blanc, Genève)
JOLANDE JACOBI — *La Psychologie de C. G. Jung* (Delachaux)
KRETSCHMER — *La Structure du Corps et le Caractère* (Payot)
RENÉ LE SENNE — *Traite de Caractérologie* (Presses Universitaires)
P. MALAPERT — *Les Eléments du Caractère et les Lois de leur Combinaison* (Alcan)
E. MOUNIER — *Traité du Caractère* (Editions de Seuil)
Th. RIBOT — *La Psychologie des Sentiments* (Alcan)
Dr PAUL CARTON — *Diagnostic et Conduite des Tempéraments — Le Diagnostic de la Mentalité par l'écriture*
J. CRÉPIEUX-JAMIN — *L'Ecriture et le Caractère* (Alcan) — *L'A.B.C. de la Graphologie* (Presses Universitaires) — *Les Eléments de l'Ecriture des Canailles* (Flammarion)
DUPARCHY-JEANNEZ — *Essai de Graphologie Scientifique* (Albin Michel)
HEGAR — *Graphologie par le Trait* (Vigot frères)
HANS JACOBY — *Analysis of Handwriting* (Allen & Unwin, London)
L. KLAGES — *L'Expression du Caractère dans l'Ecriture* (Delachaux)
MAGNAT — *Poésie de l'Ecriture* (H. Sack, éd. Genève)
J. H. MICHON — *Système de Graphologie* (réédition Payot 1947)
MAX PULVER — *Le Symbolisme de l'Ecriture* (Stock)
H. SAINT-MORAND — *Les Bases de L'Analyse de l'Ecriture* (Vigot frères) — *L'Equilibre et le Desequilibre dans l'Ecriture* (Vigot frères)
R. SAUDEK — *Experiments with Handwriting* (G. Allen, London)
ANIA TEILLARD — *L'Ame et L'Ecriture* (Stock)
L'Orientation Professionelle par la Graphologie, par un groupe de Graphologues sous la direction de P. FOIX (Payot éd.)
Bulletins de la Société de Graphologie, 28, rue Serpente, Paris VIᵉ

HANDWRITING SAMPLES

7 boulevard du Meunier
Sainte Maxime
Var

sujet de l'écriture ci-jointe
ma soeur, qui passe le plus clair
de ses journées chez ma mère
qui est agée, cherche quelqu'un
de confiance pour faire le ménage et la cuisine. Elle désirerait savoir ce qu'il faut penser
de la personne qui a posé sa
candidature et qui lui paraît à

Handwriting of Mr. A.

1. La constance est une v
il faut de bonne heure agi

2. Veuillez trouver

3. Le coeur n'est cependant
guère aux chiffons !.....

4. Je vous serais obligé de vouloir
bien me faire un service régulier de

5. Par même courrier, j'envi a .

6. Croyez que je forme
tous mes voeux pour vot .

7. de vœ perfection mes

8. remercier pour vos communications.

9. Je viens vous féliciter

10 Gaze ! est elle i Paris !
ne fais parvenir une
te / on de défauts anciens,

11 tout plus si vivement.

12 cher petite maman

13 Nous avons passé un très bon voyage.
de Paris, notre compartiment était pl
près il se vida peu à peu, et à voir

14 en étude. plus je fais attention, plus y
je pense que j'aurai été faire des patin o

14b Interrogation écrite.

---

15 Veuillez s'il vous plaît me donner l'a
de Studio de cinema voulant faire n
carrière dedans. Excusez moi des faute

16 Monsieur

Nous voici de retour et je vous [serais] bien obligé si vous pouviez de [nous] nous conserver quelques journées. ... celles je voudrais beaucoup que vous

17 57, Avenue de la Bourdonnais

18 importants qu'ils le jugeraient possible.

Agréez, cher Collègue, l'assurance de mes sentiments de haute considération

Louis de Broglie

19 je vous charge de distribuer ces invitations et dans l'intérêt

20 [illegible]

21 [illegible] ! Mais que vous y êtes gentille, encore et core, pour mil neuf cent ! merci, et toutes mes meilleures amitiés Nicole

22 sisent pour un instan
   ilme atroce qu'est la

23 Monsieur, mes meilleures salu.

24 Adhémar de la Sté je désirerais
   il savoir si la Sté a mi d

25 • Recrutement libéraire a Paris
   été faite de av avancé : en a pr
   par délégation nacla en les. Mais,
   le 1er Helolme, il ne semble pa

26 ce personnellem sus aurelle tout à fait adopté à u
   c endrais — Mles occupations ne me permettant pas

27 Je connais parfaitement la branche petrolifre
   tribukion sur le marché Parisien, d'autant mieux que j'ai de
   dans une grande société petrolifre en Roumanie. Jenis, e

28 + ur mes remerciements apriq, cher
   , l'expression de mes sentiments les meilleurs.

29 Cher Monsieur

Voulez vous m'envoyer
Cela demain samedi, ou bien
lundi, ou Mardi, dans la
matinée, avant onze heures
Et demie.

30 J'ai été a votre disposition pour
me donner toute autre permission
mais il est certain que votre

31 and he took me into see
Pouchelet, with whom I had
a brief but apparently very
satisfactory chat. That is,
he said he plans to get more

32 Paris (17ᵉ)

33 Après votre audition il m'est
venu à l'idée de vous signaler an
invention qui est exposée et présent

34

T'as vu le
jardin ? Il
est très simple
et bien entretenu
déjà.

Amitiés,
Hélène Raux

35

Je ne sais plus si j'avais bien précisé par
écrit les conclusions de notre conversation.
Dans le doute, je préfère le faire, profitant
d'un répit que j'ai ici, et m'excusant éventuellement
d'un retard.

Agréez, mon cher maître, votre dévoué

André Gide

36

Les récoltes sont rentrées, les blés en serre
maintenant nous-nous occupons de l'engrais, so.
canards et cochons ; c'est un travail de saison, très ce

37 j'espère une lettre vous d'ici
ce qui apportera une remarque
qui rappelle un peu trop

38 juillet et j'attendais de vos
nouvelles avec impatience.

39 car paralysé au regard des actionnaires

40 tellement plus beau

41 Ma chère amie, ma petite Jeanne bien-aimée,
Que Dieu te bénisse, mon cher amour, pour ta lettre si
ouce et si bienfaisante. J'en avais grand besoin, car je
uffrais durement dans mon âme et tu m'as un peu consolé.
Tu me sais malheureux, mais tu ne sais pas combien je le
uis. Je ne veux et je ne dois rien avoir de caché pour toi, désor
ais. Hier matin, il m'a fallu courir à Neuilly chez un ami dont
i me sert d'intermédiaire pour une pauvre petite combinaison
mmerciale sur laquelle je vis depuis un mois et qui est
vérité, la chose la plus douloureuse et la plus lamentable.

42 jusqu'au 15 Août) je vous
serais très reconnaissant de bien
vouloir m'indiquer quels sont

43

je suis en pourparlers avec plusieurs
personnes, mais je n'ai traité ni même
pris d'engagement avec aucune.
je crois vous avoir dit que l'été dernier
j'avais vendu verbalement la venu de
l' hôtel ou une personne qui n'a pas

44

décembre 1942 | la combinaison a été remise je dois te
bien chère petite Yvonne | ... (...
+ les bonnes lettres que tu nous a
moi, nous t'en remercions bien et
... en ...

45

comme suite à ... l'
l'amabilité de m'accorder, je me per...

46

s'il se trouve encore là, ou
s'elle se pend d'une autre
manière.
Veuillez m'excuser et
être persuadé de la plus
distinguée considération
de Votre
très dévoué serviteur
Richard Wagner
3 rue d'Aumale

47. eAttendois que vous daign
vous voyez que je n en vas
MHTe mellement —
Recevez Monsieur leurs

48. Ecrivez moi longuemen
en me disant bien
ce que vous devenez
et ce que vous

49. nous et leurs meilleures
séparés de nous. Il n'y a

50. de la guerre. Non celle d'hier, mais celle de demain
"Diplomatiquement" du Sénat ce qu'on juge cérémo
à Nuremberg. Quelle amertume! Dans ce printemps
vousvant, des enfants jouent, ces amoureux s'embra
une femme passe avec un visage sans ombre, et ce.
ne serait pas plus courbé qu'un autre jour. Mais

51. imaginer être un monarque, le
votre un auge est non moins grand,
ringer les vertus sous le couvert de la

52 Tous les renseignements

53 Le tableau est sombre . Le plus inquiétant est que nos dirigeants ne semblent pas le voir . ayant exact une fiel pessimiste, je pen—

54 Parti ce matin de Paris je solutionner en Bretagne quelques graves et importantes affaires alors que je serai pouvoir remettre ce voyage à plus tard (ce dont j'enrage!) Je ne serai de retour en la capitale que le Vendredi matin 3 Octobre.

55 Avec mes sincères remerciements . — Monsieur l'Administrateur délég

56 1 annonce parue ce dans le journal old Paris soir.

57 je vous souhaite pour nous tous et une bonne santé, que l'an

58   nous sommes liés au
     pourquoi nous ne pouvons

59   Monsieur le Directeur

60   inclus la feuille

61

62   mes meilleures salutations   63   Boulevard

64   Mademoiselle Du

64b

65   Je te signale

66   J'ai été bien

67 Madame Blanchâtrent

_____

de la part de Mr Saiget

68 Madame Simo

69 avenue

70 Paris (8ᵐᵉ eme

71 calligraphiques ou calligraphiées. leur

72 étant au quartier
— prochain samedi.

73 malgré les difficultés de toute

74 Mille pensées affectueuses

75 bien vouloir m'envoyer

76 67 Avenue de la Bourdonnais
Paris 7ᵉ

77 e chère maman -
sien. J'aurais aimé
ad aut pour Elle

78 Plusieurs exemplaires si possible des
rapports et bilan soumis à l'assemblée

79 J'ai évidemment un immense écheveau à dévider

80 mille

81 vous devez être occupée

82 au Gᵗ Hingray
Merci, amitiés

83 Mon cher Ami -

84 demoiselle,

85 m'excusez, je l'espère, d'être parti ainsi

86 bas mis [illegible] bout de compte sera fait ci

87 [illegible]

88 – pour ma documentation personnelle –

89 travail supplémentaire,
un tel besoin de [illegible]
[illegible] dont je vous ai par

90 Veux tu noter également :
[illegible] la Bastille à 8h 55 et au
8h 16. La messe commencera
– aux camarades venant par ce
~~[illegible]~~ de manquer le début.

91 étage, j'écris à Monte
le ministre de l'instruction
publique afin de mettre une

92 Je sais, que vous faites, d'habitude
» attention, et je m'excuse de cette

93 e dérangements go car je,
actuel vous devg avoir be

94 les renseignements suivants :

95 et du conseil les comptes et les bilans
1944, présentant dans leur ensemble

96 »uhainement à ce que vous
nous affutons le plus grand

97 je vous embrasse tou
eusement et encore une

98 reux ces sports d'hi-
ver. Et froid, avec
ça !!

99 sortir de ce corps par
une volonté ou mieux

100 ne donner l'adresse exacte de

101 Tom un Remerciement

102 Je vous serais très obligé de me

103 rendre compte de plus en plus ...

104 ... Bld Saint Germain
Paris

105 avec vous.

106 En vous remerciant pour l'intérêt que

107 Tout au moins dans une
banlieue éloignée de tout

108 ... le ... Guillard

109 ... que vous prouvez

110 Madame

111 huile pour pigceur
   huiles pour transformateur

113

112 4 8, Avenue des Alpes,

114 réussite

115 ; cet éloignement
   il me semble qu'il Am.

116 affectueuses félicitations

117 Je vous remercie

118 Sincèrement

119 d'hommages

120

120b bouche dans un verre d'eau
    tiède. J ajouter une pincée de
    bicarbonate de Sande.
    2; Prendre un comprimé d'
                  ! demi heure après
    l'extraction et un autre: le
    soir au moment de se

121 2 rapides courses à Lyon
Programmes sans plus

122 Recevez Monsieur, nos affectueux

123 tellement fantasque

124 merci . Chère amie .

125 Pour le moment, la Maman

126 affectueusement

127 précédemment pratiqué ce que

128 madame,

129 Encore plus ardemment

130 lettre du 5 courant m'annonçant
     par même courrier l'envoi du

131 *et abandonne aussitôt l'espoir de four-*
nir mon nom, [...] une [...] dan

132 *[...] ([...] de poids) — Je [...] de [...].*

133 *[...] d'aller habiter Paris et*
[...] après ce qui est arrivé et ce
[...] [...].   *Croyez - moi, cher*

134 *J'espère , que nous*

134b *ci joint*

135 *un tout petit peu*

136 communiquées dans votre seconde lettre.
        Je suis très heureux de savoir que votre
également de vous revoir ver les 15 Août.

137 *Personnellement,*

138 ~~MARTHE FOIS~~

139 *L. [...]*

140 Inspecteur Mécanicien du Matériel

141 vigueur. Veuillez
nos salutations

142 connaissance commerciale

143 Cher Monsieur,
Comme suite à l'entretien

144 de d'autres renseignements pour

145 une augmentation
la base d'une

146 Seriez-vous désirable

147 Bonjour, señora ! Tout
admirablement, je crois avoir
toujours sensationnels. Je pense

148 listruma

149 Par lettre du 9 Juni 1945 van

150 Monsieur le Président
Adm' Del...

151 En réponse à votre
courant, je vous informe
entièrement d'accord

152 parlant et les livres
té 24, Alex. Arnoux

153 le Comte et la Comtesse

154 Je vous prie d'agréer,
salutations.

155 mais Je ne Recommande

156 qui semble apporter un art divis..
à nos collègues. Dessin, chant, jeux
dramatiques, et par dessus tout la
sentimes qu'on s'occupe d'eux
Nous sommes dans un périod
d'action qui est très pressante, et ne
m'a pas permis de quitter la Moselle.
Pendant ce temps la ma
à la CGP a connu une tergation

157 sa mère, il le faisait au contraire
et les plus passionnés." Nous sommes

158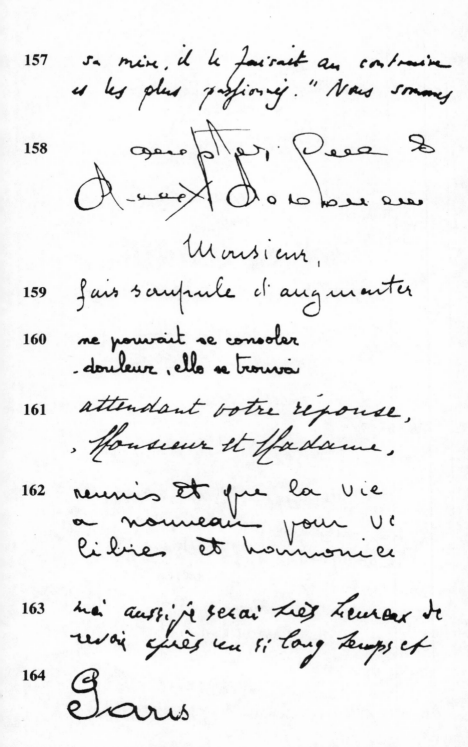

Monsieur,

159 fais scrupule d'augmenter

160 ne pouvait se consoler
. douleur, elle se trouva

161 attendant votre réponse,
, Monsieur et Madame,

162 réunis et que la vie
à nouveau pour Ve
libres et harmonice

163 moi aussi je serai très heureux de
revoir après un si long temps et

164 Paris

165 dans ses mains aussi souples qu'
attention qui remet l'optimisme
menues nouvelles du jour

166 marquait bien et. d
.pas gênant, puisque

166b conversation tomba, j'ai regardé
m'a fait penser à un Tableau,
il est peintre, cela m'a rappelé

167 sans faire la connaissance

168 autour de moi et moi
que je me suis rappelé
sur le moment je vais
de lui demandé car il
demande quel-te qui'l

169 J. E. Shepherd

170 pour l'ensemble de ma vie

171 *B. Josse* —. *voyez madame*

172 *affectueux baisers*

173 *Mussolini* *Citta*

174 *Dudley S*

175 *Marie - Mauw Tanqueray*

176 *outsideration.*

177 *H. Pion*

Jendolik

178 *— note comme 10 fine*

179 *Ac————————al*

180 *F*

181 *votre Josephine*

182

moment de ne pas écrire pour

183 Francis Carco.

184

185   186

187

188

189   190   Chopin

191   a. ampèretti

192

193

194

Je vous remercie à tous les remerciements
que vous me donnez. Je n'ai pas l'intention. Je ne
présente à votre examen et je fie l'avenir, je serai
la meni c'; mais serai tes heureux de devenir un
c'er amy Bien.

195

Réponds ?
La vie uter tes
Et le travail ?
Naturellement ;
allez, à Paris, je te fu
je crois l- te fournis
avant reprendre ; ette
an.

196

Si tu es beaucoup j'ai préféré
celui; veiller dans élément

Chère Gaby,

J'espère que Jean Pierre
a surmonté sa petite crise
morale. Jerome m'a fait

J'espère que vous ni excuserez de m'avoir pas
plus tôt. Je pouvais pouvais aller chez vous puis
cela ne les suppose. Car c'est l'erreur.
qu'ais et il y aura moins de monde dans les
serait. il possible que je vienne dans la

genre, ne familiant pas beaucoup la jeun
ma professionnelle par je convienne,

200

de nouveaux spécimens d'écriture ou de tirage
supplémentaires pour les plaques précédentes.
Je les aurais numérotés pour que puisse
m'indiquer plus facilement ce que t'intéresse.

201

si vous avez fait attendre si longtemps
demais sont que... fantaisies
rien que vous avez été fait de notre

202

Heureusement que cela finit
samedi soir chaque suivant
les 5 jours de vacances de

Ma chère maman,

Il est possible que je ne viendrai pas demain à la maison. Mais je serai là samedi, après le déjeuner : j'ai une leçon à 3 heures, comme d'habitude.

205

... usine de Torteron qui conditionne du bois,
Notre société a besoin pour cet hiver, d'une ...
de bois de chauffage pour son personnel et ...
Dans le but d'être à même de satisfaire ces ...
l'honneur de vous demander l'autorisation d'effec...

206

Chère Amie,

La personne dont vous me parlez
vient me voir demain matin Jeudi:
Je lui ferai votre commission.

207

très obligée lorsque vous aurez
de disponibles de bien vouloir
écrire, une analyse analog

Chère Simone   voici la lettre

Demande à ta tante de

me la rendre le plus vite

possible.

Merci et bonne vacance.

confiance et je vous prie de ne pas connaître [...],
essayant trop vite. J'espère que vous serez réintie
fête de Noël. Je meilleur au venant Mr.

Chère amie

J'ose vous écrire encore
car j'ai malgré tout
la conscience pure
Puis ma vie agitée,
il y a en place, pour

211

Je vous remercie vraiment et
bien voulû au peu valoir
.

212

Que sleur se parle.
affectueusement
Marie Thérèse

213

sont heureux de vous prier
part des fiancailles de leur
fils Christian avec Gabrielle

214

Vous ne m'avez donné
Magdeleine Fabonnage — réponse au sujet des deux
pays demandés pour un ami

215

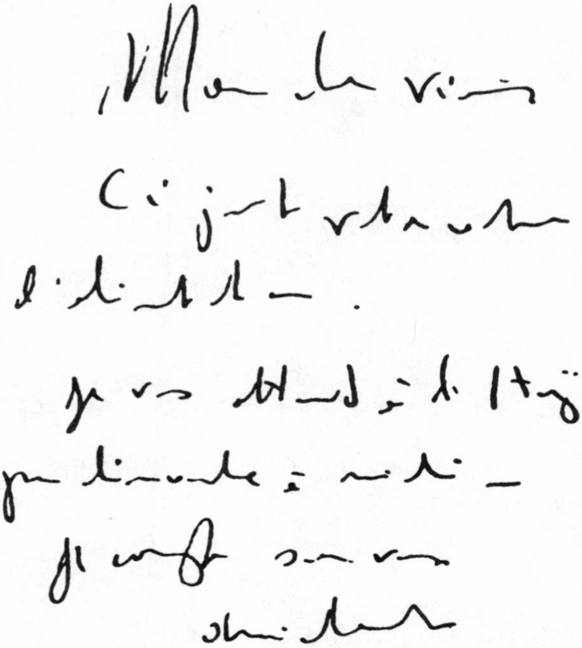

216

Chère Madame,

Je m'excuse de vous prévenir si tard que je ne pourrai venir ce soir chez vous. J'apprends seulement par téléphone que ma mère, étant souffrante, ne peut garder ma fille.

Bt le 25-1-50

Cher petit Henri,

Tu as tenu ta promesse et je t'en
félicite, à moy donc maintenant
d'en faire autant.

Nous te remercions beaucoup
de ta longue lettre, et des détails
que tu donnes. nous sommes très
heureux d'apprendre que tu t'es fait
de bons petits camarades, et que vous
vous invitez réciproquement, cela te
fait passer de bons Jeudi, avec de
bonnes choses à digérer. eh! petit
gourmand!... tâche de penser un peu
à moi lorsque tu manges ces bonnes
choses, parce que depuis que tu es parti
je n'ai plus de dessert, les Jeudis.

Maintenant parlons sérieusement.
tu ne t'ennuie pas à Paris, dont